HAMILTON'S
NAVIGATIONS

THE DEFINITIVE GUIDE TO THE NORFOLK & SUFFOLK BROADS

34th Edition

Edited by
Jamie Campbell

Published by
Hamilton Publications Ltd
9 Marine Parade
Gorleston on Sea
Norfolk NR31 6DU

British Library Cataloguing in Publication Data.
A catalogue record is available from the British Library.

ISBN 0 903094 08 8

First published in this edition in 2001
by

Hamilton Publications Ltd,
9 Marine Parade,
Gorleston on sea,
Norfolk. NR 31 6DU.

www.hamiltonpublications.com

Printed in Great Britain by Morris Printing Co. Ltd.,
58 - 61 Pitt Street,
Norwich,
Norfolk.
NR3 1DE.

Cover.   *Wisemans Mill, Oby, 1753 - Johnstone Bryden*

FOREWORD

Broads holiday makers are a changing breed and the trend towards sailing holidays has continued. Motor boats have their place and many would not venture forth without the comforting thump of a diesel beneath their feet, but a sailing boat is the real way to appreciate the Broads. Little can compare with a gentle breeze on a warm evening, maybe a startled coot rustles the reeds and even the accompaniment of a modest glass of Dr. Bells Patent Remedy. The very stuff of Arthur Ransome. The resurgence of sail seems to be desirable from all angles and to repeat a plea from the previous edition, would be hugely helped by the Broads Authority undertaking a serious programme of riverside tree felling. Most riverside trees are a relatively recent phenomena and can be decribed as a symptom of water turning itself back into dry land. Our Victorian forebears would feel that many of our upper reaches have become both unrecognisable and claustrophobic.

This edition of *Hamilton's Navigations* has again been updated and expanded. A little local knowledge can hugely increase the enjoyment of a few precious days. More photographs, including some aerial shots are used and greater detail on many places of interest, for example St. Benets Abbey. St. Benets has a fascination all of its own expressed by Lambert and Jennings in their famous work on the origins of the Broads, published in 1960. "The ruins of St. Benets Abbey, seen as one sails quietly down the Bure to Thurne Mouth looking for an evening mooring, seem at once so unaccountable and isolated that they force upon even the least sensitive, an uneasy awareness that they belong to a lost mediaeval world." The Broads are a man made phenomena and a little history helps an appreciation of just how they got to be in their current form.

We have continued to include Hamilton's Pubs and Hamilton's Restaurants with several changes for this edition. Running a riverside pub can be a precarious financial venture with all too short a season but it remains our view that too few have kept pace with the increasing expectations and standards of our visitors. First time Hamilton's Navigators will quickly realise that our ideal pub has no place for slot machines, fizzy beer, thermo plastic floor tiles or food kept nice and warm under hot lamps. Consistency is difficult with regular changes of tenant and some are insensitively managed by remote chain operators. Several of our readers

Johnstone - Bryden.

Evening Flight in a good breeze on the Norwich River

have found our suggestions helpful, whilst providing pleasurable homework for the Editor. Our choices are not commercially motivated; none of these establishments have paid for their entry and most will be unaware of their inclusion. We should point out that if, despite a lifetime of assiduous research, a particular hostelry is not included, it may simply mean that we have never visited. As always, we should be delighted to learn of others' experiences.

In East Anglia you'll be enjoying the region with the lowest rainfall in the UK., but should you be unlucky enough to have to spend a rainy day on board, we hope that *Hamilton's Navigations* will provide a helpful range of alternatives.The three main rivers of the Broads are very different and we can only recommend that a first visit includes a sample of all three.

The Broads enjoy an increasing number of visitors who enter our waters from the sea in their own boats. The plain facts are that much of the Broads are closer to Holland than London. Many of our visitors from the Low Countries have a special feeling for inland waterways surrounded by flat countryside and windmills.

All of us at Hamilton's hope that your stay with us is as enjoyable as possible and that you return to see us soon.

Jamie Campbell
Evening Flight.

Claud Hamilton.

Every edition of *Hamilton's Navigations* since 1962 has been dedicated to the founder. An editor of any work of this nature might expect to gain some knowledge of the originator but Claud just became a greater enigma. After a half a century, apocryphal stories abound but hardly a single fact about his life. The man, described by some as the scruffiest man they ever saw, could also dress the part. He was social, talented and clearly well educated. Invariably short of money, he was probably obliged to move his wherries as his debts mounted. Somehow, this did not square with his obvious intellect and academic abilities; the man who was able to hand draw all of his charts, whose French and Italian was fluent and probably also spoke Arabic and Hebrew. The founder had thrown a challenge.

Reginald Claud Matteson Hamilton was born on the 18th March 1888, in a fashionable part of London. His parents hailed from the West Country where his father, Seymour Radcliffe George Annesley Hamilton had served for a short period in the Somerset militia. His parents were married in Torquay 1886. Father Hamilton described his occupation as "esquire" whilst their address was given as a Torquay hotel.

On completion of an obviously private education, the young Claud became what was known in his day as a "remittance man" although fate continuously conspired to separate him from money. He was duly despatched to a sheep station in Australia to seek his fortune. He spent two or three years with the 17th (Prince of Wales') Light Horse Regiment but moved across the country. At the age of 27, describing himself as a "bushman" he volunteered for the Australian Imperial Force, bound for Gallipoli. It was noted that he was a good horseman and fluent in both French and Italian. Like most survivors of this appalling bloodshed, Claud spoke little of his experiences during the First World War but his records survived in Australia. Wounded at Gallipoli, he was court martialled for breaking out of hospital in Cairo and again for a day or so AWOL. He reduced himself to the rank of private but by the end of the war had been commissioned as a lieutenant. After some high jinx in Paris, Claud was again court martialled; found not guilty of drunken disorderliness but guilty and reprimanded for firing a revolver in a public place. He was returned to London where he took up residence in the RAC Club. By this time his mother had become the Marquesa Sarnelli.

Claud was still receiving an allowance but was unable to repay the Australian government sufficient to avoid repatriation to Australia. We know that he joined an American sailing ship as crew to work his passage back to Europe and that one of his ships sank under him. Within a year he had joined the Gendarmerie of the Palestine Police where the British held a Mandate.

After four years in Palestine, Claud finds himself back in Paris, where on 21st December 1926, at 38 years of age he was married in the British Consulate General to Constance Edith Merrison from Ilford. He described his occupation mysteriously as a "courier" whilst Connie was a showgirl. The dancers figure disappeared in later years, but despite her inability to swim, she stayed with Claud on their wherry until his death in 1962. Described as quiet and cutting a "Tugboat Annie" figure, she is remembered by many, rolling her own cigarettes in the Commodore PH. at Oulton Broad.

Claud was living in a bungalow in Thorpe called Anzac, marked on some of his earliest charts, when he lost his left leg in a motorcycle accident on the Dereham Road in Norwich 1933. Afterwards he rarely bothered with his artificial leg. A great writer to the local press on nautical or Broads related matters, he regularly signed himself Silver L.J.

Hamilton's Navigations was first published in 1935. Whilst he was writing his guide, he learned that Drew Miller, an Anglo American living in Dydlers Mill at Horning, was also in the process of writing a Broads guide. The two men made an agreement not to compete. Millers Guide was called "What to do on the Norfolk Broads" and they decided it would contain only diagrammatic charts and be printed on an entirely different shape of paper. Both guides survive to this day and have somehow managed to retain quite different characteristics. Claud drew all of his charts by hand, whilst soundings were carried out with a stick. Pre-war editions of Hamilton's Navigations were published by Miller Hamilton Publications

1937 found Claud renting Fleet House, on Fleet Dyke, South Walsham, which he ran as a guesthouse and teashop and sold ice creams from a small shop. The Second World War was unkind to those who made a living from tourism and Claud acquired a small bungalow at Fishley Mill. Boating was highly restricted during hostilities but he managed to obtain a licence to move about the rivers and hatched another plan to make his fortune; looking after and pumping out the yachts that had been sequestered and moored out on the Broads to prevent enemy flying boats landing. It was

Royal Flaxman collection

felt at the time that an invasion would come through the Broads and many of our fine Broads yachts perished in the interests of defence. Claud compiled the most complete list of all of the names and addresses of the owners. The pair lived at Fishley before acquiring their first wherry, *Claudian*, where Claud ran a small boat repair business immediately post war with the able professional assistance of a boat builder remembered only as Fred.

Claudian was built by probably the most famous of wherry builders, Hall of Reedham. She was said to have been the first wherry ever built exclusively for letting to visitors and was commissioned by George Smith of Wroxham, at the time landlord of the now defunct Horseshoes PH., which he used as a base for hiring boats before starting his boatyard.

A week after Claud's 65th birthday, the *Claudian* was lost during the 1953 floods. He had overlooked his mooring fees at Oulton and moved through to the salt side, into Lake Lothing. She was moored off Cleveland's breakers yard when the fast flowing floodwaters broke her bow moorings. Worrying about the many wrecks in the area, Claud cast off the stern lines in the hope of drifting clear but the wherry stuck fast on the remains of an old drifter. Claud fired shots into the air, but it took two hours for the pair of them and their two dogs to be taken off in a small boat by Russell Bessey, an eel catcher, aided by a passer by. *Claudian* was left stranded on the old drifter, her mast down and with her cabin covered in a tarpaulin and so perfectly upright that the tea the pair had been drinking was left unspilt. She spent ten weeks perched six feet above the high water mark and the local press carried several photographs of the stranded wherry. Claud claimed that *Claudian* had been launched during the same month of the same year that he had been born. It wasn't quite true but it made good copy. Attempts to drag *Claudian* clear simply broke her back and she ended her days where she foundered. After a brief spell in a houseboat on Lake Lothing, the pair were provided with the wherry *Hathor* as a replacement by the Flood Relief Fund. *Hathor* had been the Colman family wherry since she was built in 1905. Her lavish Egyptian theme was in memory of Alan Colman who had died in Egypt in 1897 on a trip down the Nile on a dahabeah called *Hathor*. The trip had been planned as a cure for the young mans tuberculosis. She too was built by Halls at Reedham. Her hull is recorded as costing £575 but the interior fitting out and the elaborate marquetry depicting mythical Egyptian creatures, cost a further £1,057. The total cost of fitting out came to a total of £1,464 with a final bill for the completed vessel of £2,039:5s:4d; a considerable sum in 1905. It is a source of regret that Claud's permanent state of pecuniary cramp caused him to pillage his new acquisition. The porcelain and the gold leaf basins left on board were all sold.

At Oulton, he had been moored off Richardson's yard but in 1954 he took Hathor to Geldeston. From Geldeston, he moved her to Acle Weybridge, where he is believed to have fallen out with the owner of what was then known as the Bridge Hotel. He moved the wherry upstream beside his bungalow at Fishley Mill and his custom to the Hermitage. The two of them lived on board with Claud's golden retriever, always called Lady and Connie's Pekinese. When the stream was cut off at Fishley, he stored fresh water in his dinghy. *Hathor* usually flew the Australian ensign during Claud's stewardship.

Claud Hamilton's schemes to raise cash were inventive, if never actually successful. One photograph shows him with one leg and a yachting cap scrubbing Hathor on Breydon at low water; appropriately with a packet of Tide perched on the mud. Procter & Gamble failed to grasp the opportunity. Hamilton kept *Hathor's* quant poles crossed over the bow in traditional wherry fashion at Fishley. They stuck out into the river and were constantly broken by the hire craft of the day. He would hop on deck and demand reimbursement for a replacement; glueing the broken pole together and waiting for the inevitable repeat performance. In the early fifties, Gordon Money from Oulton Broad was his partner in Hamilton

Publications. Claud was despatched in a motor boat with an echo sounder and a young sound engineer called John Soutar to update their charts. John was given explicit instructions not to let Claud anywhere near the money.

After a long illness, Claud was taken to the Norfolk and Norwich Hospital and later moved to Addenbrooke's Hospital in Cambridge where he died on 6th January 1962 at 73 years of age.

Personally I am sorry never to have raised a jar with this talented man, which I am confident would have been to my account. I am absolutely certain he would have enjoyed the run around he has provided in trying to find out more about him but I like to hope he might not have considered the current generation too unkind to his handiwork.

J.O.C.

CONTENTS.

	Page
Foreword.	3
Claud Hamilton	8
Introduction.	
Origins of the Broads.	15
Local Sailing Craft.	18
Part Two. Navigational Index.	
General Information	28
Bridges	34
Distances	37
Tides	42
Passage through Great Yarmouth	47
Great Yarmouth from the sea	49
Waveney	54
Lowestoft from the sea	67
River Yare	78
River Wensum	101
Norwich	102
River Bure	113
Great Yarmouth	113
River Ant	150
River Thurne	162
Southwold	172

Appendices
>   Navigation Byelaws 1995.
>   Speed Limit Byelaws 1992.
>   Size Byelaws.
>   Useful Telephone Numbers.

Origins of the Broads.

The Broads were long thought to have been the freshwater relics of a time when the area was a huge estuary; simply peaty hollows left by a retreating sea. It was not until the work of Lambert and Jennings in the early 1960's that it was generally accepted that most of the Broads owed their origins to Mediaeval peat diggings. Dr. Joyce Lambert turned 2000 trial bores by hand, to show that these peaty hollows had vertical walls, which over the years had become concealed by marginal vegetation. The floors were found to be largely flat and not concave as would have been expected had the Broads evolved naturally.

Local forests had been cleared before the Domesday Book, and the area has no natural stone, bar the flint found in chalk. As a result, wood became too precious for burning and had to be used for building. Peat was left as the only economic source of energy.

Dr. Lambert and her co-workers calculated that the amount of peat required to be dug out to create the Broads would have to cover 2611 acres (1057 hectares) to an average depth of 2.4m (8'). C.T. Smith calculated in this report that some 9 million cubic feet must have been removed and that this could have been achieved over a 350 year period.

During the Middle Ages, Norfolk and Suffolk were the most densely populated parts of England and the prosperity of local establishments such as St. Benets, Norwich Cathedral, and the Great Hospital was enormous. The account rolls for Norwich Cathedral Priory show their kitchen alone using 400,000 turves in a single year during the late thirteenth and fourteenth centuries. Salt production had been a major local industry for centuries and would also have used a huge amount of fuel. Despite the volume of local production, we also know that Norwich bought peat from other areas. A source of fuel was as crucial then as now and there are many examples of rights of access being jealously guarded. The parish boundaries of Hickling, Catfield and Potter Heigham across Hickling Broad are arranged to allow all three parishes had access to the peat deposits.

The peat diggings were deliberately separated from the rivers by baulks of peat left undug to prevent flooding. There is further evidence of this in the photograph below. Barton Broad was extensively dredged in the 1960s, largely as a result of Herbert Woods' enthusiasm. The aerial photograph of Barton taken in 1951 provides a good example and the one used by Lambert and Jennings et al. to illustrate how the peat was removed. Pleasure Hill Island in the middle of the Broad forms the old parish boundary between Irstead and Barton Turf. The format of the strips is clearly visible; whilst the Barton side chose to lay out their residual strips in a clearly different pattern to their neighbours in Irstead. Since these ridges were shallower when the workings flooded, they more quickly became colonised by reeds and waterside plants, forming peninsulas.

Aerofilms of Boreham Wood.

In 1209 a reference was made to "Alderfen Pyttes" on the site of what we now know as Alderfen Broad. By 1287 there is an account by John of Oxenedes, one of the monks of St. Benets, of large scale flooding when the sea broke into the area. This may have been a crucial period after which peat production became gradually more difficult. As the flooding increased, the method of cutting the turf changed and latterly the turf was won by dredging from a boat, just as it was in Holland. There is little evidence of turf cutting much after 1500 and most if not all of the turbaries were flooded by the fifteenth century.

The first reference to anything approaching a "broad" was not until the early 16th century when a "Brodingge" was described at South Walsham. Lambert, Smith and Jennings noted in 1965 that "by the end of the fourteenth century, turf production had ceased entirely, the reed beds of the Abbot of St. Benets in South Walsham could not be cut as they were flooded with water....".

LOCAL SAILING CRAFT.

The Norfolk Broads are unique in having so many differing sailing craft that have developed specifically to sail on inland waters. All local boats have lowering masts, usually with a tabernacle and a large counterbalance weight. Gaff rig, unfashionable offshore for decades is usual. A "square" sail above the trees, particularly with a topsail set, can catch enough breeze on a calm day to move many times faster than its more fashionable Bermudan counterpart.

The largest vessel unique to the Broads is a Norfolk Wherry. These developed through centuries as trading vessels. Before the advent of railways or a proper road system, the rivers were used as public highways between local ports, the market towns and the villages. Sailed by a man and a boy, they have neither keel nor leeboard, but manage to use the pressure of the water between their great length and the leeward bank to stop them making too much leeway. There were hundreds of wherries and their precursor, the larger keels, plying these rivers. The very large Dutch population of religious refugees in the early seventeenth century are credited with adding the single, fore and aft, gaff sail that completed the development from square rigged keel to early Norfolk Wherry.

The Norfolk Wherry Trust (a registered charity) was founded in 1949 to rescue the *Albion,* as she was about to be broken up at the end of her working life with Colman's Mustard. This act of economic folly prevented the entire disappearance of an essential part of a traditional Norfolk landscape. Even in 1949, a black sailed trader had not graced these rivers for ten years.

William Brighton built *Albion* at Oulton Broad in 1898. She is not quite typical, as her hull is carvel (smooth) and not clinker (planks laid on top of each other), like most wherries. She was once known as *Plane* for her smooth hull. Typical is not an easy definition, as wherries were all different, short, long, fast, slow, some had transoms and all were built by eye. Happily, the *Albion* has become a common sight on the rivers. The Norfolk Wherry Trust also own the wherry *Lord Roberts*, which whilst currently resting, may one day justify the funds for rebuilding. The *Albion* has no engine and the only alterations made to her since her trading days has been the addition of basic accommodation in the hold. The Norfolk

Wherry Trust can be contacted through their Membership Secretaries J & D Cooper, 20 Latchmoor Park, Ludham, Norfolk NR29 5RD. Tel: (01692) - 678630. The *Albion* is available for charter with a skipper and mate by arrangement with Mrs. Judy Blackwell, Victoria House, 49 White Street, Martham, NR29 4DQ. Tel: (01493) - 740140. E mail:jjay@cwcom.net

The *Maud* has recently rejoined the *Albion*. She has fine lines and a traditional hull. Her owners Vincent and Linda Pargeter raised her from Ranworth Broad during the late seventies; where for some years she had done a fine job of supporting the banks. Mr Pargeter is an Essex millwright and the couple have spent years rebuilding her. It is still not at all uncommon to see the remains of a wherry rotting in a dyke off one of the main rivers.

As the Broads grew ever more popular with Victorian tourists, it was not long before enterprising locals began to convert the wherries that were being outmoded by the very railways that were bringing the tourists. Nicholas Everitt credits the first conversion in 1880 of a trading wherry for charter use: "Messrs Press Bros. of North Walsham conceived the idea of raising the hatches of a trading wherry and filling the vacancy with glass windows, partitioning off her hold into several cabins and upholstering the interior with some idea of comfort." Wherries were soon built purely as pleasure craft. *Hathor* and *Solace* are examples built by Hall of Reedham (as was *Maud*.) all of which may be seen sailing today.

The Victorians, unsatisfied with replicas of mere working boats, developed the Wherry Yacht, and of these the *Olive*, *White Moth* and *Norada* are all still sailing. They have a similar, single sailed rig to a trading wherry but carry a white sail and have a large, white carvel (smooth) hull with a counter (overhanging) stern. The last wherry to be built was a wherry yacht, the *Ardea*, finished in record time by Leo. Robinson at Oulton Broad. The vessel was funded by a notable local benefactor, Mr. Howard Hollingsworth (he had a shop in Oxford St. W1 with a Mr. Bourne.) as a job creation scheme during the depression. She was built of teak and said not to enjoy the sweet lines of a traditional oak wherry. She can still be seen today, varnished and with a superstructure over her cockpit, moored just outside Paris where an owner took her in the late 1950's to solve his housing problem. Somehow *Ardea* wants to come home.

Several of these wherries are now available for charter groups or corporate entertaining or simply a party, and come complete with skipper:-

White Moth is a wherry yacht suitable for up to 12 people; contact Mike Barnes of Norfolk Broads Yachting Co., Southgates Yacht Station, Lower Street Horning. Tel: (01692) - 631330. email: mike@nbyco.com

Norada and *Olive* are wherry yachts whilst *Hathor* is a pleasure wherry. Contact Peter Bower, Wherry Yacht Charter, Barton House, Hartwell Rd. Wroxham. NR12 8TL. Tel: (01603) - 782470.

Broads River Cruisers. There are over 300 boats registered in this class, which provides a great deal of family fun, together with handicap racing of sorts. Hardly two of these boats are identical, but generally they have low freeboard, shallow draught, with masts lowering in tabernacles and often lifting cabin tops with canvas sides to provide better access to some fairly basic living accommodation. Many of the class carry too much sail and races often provide a great spectacle. A visit from the fleet for a regatta usually fills the river and represents an early Christmas for riverside landlords. *Evening Flight,* shown on page 6 was the second boat to be registered in the class.

Brown boat number 50.   *Knights*

Brown boats or Broads One Designs, as they are properly known, are the oldest of the local one design classes and the only one to be equally at home at sea or inland. They were designed by the famous Victorian naval architect, Linton Hope. These elegant, spoon bowed, 24 foot long boats were originally built in Burnham on Crouch in 1901 by the Burnham Yacht Building Company and the first few boats planked with cedar. The designer offered £5 to anyone who could capsize one and there was a tradition amongst watermen that Mr. Russell Colman would give £50 for such a feat. No-one has managed yet, although collection of the wager might prove problematical. The class has retained its gaff rig, changes have been very few and only two boats have been lost to the class. The boats were required to be varnished and over the years many have been rebuilt, although few to the standards or extent that Nick Truman of Oulton Broad has achieved with both *Spoonbill* and *Goldeneye*, both of which were first built in the early 1920's. Some of the early boats were beginning to show signs of wear in rough weather and their owners had become reluctant to take them to sea. The class was rejuvenated by the development of a glass fibre Brown boat and to date about twenty new boats have been built to bring the numbers in the class to over fifty. In the meantime, the rest of us are faced with the confusion of white and blue Brown boats.

Yare and Bure O.D.   *Johnstone Bryden*

Yare and Bure One Designs, known as White boats are twenty foot, half deckers, carrying a 211 square foot of mainsail. They were first built by Ernest Woods in 1908, whose yard was then at Cantley on the River Yare, to the order of the Yare and Bure Sailing Club. This is numerically the largest of the local one design classes, consisting of some 120 boats. Glass fibre is now used for construction but a casual observer would be pushed to notice.

A visitor to the area would do well to spot one of a small number of Yarmouth One Designs, another half decker, but unique in their lug sails and drop keels. Only six were ever built; four are known to survive and two of these are based on Hickling Broad.

Waveney O.D.   *Johnstone Bryden*

Waveney One Designs, known locally simply as Waveneys, are not dissimilar to White boats but are numerically a much smaller class of some 27 boats dating from 1924. Waveneys carry the letter W in red on their sails and the class is based at Oulton Broad, where racing is held. They too, are now produced in glassfibre.

Norfolk Punt   *Johnstone Bryden*

Norfolk Punts are direct descendants of Broads gun punts, used by traditional "market gunning" wildfowlers. There are nearly a hundred punts registered in the class. Since it is a restricted class, permitting limited changes and development, many of the old boats would not now race even with the advantage of a large handicap. They have retained the original low freeboard and double ends (sharp at both ends!) but that is where resemblance ceases and newer punts sport two trapezes, spinnakers and can be very fast, athletic and latterly, quite expensive.

Norfolk Dinghy   *Johnstone Bryden*

About the only local class untouched by glass fibre is the Norfolk Dinghy. Several fourteen foot local one designs were used in 1923 as the basis of new rules to form a National Fourteen Foot Class, which of course became the International Fourteen. A precursor of our current Norfolk Dinghy was one of these, also known at the time as a Norfolk Dinghy; but a development class, carrying a lug sail and originally built to the rules of the Yare Sailing Club. By 1931 the cost of an International Fourteen, about to become the first planing dinghy in the world, had soared to over 150 guineas. Herbert Woods of Potter Heigham produced his new one design dinghy to sell for 65 guineas. The Broads Motor Boat and Sailing Club and the Royal Norfolk and Suffolk Yacht Club adopted the new class. A total of 86 boats have been built, with only four unaccounted for over nearly seventy years. Norfolks are built from copper clenched, clinker mahogany, all varnished and carry a red letter "B" on their sails.

REGATTAS.

Racing is organised by local clubs over most summer weekends but many hold Open Regattas which are often the direct descendants of the old village regattas and waterfrolics. They can provide quite a spectacle but skippers should be advised that the larger regattas cause some congestion on the river for the duration of races. The Broads are not overcrowded; in fact the number of boats available for hire has halved in about ten years. However, if you seek peace and tranquility and go to an area holding a major regatta on a Bank Holiday weekend, the result will be the same as in any other tourist area of the British Isles. The dates of these regattas change annually but usually fit in to a pattern accepted between the various clubs. The Norfolk and Suffolk Yachting Association co-ordinates these fixtures to try and prevent clashes.

Thurne Mouth Open Regatta. Spring Bank Holiday (May). East Anglian Cruising Club.

Three Rivers Race. Horning Sailing Club. The first weekend in June. All competitors start at Horning at Saturday lunch time. They then usually sail to Hickling Broad, South Walsham Broad, and to a buoy on the Lower Bure, often down by the Stracey Arms. Competitors may take the buoys in any order they think will give them the best tidal advantage. This involves overnight sailing and lowering of masts. Potter Heigham Bridge is a good place to spectate but the Northern Rivers seem busy with sailing boats all night.

Wroxham Broad. Norfolk Broads Yacht Club, Wroxham Week is usually held during the last week in July. There are two River Cruiser events over the preceding three weekends, which are well attended. Club regattas are held over most summer weekends.

Horning Week. Horning Sailing Club. Usually the first week in August.

Beccles Regatta. Beccles Amateur Sailing Club. Early August.

Hickling Regatta. Hickling Broad Sailing Club. Early August.

Oulton Week. Waveney and Oulton Broad Yacht Club usually hold their regatta during the week preceding August Bank Holiday.

Barton Open Regatta. Norfolk Punt Club and Barton Open Regatta Committee; held over August Bank Holiday weekend.

Yare Navigation Race. Coldham Hall Sailing Club. This is the largest gathering of traditional sail anywhere in the British Isles. Over seventy Broads River Cruisers sail from Coldham Hall to Breydon Water and back. Competitors choose their own starting times to take the most favourable effects of wind and tide. Reedham is a very central and quite busy place to watch the race. The Yare Navigation Race takes place in September.

Sailing isn't difficult to learn but the inexperienced or newcomers to the sport may wish to take a short course of sailing lessons in a controlled environment, from home, prior to their holiday. Exhaustive national lists are inevitably outdated but the Royal Yachting Association, the controlling body for the sport, are extremely helpful. They are based at RYA House, Romsey Road, Eastleigh, Hants. SO5 4YA. Telephone: (01703) - 629962. Fax: (01703) - 629924. RYA recognition of a school guarantees certain standards and will be a helpful accreditation for those less familiar with the area. It is particularly important for youngsters learning to sail that when they have completed their course, they receive a nationally recognised piece of paper. The English have a long tradition of freedom of the seas and no paper qualifications have historically been required of skippers, with the obvious exception of commercial and passenger vessels and for insurance purposes on some very large yachts. The EEC is likely to change all of this, and Certificates of Competence are now required to visit most countries of Europe. The paper itself may be meaningless and most learned the hard way, swimming round dinghies and crewing for adults. Regrettably these qualifications are likely to be increasingly necessary to enjoy our sport.

Sailing lessons are available locally from the following RYA recognised schools:

Horstead Centre, residential / activity centre. Horstead, Norwich NR12 7EP. Tel: (01603) - 737215.

Lallagullis Sailing. Riverside, Brundall, Tel: (01603) - 716317/410989.

Norfolk Broads School of Sailing, c/o Camelot Craft, The Rhond, Hoveton, Norfolk. NR12 8UE. Tel: (01603) - 783096.

NYCS, (Norfolk County Council, Education), Main Road, Filby, Norfolk. NR29 3AA. Tel: (01493) - 368129.

Sailon, based on Oulton Broad. 8 Gunton Cliff, Lowestoft, NR32 4PE. Tel: (01502) - 572014.

Norfolk School of Canoeing. Approved by British Canoe Union. Randalls Yard, Mill Road, Horstead, Norfolk. Courses and guided trails through the Broads. Tel: (01603) - 737456.

Water - skiing is still permitted on some stretches of the Rivers Yare and Waveney. These are marked on the relevant charts. Skippers should keep a special look-out for fast approaching boats and wide or overtaking skiers in these stretches. A special licence or water ski permit is required which may be obtained by application to the Broads Authority. Skiing is limited to these stretches and certain times and days. A boat may only exceed the speed limit when towing a skier. Precise details of the regulations are contained in the Speed Limit Bye Laws at the back of this edition.

Part Two.

Broads Navigational Index.

GENERAL INFORMATION.

This section of *Hamilton's Navigations* contains information designed to help both private owners and hirers of either motor or sailing yachts, get the best out of their time on the Norfolk and Suffolk Broads. Inevitably, a large part consists of do's and don'ts and general advice on the area. If some of this appears a little basic or unnecessary to more experienced brethren, then we make few apologies. The Broads are a great place to start a lifetime's obsession with small boats and we have a large number of visitors anxious to try their hands.

In the text and on the charts, the rivers and broads are divided into half-mile sections, each with a reference number, starting from the mouth of the river and ending with the upper navigable limit. The prefix simply stands for the name of the River; for example W stands for Waveney and TH for Thurne.

Good moorings are described as such, only when they have a sufficient depth of water, combined with a bank which provides a firm landing and should not damage moored craft. Quay heading is subject to both damage and deterioration, so skippers should always be sure to satisfy themselves of their vessels' safety. Banks marked red on the enclosed charts should be avoided. An Emergency Mooring (EM) is not a good mooring but one that might be used, not from choice but for example, in the event of a breakdown. Banks not shown as definitely good or bad do not fulfil all of the above requirements, but may well be used with care.

Reaches are stretches of water between bends. They will not precisely coincide with the numbered half-mile sections, but the name is given in the section containing the greatest proportion. We have preserved as many as possible of the traditional names of reaches, most of which date back to the days when these rivers were the major local highways. As far as we are aware, *Hamilton's Navigations* is now the only published source of these names.

Notes for visitors to the Broads entering by sea are included under the relevant sections on Gt. Yarmouth, Lowestoft and a small section on Southwold. These notes are intended to provide useful information, but under no circumstances should they be taken to replace the use of properly updated charts for these ports. It should be noted that yachts with a draught much in excess of 1.5m (5') will find themselves considerably restricted on these waterways.

Children should wear a lifejacket at all times when afloat. Adults might be expected to take their own decision.

Particular care should be taken with overhead power lines by skippers of yachts with tall masts or dinghies on trailers. There are several reasons for this. The authorities seem reluctant to give clearance details, as the height of the larger power cables can apparently vary by up to ten feet, depending on the temperature. In some weather conditions power cables are capable of arcing - your mast does not have to touch the cable; the current can jump a considerable distance. Best to be safe and stay well clear.

Most boats are now diesel powered, in fact petrol has become difficult to obtain beside the river. Spills of petrol and leaks of gas represent a significant danger of fire and explosion. In such an event, all naked lights or sources of ignition should be removed and as much ventilation as possible should be provided through the bilge of the boat concerned. Anyone who is remotely concerned about such an incident would do well to call the local Fire Brigade and seek their advice.

Do leave your boat as secure as possible when unattended. The Broads area is not notably prone to thieving, but remember to lock your boat and raise the canopy before you leave it, hiding all valuables, including fishing tackle. Whilst boats are relatively difficult to secure, most thefts are opportunistic and a little forethought can save an incident that might otherwise spoil your holiday.

The local Police request that anything suspicious be reported to their central numbers: -

Norfolk Police Control, Norwich: - (01603) - 768769.
Suffolk Police Control,
(Central Switchboard, Martlesham.): - (01986) - 835300.

Craft visiting the broads for up to 28 days in the toll year must pay a short visit toll and display their short visit number. Short visit licences can be obtained from the Broads Authority, 8 Colegate, Norwich, Norfolk. NR3 1BQ. Tel: (01603) - 610734. Craft remaining on the Broads for a period in excess of 28 days must register with the Broads Authority, pay the annual registration toll and display their registration number.

There are two major public footpaths running for long distances beside or close to these rivers. The Weavers Way crosses the area of the north rivers many times. It runs for 250 miles over its whole length, from Cromer to Great Yarmouth. From North Walsham to Stalham and Hickling the footpath finally gets close to the water and runs for a short distance alongside the southern half of Hickling Broad and alongside Heigham Sound. Before Candle Dyke it turns to Potter Heigham and crosses the old bridge. Weavers Way then follows the south bank of the Thurne downstream; at the village of Thurne it skirts inland briefly but returns to follow the banks of the Bure to Acle bridge. Crossing Acle bridge the footpath continues along the west bank of the Bure to Acle Dyke. The river is left behind for some distance as Weavers Way heads inland through Halvergate to rejoin the River Yare at the Berney Arms. It follows the northern shore of Breydon water to Yarmouth.

The Angles Way runs from Great Yarmouth, along the south bank of Breydon Water. Leaving the banks of the Waveney at Burgh Castle. The footpath passes through Somerleyton and round Oulton Broad. It does not regain the banks of the Waveney until Share Mill just upstream of Oulton Dyke and follows the south bank to Beccles. It then leaves the river and meanders through the river valley until it ends in Knettishall Country Park, upstream of Diss.

The representations in the charts or text of a road, track, mooring or footpath should not be taken as evidence of a right of way.

Generally, the lower reaches of the rivers are deepest on the outside of bends. At low water, the lower reaches of the Bure particularly, are now quite shallow on some inside bends. It is much better for a yacht to tack early, than go aground; especially on a falling tide. Except in the case of public quays, piling or quay heading is often purely to stop bank erosion and there is no guarantee of a suitable mooring. Skippers should watch carefully for projecting bolts, flint banks or similar obstructions. When moored, test that there is sufficient depth to ensure you will not be aground at low water.

It is usually helpful if the skippers of sailing boats are able to politely indicate to motor boats which side they would like them to pass. A "thank you" is rarely taken amiss. In high winds you will sail faster and be more under control with a reef or two. Reefing a sailing boat is seamanship rather than a sign of cowardice. A collision can spoil anyone's holiday.

Sailing or Yacht Clubs on the Broads are included in the navigational notes, together with the names of their secretaries, but these are prone to regular changes. Whilst these are private clubs, most run open regattas at some point over the year. A quiet word usually ensures a welcome for a visiting member of another club.

The Broads are considered by many to be at their finest over the winter. The fishing is at its best, our many migratory birds are present and the rivers are largely empty. Most of the Broads are freshwater and sometimes freeze. If a winter outing should appeal; a word of warning about ice may be timely. Pushing a boat through ice, particularly a glassfibre hull is a remarkably quick way to sink the boat. Surrounded by ice in the winter, it may take a long while for anyone to find you.

The basic "rules of the road" are simple: Keep to the right (starboard); overtake in the middle of the river only when it is safe and clear. Hire craft are forbidden to navigate after sunset, as they are not equipped with navigation lights. Motor powered craft give way to sailing craft, whilst all pleasure craft are expected to keep clear of working vessels.

The Broads were popularised by the Victorians, many of whom were overtly in search of their fortunes by opening the hinterland to the railway. Sir Samuel Morton Peto for example developed much of South Lowestoft, when he brought the railway from Reedham. He was able to build himself Somerleyton Hall on the proceeds. The Broads area contains a huge amount of history, one of John Payne Jennings photographs; coincidentally commissioned by the Great Eastern Railway is used in this edition.

Christopher Davies, known as "the man who found the Broads" published a list of "hitherto unwritten rules of the Rivers and Broads" in his Handbook to the Rivers and Broads of Norfolk and Suffolk, first published in 1883. Much of this is charming and bears repetition.

"I therefore beg the large unknown public (of whose friendliness to me as an author I have had so many proofs), when they visit the Broads, not to allow the exhilaration of an enjoyable holiday to interfere with a due propriety of behaviour.

Do not, in the neighbourhood of other yachts or houses, indulge in songs or revelry after eleven p.m., even at regatta times.

Bathe only before eight in the morning, if in sight of other vessels or moored in a frequented part of the river. Ladies are not expected to turn out before eight, but after that time they are entitled to be free from any annoyance. Young men who lounge in a nude state on boats whilst ladies are passing (and I have known Norwich youths do this) may be saluted with dust shot or the end of a quant.

Adhere strictly to the rule of the road when boating, according to the instructions contained in a subsequent chapter, and when angling moor out of the way of sailing craft, as afterwards explained.

Do not throw straw or paper overboard to float to leeward and become offensive; but burn, or take care to sink all rubbish.

Do not light fires, place stoves or throw refuse on the banks in the path of others, whose yachts may be moored to the same bank .

Steam launches must not run at full speed past yachts moored to the bank, particularly when the occupants of the latter have things spread out for a meal.

Don't take guns on board, unless you have leave to shoot on somebody's land.

Remember that sound travels a long way on the water, and do not criticise the people you may encounter with too loud a voice.

Don't go on a friends yacht with nailed shoes. (the commodore of a Thames sailing club once came on board mine in cricket shoes armed with spikes.) Don't knock the ashes of your pipe out into his boat and don't catch small fish and litter his deck with them, leaving them for him to clean up after you.

Don't moor up outside another yacht without the permission of its owner. Ladies, please don't gather armfuls of flowers, berries, and grasses which, when faded, you leave in the boat for the unfortunate skipper to clear up. Don't play the piano in season and out of season, (the reed birds song is sweeter.); and don't turn out before eight o'clock in the morning when other yachts are near.

Observing these simple maxims, any number of visitors will find plenty of room for their own enjoyment without offence to anyone."

It might have been nice if such advice as to gentlemanly behaviour had currently been considered sufficient. The current Byelaws are reproduced at the back of this edition of *Hamilton's Navigations*. The Editor, who might be considered an experienced yachtsman, has to express some exasperation as to how he or anyone else is supposed to differentiate between 4 mph and 5 mph - and speed over ground at that, on tidal waters and usually in a vessel without instrumentation.

The increasing desire of the authorities to legislate, in most respects misses the spirit of the place, epitomised by that quintessential English author Arthur Ransome. The English have long held sacred an unfettered public right of navigation over tidal waters; whilst a boy's first experience of sailing is often in a small and inadequate boat, used and abused in the unsuspected safety of confined waters. That first boat lives for ever as a rosy memory. Equally a rowing dinghy with an outboard motor can be the first piece of mechanical equipment that a child is allowed to control alone. Whilst there is an element of danger attached to anything that qualifies as fun, the Broads are incredibly safe for children; usually the worst accident to befall them involves blowing up into the reeds. We all survived. These freedoms given at a young age have proved invaluable to the many thousands of children who have developed into self reliant, mature adults, learning to handle small boats on the Broads. This is now described as Navigation by Minors.

Radio Weather forecasts are available:-
National Shipping Forecasts; sea areas Thames / Humber.
There are two local radio stations; BBC Radio Norfolk FM 95.1 104.4MHz/MW855, 873KHz. or Radio Broadland FM102.4 MHz/MW 152KHz .

BRIDGES.

Hathor under Vauxhall Bridge   *Johnstone Bryden*

Clearance is given at Average High Water during summer months.This is intended to represent an average minimum; precise clearance will vary with the tides and other variable factors such as rainfall.

Bridge clearance table

Bridge name	Clearance (metric)	Clearance (imp.)	Width (metric)	Width (imp.)	Description
Acle	4.00	13'	23.7	78'	Fixed road
Beccles Road* +	1.98	6.5'	12.6	41.5'	Fixed road
Beccles Bypass	4.27	14'	28.9	95'	Fixed road
Breydon Road	3.96	13'			Fixed side spans
Breydon Road	3.5	11.5'			Lifting span
Carlton, Lake Lothing	4.57	15.1'			Swing rail
Haddiscoe New Cut	7.32	24'	12.1	40'	Fixed road
Ludham	2.6	8.5'	5.4	18'	Fixed road
Norwich, Postwick	10.7	35'			Fixed road
Norwich, Carrow	4.27	14'	9.1	30'	Lifting road
Norwich, Foundry	3.05	10'	16.4	54'	Fixed road
Norwich, Trowse	3.05	10'	9.1	30'	Swing rail
Potter Heigham, bypass	2.36	7.75'			Fixed road
Potter Heigham, road*+	2.03	6.75'	22.4	73.5'	Fixed road
Oulton Broad, Mutford	2.4	7.9'	6.4	21'	Swing road
Reedham+	3.05	10'	16.6	54.5'	Swing rail
St. Olaves+	2.44	8'	23.9	78.5'	Fixed road
Somerleyton	2.6	8.5'	16.4	54	Swing rail
Thorpe rail (each)+	1.83	6'			Fixed rail
Tonnage	2.44	8'			Fixed road
Wayford+	2.13	7'	6.1	20'	Fixed road
Wroxham, rail	4.57	15'	14.3	47'	Fixed rail
Wroxham, road*+	2.34	7.75'	8	26.5	Fixed road
Yarmouth, Haven	2.9	9.5'	26.8	88'	Lifting road
Yarmouth, A47+	2.13	7'	21.3	70'	Fixed road
Yarmouth, Vauxhall+	2.13	7'	30.4	100'	Fixed foot

Bridges marked with an asterisk* are arched and clearance measuremnts refer to the centre of the arch. Skippers should remeber the beam of their boat as clearance will be less at the edges of the bridges. The old bridge at Potter Heigham is particularly difficult and most hired craft are required to take a pilot. Many old bridges were not built at right angles to the river.

Bridges marked + have a gauge on their approach giving the clearance curently available. Hamilton's suggest that these are treated with some caution. Not only is there a natural inclination towards pessimism but the wooden gauges have usually been hit by passing boats on several occasions.

Skippers of sailing craft without auxilliary power should note that many of the older bridges cause a constriction in the flow of the river.This results in a swifter current which scours the river bed to a much greater depth than the immediate area. If it is not possible to moor close by the bridge to raise and lower masts then skippers should consider that their quant poles may not be long enough to make contact with the bottom. St Olaves and Acle Bridges are good examples of this, as is the western side of the channel downstream of Wroxham Bridge.

If your boat is a "tight fit" through a bridge at low water; keep an eye on the weather forecast. A heavy rain could raise the water level and leave you stuck upstream of the bridge; waiting like Noah for the waters to recede.

There are times for a statement of the obvious; canopies and masts should of course be lowered when appropriate for bridges. Skippers should ensure that all the crew are in the cockpit where they can be seen and if towing a sailing dinghy it's no bad thing to remember to take that mast down too.

Dimensions of bridges above Bishop Bridge in Norwich are given in the relevant section, as is Waxham New Cut bridge.

Owners of larger yachts are often concerned that if they have sufficient air draught to clear Vauxhall Bridge, Great Yarmouth, they may be left with insufficient depth of water. At the time of going to press the clearance between the bottom of Vauxhall Bridge and the river bed was 6.4m (21') The A47 road bridge has a greater depth of water. It must be emphasissed that this measurement will be subject to change and skippers close to tolerance should make their own checks.

River Ant Distances

River Ant	Chart Ref.	Bradford (source)	North Walsham	Briggate Mill	Honing Lock	Dilham	Wayford Bridge	Sutton Broad	Barton Turf	Neatishead	Irstead	Ludham Bridge
Bradford (source)												
N.Walsham		4.5										
Briggate Mill		7.5	3.0									
Honing lock	A21	8.5	4.0	1.0								
Dilham	AD1											
Wayford Bridge	A16	10.5	6.0	3.0	2.0	1.1						
Sutton Broad	A13	12.5	8.0	5.0	4	2.4	1.3					
Barton Turf	A11	14.3	8.5	5.5	4.5	3.1	2.0	.5				
Neatishead	AB2	14.3	9.8	6.8	5.8	4.9	3.8	2.3	1.9			
Irstead	A9	14.3	10.0	7.0	6	4.6	3.5	2.0	1.5	1.5		
Ludham Bridge	A2	17.3	13.5	10.5	9.5	8.1	7	5.5	5.0	5.0	3.5	
Ant Mouth	A1	18.5	14	11	10.3	8.9	7.8	6.3	5.8	5.8	4.3	.75

Ant to Stalham (AS 4) is 1.25 miles.   Ant to Sutton (AS 5) is 1.25 miles.

distance in miles.

River Waveney Distances

River Waveney	Geldeston	Beccles	Aldeby	6 Mile Corner	Waveney Staithe	Oulton Dyke	Somerleyton	Haddiscoe	New Cut	St. Olaves	R. Yare (Breydon)	Yarmouth Yacht Stn.
Chart Ref.	W 42	W 36	W 32	W 27	W 22	W 20	W 15	W 11	W 11	W 10	Y 1	B 1
Geldeston Lock		3	4.75	7.25	10	10.75	13.5	15	15.25	15.5	20.75	25
Beccles			1.75	4.25	7	7.75	10.5	12	12.25	12.5	17.75	22
Aldeby				2.5	5.25	6	8.75	10.25	10.5	10.75	16	20.25
6 Mile Corner					2.75	3.5	6.25	7.75	8	8.25	13.5	17.75
Waveney Staithe						.75	3.5	5	5.25	5.5	10.75	15
Oulton Dyke							2.75	4.25	4.25	4.75	10	14.25
Somerleyton								1.5	1.75	2	7.25	11.5
Haddiscoe									.25	.5	5.75	10
New Cut										.25	5.5	9.75
St. Olaves											5.25	9.5
R.Yare Breydon												4.25

Oulton Broad

	Oulton Dyke	R. Waveney	Oulton Broad	Oulton Broad Yacht Station
Chart ref.	W 20	O 3	O 4	
River Waveney		1.25	2.25	
Oulton Broad			1	

distance in miles

River Yare Distances

River Yare	Chart Ref.	Norwich	Thorpe	Bramerton Woods End	Surlingham Ferry	Brundall	Buckenham Ferry	Langley Dyke	Cantley	Hardley Cross	Reedham	New Cut	Mouth of Waveney
Norwich	WM3												
Thorpe	Y43	2											
Bramerton Woods End	Y37	5	3										
Surlingham Ferry	Y33	6.7	4.7	1.7									
Coldham Hall	Y30	8.2	6.2	3.2	1.5								
Buckenham Ferry	Y24	11.2	9.2	6.2	4.5	3							
Langley Dyke	Y20	13	11	8	6.2	4.7	1.7						
Cantley	Y18	14	12	9	7.2	5.7	2.7	1					
Hardley Cross	Y13	15.5	13.5	10.5	8.7	7.2	4.2	2.5	1.5				
Reedham	Y11	17	15	12	10.2	8.7	5.7	4	3	1.5			
New Cut	Y10	17.5	15.5	12.5	10.7	9.2	6.2	4.5	3.5	2	.5		
Mouth of Waveney	Y1	22	20	17	15.2	13.7	10.7	9	8	6.5	5	4.2	
Yarmouth Yacht Stn.	B1	26.2	24.2	21.2	19.5	18	15	13.2	12.2	10.7	9.2	8.7	4.2

distance in miles

The River Chet is approximately 3.5 miles long.

River Bure Distances

distance in miles.

River Bure	Chart Ref.	Coltishall Lock	Belaugh	Wroxham	Wroxham Broad	Salhouse	Horning	Ranworth Dam	Ant Mouth	Thurne Mouth	Acle Bridge	Stokesby Ferry	Stracey Arms	Mautby Swim
Coltishall Lock	B62													
Belaugh	B57	2.7												
Wroxham	B49	6.7	4											
Wroxham Broad	B47	8	5.2	1.2										
Salhouse	B45	9.2	6.2	2.5	1.2									
Horning	B40	11.2	8.2	4.5	3.2	2								
Ranworth	B35	13.2	10.2	6.5	5.2	4	2							
Ant Mouth	B33	14.2	11.5	7.5	6.2	5	3	1						
Thurne Mouth	B29	16.2	13.5	9.5	8.2	7	5	3	2					
Acle	B23	19.2	16.5	12.5	11.2	10	8	6	5	3				
Stokesby	B19	21.2	18.5	14.5	13.2	12	10	8	7	5	2			
Stracey Arms	B16	22.7	20	16	14.7	13.5	11.5	9.5	8.5	6.5	3.5	1.5		
Mautby Farm	B9	26.5	23.7	19.7	18.5	17.2	15.2	13.2	12.2	10.2	7.2	5.2	3.7	
Yarmouth Y.S.	B1	30.2	27.5	23.5	22.2	21	19	17	16	14	11	9	7.5	3.7

Hamilton's Broads
Tide Calculator and Slack Water Calculators.

Hamilton's Broads tidal calculators are sold as a pair in a vinyl case and are available from all good yacht chandlers or direct from the publishers: Hamilton Publications Ltd., 9 Marine Parade, Gorleston on sea, Norfolk. NR31 6DU. Price £3.45 including post and packing.

Halvergate Sunset

TIDES.

The whole of the Broads empty into the sea at Great Yarmouth; and the nearer to Great Yarmouth, the stronger the tide. It is helpful for all skippers to use the tide to their advantage but essential for sailing boats. Even the fastest yachts would be quite unable to beat against the tide through Great Yarmouth and might equally experience difficulty battling a full tide through Reedham Swing Bridge. Motor boats are usually able to "punch" a tide, but at a considerable cost in both terms of fuel used per mile and time taken for the journey.

The tide is a periodical rise and fall in the sea level caused by the gravitational attraction of the moon and, to a lesser extent, the sun.

When the moon is over an ocean, the water is pulled towards it. The "pull" of the Moon is not equal and the points on the earth's surface closest and furthest away from the moon experience the greatest pull and therefore the highest water. When the Sun and Moon are in line, we experience the greatest tides, called Spring Tides that occur about three days after full and new moons. Tides wax and wane from Springs to Neap tides (smallest) and fall back to Springs approximately every 14 1/2 days. A lunar day (the time between two successive passes of the moon over the same meridian) is a period of about 12 hours 50 minutes. As a rule of thumb, tides are about an hour later every day.

Both Springs and Neaps have a marked effect on depth of water and clearance at bridges. At Low Water Springs there will be more clearance at bridges, but less depth, whilst the reverse will apply for Neap tides. The term Mean applied to tides, as in Mean High Water Springs or Mean Low water Neaps, will be familiar to sea going navigators and is defined precisely. Hamilton's use Average High Water (AHW) or Average Low Water (ALW) to provide data that we believe is more relevant and generally helpful to summer visitors to these waters, without the constraints of an official definition. Soundings are given in metres (feet). The term Mean has only been used in this publication in relation to the seaports of Yarmouth, Lowestoft and Southwold, where the relevant Harbour Authority has supplied the data.

The tidal stream at Gorleston Bar controls all tides on the Broads but the times of tides at Yarmouth Yacht Station are the most useful reference point for inland navigation. Hamilton's Tide Tables are calculated at the time of Low Water at Gt. Yarmouth Yacht Station and are corrected to British Summer time, where appropriate. Skippers should use the *Hamilton's Tide Calculator* for easy and accurate calculation of the times of High or Low Water at other locations on the Broads or *Hamilton's Slack Water Calculator* to calculate departure times to ensure making the recommended slack water passage thorough Gt. Yarmouth.

On the coast at Great Yarmouth, the tides flood to the south and ebb to the North. In most cases, particularly in official nautical publications High Water Gt. Yarmouth, means High Water Gorleston Bar. The tides along the coast change inshore first and this can mean up to an hour's difference for craft near the beach against one in the main channel beyond the sandbanks.

* Official tide tables are published in Greenwich Mean Time and require one hours adjustment for British Summer Time.

* High Water Gorleston Bar is given as two hours twenty one minutes before HW Dover.

* Yarmouth Yacht Station averages from 3/4 hour to one hour later than Gorleston Bar. The current still runs out past Yarmouth Yacht Station for 11/4 to 11/2 hours after the water level has been rising.

The flood comes in as a "salt water wedge" on the riverbed, below the fresh water at the surface still flowing towards the sea. This may prove crucial to yachts with a large air draught that need to take the low bridges at Yarmouth at dead low water. Further upstream at Stokesby, the water starts to fall long before the flood has ceased to run.

Tides on the Broads usually flood for about five hours and ebb for seven hours. Speed of the current varies according to the distance from the sea, but ranges between .5 mph in the upper reaches to a regular 5-mph on the River Bure at Gt. Yarmouth. The ebb generally runs about .5mph faster than the flood. Whilst both current and rise and fall is slight in the upper reaches of the Bure, simultaneous readings by Anglian Water in April 1980, identified a very clear tidal pattern up as far as Hoveton.

The Confluence of The River Yare & Bure at Great Yarmouth
Norfolk Museums Service

Constriction at Great Yarmouth causes the Bure to ebb for about an hour longer than the Yare, whilst the North Rivers have about half the amount of tidal rise and fall of the Rivers Yare and Waveney at similar distances from the sea.

It is most important to realise that the timing of tides is imprecise and subject to many outside influences. Whilst it is possible to accurately predict lunar activity, the North Sea particularly and consequently the Broads, are subject to a range of additional outside influences which can have considerable effect on both time and range.

* Barometric pressure affects the sea level in the North Sea and hence the height of our tides.
* Wind direction raises the water level on the lee shore. Any Northerly wind can hold back the ebb in the North Sea.
* Storm surges affect both times and levels.
* Otherwise unconsidered weather patterns on the West Coast or around Iceland can also affect the passage of water out of the North Sea and hence our Broads tides.
* Rain and drainage from the marshes upriver also have their influence; these effects are particularly noticeable where the Rivers are constricted, such as the Bure at Yarmouth or the Waveney at Beccles. The Upper Broads drain huge areas of land.

Add to the time of Low Water at Yarmouth Yacht Station for: -

	High Water	Low Water	Av. Summer Springs Range metres
Acle Bridge	7.5 hours	2.5	.5
Barton Broad	-	-	
Beccles	8	3	.6
Burgh Castle	5	.5	1.2
Brundall	8	3	.3
Buckenham	7.5	2.5	
Horning	8	3	.2
Hickling Broad	-	-	
Horning	8	3	.2
Loddon	7.5	2.5	.76
Norwich	8.5	3.5	.6
Oulton Broad	8	3	.8
Potter Heigham	8	3	.4
Reedham	6.5	1.5	.9
St. Olaves	6.5	1.5 hours	.9

TIDES for Gt. YARMOUTH.

Johnstone - Bryden.

Nowhere on the Broads is it more important to get the tide right than for a passage through Yarmouth. Tides should not be a cause for concern - with just a little attention they can be a great help.

Yarmouth Yacht Station, the Broads Authority moorings (free) and the Port of Yarmouth Marina (which have little depth for sailing boats) are the only moorings available for several miles between the western end of Breydon Water at Burgh Castle or the Berney Arms and the Stracey Arms, probably an hour and a half steaming up the River Bure.

If a skipper is at all unsure of the state or timing of a tide, it is advisable to telephone the Broads Authority Quay Attendant at Great Yarmouth (01493) - 332314 from Reedham, Acle or St. Olaves to confirm how the tides are running. We cannot over emphasise the danger to craft in going through or stopping at Gt. Yarmouth with the tide at full ebb or flood.

TIMING A PASSAGE THROUGH GREAT YARMOUTH.

From the North River.

Power boats are best to go through Yarmouth at slack water or up to 2 hours after. "Punching" a slow flooding current gives better control of the boat for stopping or mooring, but skippers of boats requiring a large clearance at the two very low bridges over the Bure in Yarmouth may well be obliged to make passage at dead low water.

For sailing craft without power.

The best advice available to any sailing craft, without auxiliary power and considering a passage through Yarmouth is not to try without a tow, which can usually be arranged through either Yarmouth Yacht Station or the Broads Authority Quay Attendant. Unless you are VERY experienced, it is likely that you will at some point find yourself aground and swept across the river by the strong tides, causing a blockage to the river that other boats will be unable to avoid. This will almost certainly damage your paintwork and there is a possibility of major damage to your mast, particularly if it hangs a long way over the stern. If you have absolutely no option, here is the method that was used by wherrymen travelling to the South Rivers. They too had no engines, but the rivers carried significantly less traffic:-

Skippers intending to pass straight through Yarmouth should time their arrival at Yarmouth Yacht Station for Low Water. There will still be an hour of the current running down the Bure to take you past the Yacht Station and the tide will already be making quite strongly through Breydon when you reach the Yare. Sails should be stowed no later than Section B2 on Chart C. Downstream, the river narrows and there are shoals and posts on both sides that do not allow sufficient searoom to turn under sail. Buildings shelter the river and increase the risk of a loss of steerage way, which could result in the tide carrying the boat under the road bridge. Two quant poles might be helpful for this passage.

In a part of the river where there is sufficient space and preferably no motor boats to confuse, turn the boats bow upstream and into the current. From the bow, lower your mudweight. When it "holds" shorten the line so the mudweight is just brushing the bottom. (The wherries used chain for this.) You will find that you can steer with the rudder as the boat travels steadily backwards. If you intend mooring at the quay just before the first bridge, you should have a line coiled and ready to throw from your bow. If no one is on the quay to take your line, pay out on your weight and steer into the quay. When the boat is moored, the mudweight can come back on board.Trailing a mudweight over the stern of a boat is not as effective. When the stern is unable to swing, the rudder becomes useless, whilst any dinghies towed astern will hang over a quarter.

The Editor admits to a personal penchant for taking Great Yarmouth at Low Water during the small hours. This could not be recommended for any but the most experienced (and is both illegal and forbidden for hire boats, which are not fitted with navigation lights.) but for a particularly long tow or a yacht with an unwieldy mast, it almost guarantees the absence of other traffic.There would also have to be an admission of a fascination with Breydon's emptiness and bird life. A word of warning to the like minded. If Low Water happens to coincide with dawn (in any case a magical time to be on the river) then travelling upstream across Breydon and away from the rising sun, you will be heading into complete and utter blackness.

From the South Rivers:
Power boats should reach the Bure not later than Low Water. There will a weak ebb to stem through Yarmouth which will give more control of the boat for mooring or stopping in the event of another boat pulling across their bows.

Sailing craft should time their arrival at Yarmouth for approximately one hour after Low Water at Yarmouth Yacht Station. You may have to punch a slight flood half way across Breydon, but there is very little current at the beginning of the flood. This timing enables you to reach the mouth of the Bure just as the tide is changing and gives the reassuring feeling that should you have the misfortune to go aground, the tide will soon refloat you. Always pass to the south of the dolphin, to the north is a very shallow bank known as the Knowle. Should a skipper find the current still flowing down the Bure, moor before the the first bridge (Vauxhall). Commercial vessels often use Bowling Green Quay on the starboard bank. It is also possible to wait by hanging off the dolphin at the confluence of the rivers. (See aerial photograph page 44).

The new road bridge across Breydon Water has made passage for sailing boats without engines significantly more difficult in this direction. Skippers have two options; either to follow the above suggestion and raise and lower their masts between Breydon Bridge and the mouth of the Bure and sail (or try to quant) the short distance involved, or take the ebb down the Yare and wait for a while at the dolphin or one of the green mooring posts for the tide to change in the Bure. The Port Authority is reluctant to open Breydon Bridge for sailing boats able to lower their masts, as this causes considerable disruption to road traffic above.

Breydon Bridge at Sunset   *Johnstone - Bryden*

GREAT YARMOUTH - from the sea.

There are no good harbours to the north of Great Yarmouth until Hull on the River Humber. Facilities and moorings for yachtsmen at Great Yarmouth, either sheltering or entering the Broads from the sea are virtually non-existent and given freedom of choice a skipper would be best advised to make for Lowestoft. The bar across Gt. Yarmouth harbour (61m wide) can be choppy, particularly with a strong south easterly wind and an ebb tide. Yachts with low power are advised to enter harbour on slack water, as there are strong eddies and currents at the entrance.

Vessels unable to lower their masts or with excessive air draft (see clearance under bridges.) will not be able to gain access to the River Bure, but can, when bridges are lifted, travel up the River Yare as far as the Postwick Bridge (about 23 miles), if their air draft is greater than 10.67m (35'). All remaining bridges to Norwich some 26 miles away will open - eventually. If the yacht's air draught is less than 7.5m (24ft.), Haddiscoe New Cut provides access to a further 25 miles of cruising on the River Waveney to Beccles and Oulton Broad amongst some of the most picturesque scenery on the Broads. Arrangements can be made at most local boatyards to crane out the mast of a sea going sailing boat.

In the event of a delayed entrance, Yarmouth Port Authority suggests anchoring in any part of Caister or Yarmouth Roads; small craft will find the best anchorage to the west of Caister shoal. In easterly winds, the sea conditions can be unpleasant and the best anchorages will be found close to the shallowest part of the banks, indicated by the heaviest breakers. It is not uncommon to find commercial traffic anchored off the harbour mouth, whilst anchoring is requested well away from the approaches to the port. If you are obliged to lie uncomfortably to anchor in rough weather, an erudite crewmember may point out that Daniel Defoe described Robinson Crusoe's adventures, starting from an anchorage in Yarmouth Roads.

Yachts entering or leaving the harbour are requested to make early contact with the Port Authority either on VHF Channel 12 or by mobile phone: (01493) - 335500. Traffic signals are exhibited on the red brick building on the east end of the South Pier. Vessels shall not enter the harbour when three red lights are disposed vertically. Should these lights fail at night, the Brush Light, the leading lights and the South Piers lights will be extinguished or vessels will be informed by Yarmouth Port Radio. When three red lights disposed vertically are exhibited from the north side of the Port Control Office at the root of South Pier, then vessels heading back to sea, shall not pass south of the lifeboat house which is approximately 400m metres NW of Brush Bend.

There are slipways near Gorleston Lifeboat house on Riverside. Potential users should beware of launching near Low Water, as these slips seem to end without warning. Yarmouth's new power station immediately to the north of the harbour makes a useful landmark.

Yarmouth is a commercial harbour and skippers should keep a look out for such traffic. The River Yare is narrow enough to cause larger ships to leave the harbour astern, whilst ships able to turn can fill the whole river. Moorings are available within the harbour for pleasure craft on Town Quay but it must be pointed out that these provide no facilities for yachtsmen. The disabled, elderly or very young will experience great difficulty getting ashore at low water. Should you be obliged to moor in Great Yarmouth, Hamilton's Restaurant is down a narrow "Row" just behind the Town Hall. Lazzarella is a small Italian Restaurant with a choice of either a very small dining room or al fresco eating on tables in the courtyard, two minutes walk away. Credit Cards are not accepted.

Lazzarella, No3, Row 75, Howard St. North, Great Yarmouth. Norfolk.
NR20 2PU. Tel: (01493) - 330622. Hamilton's other restaurants in Great
Yarmouth are found in the other section on the town at the head of the
River Bure index (page 113).

Great Yarmouth Port Authority is located at 20 - 21 South Quay, Great
Yarmouth, Norfolk. NR30 2RE. Tel: (01493) - 335500.

Navigational charts of Gt. Yarmouth Harbour and its entrance are not
provided with this publication and good pilotage information is
recommended. Charts and harbour information should be checked as
the offshore sands are constantly moving and details are subject to
modification. Easterly gales can cause temporary shoaling.

MHWS 2.4m MLWS 0.5m.
MHWN 2.0m MLWN 1.0m.
Depth at Bar 6.25m (20') Neaps 6.63m (18').
High tide is given as two hours twenty-one minutes before HW Dover.

Haven Bridge. Great Yarmouth. Beyond the limits of navigation for
Broads hire craft. Tide; add 45 minutes to Yarmouth Bar. Rise and fall:
Springs 2.03m (6.5') Neaps 1.72 (5.5'). The rate of ebb at Haven Bridge of
ordinary tides is 2 knots neaps and 3.5 knots springs, whilst the rate of
flood is 1.5 knots neaps and 3 knots springs. Haven bridge has over 2.9
metres (9.5') clearance at Average High Water and over 4.37m (14') at low
water. Width of the bridge is 26.8m (88'). This bridge is no longer manned
and craft requiring bridge lifts should make prior arrangements through
the Harbour Office on (01493) - 335500. Weekend lifts should be

arranged before 1500 hours the previous Friday. When vessels requiring bridge lifts are approaching from opposite sides, the vessel which is running with the tide will have priority over the vessel stemming the tide.

The south bank of the River Yare at Great Yarmouth is properly known as Gorleston. There is a large sandy beach and Hamilton's Navigators may care to try another of our recommended restaurants:-

Piccolos, a very small Italian Restaurant at 16 Beach Road, close to Brush Light in Gorleston. Tel: (01493) - 668642. Booking is essential.

More economically priced is Cozies Restaurant, (named after the wooden "snugs" set in the old pier at Gorleston.) at 28 Baker St., Gorleston. Tel: (01493) - 651065. Again, a reservation is recommended. Credit cards are accepted. Monsieur le patron, Philip Grapes runs a good restaurant where you can dine under the gaze of film stars your children won't remember.

Hamilton's pub is the Dock Tavern, right down on Riverside, beside Somerfield's store. A "must visit" for the real ale enthusiast - no food and no juke box but at last count, sixteen real ales. The Dock Tavern, Dock Tavern Lane, Gorleston. Tel: (01493) - 442255.

Dinghy racing is held by the Great Yarmouth and Gorleston Sailing Club from Gorleston beach, just to the South of the harbour mouth. Secretary: Thomas Carr, 9 Corton Road, Norwich NR1 3BP. (01603) - 612035.

Boatyards.

Gorleston Marine Ltd., Beach Road, Gorleston. Tel: (01493) - 661883. Fax: (01493) - 657441. Outboard motor specialist and Yamaha agent.

Bure Marine. Breydon Road, Gt. Yarmouth. Tel: (01493) - 656996.
Bure Marine is the nearest yard facilities for yachts from the North Sea.

Beside and upstream of the Haven Bridge at *Stonecutters Quay* is a day trip company:
Mermaid Cruises. Tel: (01493) - 728876.

Broads Hire Craft are not permitted downstream of the confluence of the rivers Yare and Bure.

BREYDON WATER. Chart C. BN1 to BN7

Some approach Breydon with apprehension, but provided skippers make certain of their tides at Gt. Yarmouth beforehand, there really should be no difficulties.

Breydon Water falls under the jurisdiction of the Great Yarmouth Port Authority. Breydon Bridge (01493) - 651275 will lift, although craft that have to lower masts etc. for the Bure, should also leave them down for this bridge. Clearance is 3.96m (13.25') and 3.50m (11.5') for the fixed side spans and 3.50m (11.5') for the lifting span. The bridge monitors VHF Channel 12 and is manned from 0600 - 2200 from mid April to mid October and from 0800 - 1700 during the winter. Pleasure craft should pass through the starboard (right hand) span in either direction. All craft should keep clear of the central lifting section if three vertical red "stop" lights are showing as this will usually mean that a large vessel, which may be unseen, is about to pass through the bridge. Lockgate Mill, preserved under a shiny aluminium cap, is visible for some distance on the north bank when approaching the Berney Arms.

Breydon Water is approximately four miles long and is the remnant of a vast estuary flowing into the North Sea that included the Rivers from Beccles to Norwich and opened out between the Roman castle at Burgh Castle and the Roman town at Caister. The Romans knew this estuary as Gariensus Ostium. What is now Great Yarmouth, was probably little more than an area of mid channel silting. The Ant joined the Thurne, which then flowed the other way, into the sea near Winterton, whilst the Bure joined the sea just north of Caister.

The tidal flow is uneven at the confluence of the Rivers Waveney and Yare at the western end of Breydon Water. The flooding tide slows and almost stops when it reaches the level of the mud flats. After the flats have filled, the current continues to flow on, up the respective rivers.

Red posts mark the port (left) side of the channel travelling upstream towards Norwich, whilst green posts with white tops mark the starboard side. In poor visibility, yachts fitted with radar will find the posts very visible with the radar set on a quarter of a mile. Fog is a particular hazard on Breydon and can be totally disorientating. If fog descends quickly, the best advice is to lower the mudweight as soon as possible and wait for the fog to lift. In this event, a good lookout should be kept for other, particularly commercial vessels. There is no speed limit signed on Breydon Water, but safe navigation speeds are defined in the International Collision Regulations. The Editor would like to enter a personal plea that large motor yachts travelling at twenty knots past a sailing cruiser with her mast down, can cause a considerable amount of damage when the mast is rolled out of its crutch or at very least spill the beer.

Keep strictly between the posts and in the channel, where there is an average of 3.75m (12') of water at ALW. Outside the channel are mud flats beyond the posts and there are no "shortcuts." A trip over Breydon at dusk and low tide, is a treat for anyone remotely interested in bird life. Most of the area now comprises the Breydon Water Nature Reserve.

There are no safe moorings on Breydon, so it's a good idea to keep the mudweight on deck and cleated, to prevent blowing onto the mud in case of a power failure. Should you be unlucky enough to stray from the channel and ground, you have a limited number of options. Lower your mudweight as quickly as possible and note the time. If the tide is falling, work out how long it is till the tide turns. For example, if there are 3 hours till the tide changes, then the tide will also have to make for at least another 3.5 hours for you to refloat. In this case you would be stuck fast for about six and a half hours. Hamilton's Navigators aim to take Great Yarmouth at Low or Slack Water; whilst they may be a little tide to punch after your mishap, you will never have long to wait to refloat. The nearest safe moorings are at Burgh Castle or the Berney Arms on the Yare.

If you do go aground, always check for leaks and don't forget to check your water filter for mud when you refloat.

RIVER WAVENEY. Charts A & B
(Saxon "Waifen" meaning waving or troubled waters.)

The sections of the River Waveney are numbered from the point where the mud flats of Breydon Water cease. The strong tide on the Waveney calls for careful navigation, but the river has deep water and comparatively few trees. It is a good sailing river, with particularly attractive upper reaches. The late James Wentworth Day described the Waveney as "a gentlemanly sort of river. Quiet, peaceful, lit with beauty, born in the deep heart of East Anglia, enriched by history and alive with birds and fish." It is an historic river, much less subjected to the changes the northern rivers have undergone, with no less than three castles along its length. Downstream of St. Olaves, at Herringfleet the Waveney provides the county boundary of Norfolk and Suffolk.

The Waveney is not usually a fast flowing river; surveys report a fall of 20m (67') between Hoxne (pronounced Hoxen and some miles upstream of the end of navigation.) and Beccles, a distance of 25 miles, whilst the fall between Hoxne and Great Yarmouth is recorded as 24.25m (80').

BURGH CASTLE. Chart A

Special Notice. If you are leaving Burgh Castle for Great Yarmouth, make sure that you will be going down with the last of the Ebb Tide. Low Water at Burgh Castle is 1/2 hour later than at Yarmouth Yacht Station. Slack Water at low tide is 1 hour after Low Water at Yarmouth Yacht Station. Average rise and fall of Summer Spring Tides at Burgh Castle is 1.2m (4').

The most immediately noticeable feature of Burgh Castle is the Roman Fort of Gariannonum, built to keep out troublesome Saxons, which can be clearly seen from the river. The roman fort was built on the south bank of a large estuary, although the west wall has collapsed into the river. At Caister, on the north bank of this large estuary, there is evidence of a further walled Roman and Saxon town covering 35 acres. Caistor by Norwich (not to be confused with Caister, near Great Yarmouth.) was the Roman regional capital, Venta Icenorum. There are also believed to have been Roman settlements at Reedham, Brundall and Thorpe. After the retreat of the Romans, an Irish missionary, Fursey established a monastery at Burgh Castle, although none of Fursey's monastic building remains. Fursey was canonised in the middle ages and his nine monks were alleged to have witnessed extraordinary happenings. These ranged from reviving a dead youth with the tolling of a bell given to Fursey by an angel and sucessfully growing a field of corn in three days at a time of local famine. St. Fursey's visions were also diverse and ranged from angels in full song, to a manifestation of the terrors of hell.

W 1R. A five-mph speed limit is imposed about 100m upstream of the Fisherman's Bar. There are free moorings for patrons outside the Fisherman's Bar. Tel: (01493) - 780729 and a footpath runs along the riverbank, in front of the bar to the Roman fort. There are no safe moorings downstream, with many underwater obstructions. There was a Portland Cement factory here from 1859 to 1880, which used chalk from Norwich and mud dredged from the river.

Burgh Castle   *Norfolk Museums Service*

Boatyards.

Goodchild Marine Services, Butt Lane, Burgh Castle, Gt. Yarmouth NR31 9PZ. Tel: (01493) - 782301. Fax: (01493) - 782306, carry out necessary service and repairs for both Blakes and Hoseasons boats. Moorings are available by arrangement.

Burgh Castle Marina, Burgh Castle, Norfolk. NR31 9PZ.Tel: (01493) - 780331, email: rdw-chesham@compuserve.com, just upstream have moorings and also a large residential caravan site, with heated pool, play area, laundry facilities, etc. Minimum depth in both these moorings is now 1.2m(4').

There are free 24 hour moorings on the riverbank, just upstream.

Jurisdiction over the river changes from Gt. Yarmouth Port Authority to the Broads Authority about 229 metres downstream of the entrance to Burgh Castle Marina, where the speed limit increases to 6mph.

W 2L *Belton Short Reach.* These banks are substantially eroded and unfit for mooring.

W 2R The banks have been piled but there is a mud bank which is exposed at low water runs about 5m (16') out from the bank. On a swift ebb, a boat can be irretrievably aground almost as soon as she touches. Average tidal rise and fall here is .93m (3') to 1.25 (4')

W 3L. *Dolers Reach.* No moorings on either bank.

W 4R. Black Mill lies some distance back from the river beyond the reeds. This mill was built in 1830 and was said to shake when working.

W 4L & R. *Bowling Alley Reach.* No moorings on either bank.

W 5L. No moorings. Towards the end of this section lays some dangerous old piling and stakes.

W 5R. A small, shallow emergency mooring by Caldecott Mill (also known as Bell Hill Mill) at the end of this section is available, with access to Belton.

W 6L *Seven Mile Reach.* Pettingill's Mill lies downstream of Seven Mile House in this section.

W 6R On this bank, though erosion has occurred, moorings can be found with a depth alongside of .93m (3') to 1.25m (4') ALW. All of this bank is liable to flooding at AHW.

Close to the bank of sections W7, 8 & 9, lumps of the bank (described locally as "hovers") break off; some are only .9m (3') below the surface at ALW, but they are not very far out and soft.

W 7. *Wiggs Mill Reach.* No moorings on either bank. Wiggs Mill has disappeared.

W 8L. *Humberley Reach.* No moorings on either bank. Toft Monks Mill. This mill has a cap, but has been converted to a summer residence. The speed limit is increased from 5 to 6mph.

W 8R

W 9L. *Leathes Reach.* No moorings on either bank. High Pylons cross the river in this section, clearance at AHW is 28m (92').

W 9R. Fritton Marsh Drainage Mill. Currently fitted with a black, corrugated, triangular cap.

W 10L *St. Olaves Reach.* Just around the bend is the village of St. Olaves. St. Olaves Mill. is a small, boarded, trestle mill. The Post Office in the village holds the key to the mill, which is open all year. Just around the bend there is a fixed iron road bridge with a clearance of 2.5m (8') AHW. Width is 23.9m (78.6').

The tide is still very strong in this reach and it is inadvisable to try and moor in the same direction as the current - turn into the current to maintain manoeuvrability. The speed limit reduces to 5 mph for the village.

W 10R From the end of the reeds to the windmill, there is about 160m of free 24 hour moorings with 1.56m (5') at ALW. Beside the mill is the exit of Blocka Run, which is not navigable but connects Fritton Decoy to the Waveney.

St. OLAVES.
(named after King Olaf of Norway. d1030)

If you intend to make passage through Gt. Yarmouth, St. Olaves is a good point from which to telephone the Broads Authority Great Yarmouth Quay Attendant Tel: (01493) - 332314 to enquire about the tides. Average rise and fall of summer Spring tides at St. Olaves is .9m (3') whilst High Water is approximately 1 1/2 hours later than Yarmouth Yacht Station.

St. Olaves is a pretty village, on the borders of Norfolk and Suffolk, seven miles from Gt. Yarmouth and nine miles from Lowestoft.

The remains of St. Olaves Priory, dating from 1216, have been excavated, partially restored and are now owned by English Heritage. The village of Blundeston is not far away and may be recalled from Charles Dickens' novel David Copperfield; but is more likely to be remembered as providing temporary home accommodation for John Stonehouse.

Fritton Decoy is a mile along the A143 from St. Olaves. Fritton Lake Country World covers 250 acres and has many attractions. It is open daily

from April to September. Tel: (01493) - 488288/488208.
Petrol is available from a filling station in the village, whilst there are public toilets and a pay phone near the filling station.

St. Olaves is served by Haddiscoe Station, which is almost thirty minutes walk from the village.

St. Olaves Bridge.

Hamilton's Pub is on the south bank, just upstream of the bridge and is The Bell (Tel: 01493 - 488249). This is a 15th century inn, open all day during the summer (which includes breakfast) and has both an a la carte restaurant and bar foods, The pub's moorings are free to patrons. The pub signs claim it is the oldest Inn on the Broads. It probably wouldn't pay to ask the landlord about the Adam & Eve in Norwich.

Hamilton's Restaurant is The Priory. Good food is prepared by Stephen Teasdale the chef/proprietor. A sensibly priced wine list is worthy of mention. Well worth the short walk up the hill from the river. Children are welcome but reservations avoid a disapointment at weekends. Mastercard, Visa and American Express cards accepted. Telephone: - (01493) - 488432.

Boatyards

Alpha Craft, (Hoseasons) Tel: (01493) - 488254.
Castle Craft, (Blakes). Tel: (01493) - 488675.
South River Marine. Repairs and maintenance, craneage. Tel: (01493) - 488469.

Waveney Valley Boats, St. Olaves Marina. Private Moorings.

W 11L   *Herringfleet Reach.* There is a shoal, (.9m {3'} to 1.25m {4'}
ALW) across the Waveney entrance to Haddiscoe New Cut which is shallowest
up against the St. Olaves Bank. The River Waveney has a deep section at
the point where the New Cut is joined. The current can run quickly here,
as the New Cut joins the tidal influences of both the Yare and the
Waveney. Crossing the mouth of the New Cut there are no moorings for
some distance. Beyond the New Cut, is a base for the Environment
Agencies operations.

Haddiscoe New Cut (see Chart C for Northern section.) was dug on
behalf of Lowestoft traders to make their town more accessible to
Norwich. Unfortunately the Lowestoft to Norwich Navigation
Company, which opened in 1822, was bankrupt by 1834. Prior to the
extension of the railway from Reedham to Lowestoft, Great Yarmouth
was always a more successful port than its rival. Lowestoft then had no
harbour, whilst Yarmouth was always much deeper and could accommodate
the largest ships. The Lowestoft company had hugely underestimated the
cost of keeping the sand bar at Kirkley Gap dredged to maintain access to
the sea.

Some 2 3/4 miles long, the New Cut is now quite shallow having an average
depth of 1.25m (4') at ALW. Haddiscoe Bridge spans the New Cut at its
southern end and has a clearance of 7.5m (24') at AHW. This bridge looks
high, but all but the smallest sailing boats will have to lower their masts;
there are suitable mast lowering moorings north and south of the bridge
on the east bank. The New Cut narrows considerably under the bridge to
12.1m (40').

Spinnakers Restaurant is beside Haddiscoe Bridge.

There are no other moorings on the New Cut, whilst nearly the whole
length is piled, much is old and broken, whilst the edges are very shallow
with submerged obstructions. There is a speed limit of 5 mph along the
whole length. The tidal rise and fall is .9m (3') at average summer spring
tides.

About midway, Haddiscoe New Cut is crossed by power lines. These have
a clearance of 28m (92'), so all broads sailing craft will be able to pass
under without having to lower their masts. None but the smallest sailing

craft would enjoy having to tack up a narrow waterway like the New Cut, but the prevailing wind often makes for a pleasant reach down the whole length.

W 11R From the private dyke upstream of the Bell, there are no moorings for about 1/4 mile until upstream of the centre pier of the old railway bridge. At the old pier, the speed limit is increased to 6 mph. Herringfleet Hills lie behind this reach.

W 12L *Hole o' the Hill Reach.* There are no moorings in this section.

W 12R There are a series of private quay headings on this bank. There is a disused central pier of a railway bridge in the midle of the river.

W 13L *St. Thomas' Reach.* Provides reedy moorings but the rise and fall of the tide is quite considerable, so care is needed.

W 13R Provides no moorings, reedy. Herringfleet Mill is the only remaining smock mill in the region in working condition. Suffolk County Council staff, on two or three advertised days a year rig its canvas (known as common) sails and give a working demonstration.

W 14L Mostly reed banks.

W14R From the end of the reeds and the bend up to Somerleyton Dyke, there are good, free, 24 hour moorings. The speed limit reduces to 5 mph. The moorings in the dyke are maintained by Crown Cruisers and there are no moorings between the boatyard and the bridge. The boatyard occupies the site of a former brickyard, owned for a while by Morton Peto but shortly leased to Lucas brothers of Vauxhall in London. Their bricks were used to build much of South Lowestoft, the model village at Somerleyton and Liverpool Street station. The brickyard closed in 1939 but the dyke is sometimes known as *Brickfield Dyke.*

SOMERLEYTON

The picturesque village of Somerleyton has a shop and a Post Office about half a mile away from the river, whilst the Dukes Head Inn is only 1/4 mile away. Somerleyton Hall was built between 1844 and 1851 at the wish of Sir Samuel Morton Peto, one of the great Victorian railway builders. He employed the architect John Thomas, formerly a sculptor and ornamental mason, who had previously worked for Peto when he was the building contractor for the Houses of Parliament. Thomas was to transform the 16th century hall of Sir John Janegan into a Jacobean mansion, "more Jacobean than any original Jacobean house" according to Pevsner. The Illustrated London News at the time referred to "the fairy - like qualities of the exterior and the scene of enchantment within" whilst Robert Kerr wrote in "The Gentleman's House" in 1864 of "a design characterised by a good deal of pretentiousness and that of an unsuccessful kind". Hamilton's Navigators are able to judge for themselves, as Lord Somerleyton's home and its 12 acres of gardens, including a famous maze, are open from Easter to the end of September on Thursdays, Sundays and Bank holidays from 1230 to 1730. During July and August the Hall is open for the same hours but for Tuesday, Wednesday, Thursday, Sunday and Bank Holidays. Tel: (01502) - 730224.

The attractive estate village is based on Blaise Hamlet, near Bristol, an English Model village, designed by John Nash.

There is a train service from Somerleyton to both Norwich and Lowestoft.

W 15L *Somerleyton Reach or Whitehouse Reach.* Somerleyton Swing Bridge will open on request. The "bridge will open" sign is fixed and the bridge keepers put out a board giving the number of minutes to wait, if a train is expected. Three short blasts signals a request to open the bridge, but these are not generally necessary. One red flag means the bridge is operational, two red flags means the bridge will not open. The clearance on this bridge is 2.6m (8.5') AHW. Width available is 16.4m (54'). This bridge has no telephone or VHF communication, but is manned on a 24 hr. basis. There is a strong tide, with a rise and fall of .91m (3'). The speed limit is once again increased to 6 mph upstream of the bridge.

W 15R No moorings in this section, either below or above the bridge. Reedy with a strong current.

W 16L *Barber's Pole Reach.* Reed Banks and saltings. The Black Mill dyke is not recommended for moorings and has no footpath. The ivy covered remains of the steam pump chimney can be seen. Black Mill and Strumpshaw, on the Yare are the only steam pump chimneys remaining intact.

W 16R   Opposite Black Mill, is an outlet that may make an emergency mooring. Somerleyton village is about a mile by a footpath.

W 17L   Reedy moorings best used on a rising tide.

W 18L   *Long Galley Reach.*

W 18R   Reedy moorings with a rise and fall of .93m (3').

Change to Chart B going upstream, Chart A going downstream.

W 19L   *Short Galley Reach.* Reedy moorings, care should be taken over the state of the tide.

W 19R   No moorings.

W 20L   *Carvers Reach.* Reedy moorings with bad landings and no access.

W 20R   There is an emergency mooring in this section with a footpath to Oulton Broad.

OULTON DYKE joins the River Waveney. Oulton Dyke was dug out on behalf of Lowestoft traders to complete the access by river to Norwich from Lowestoft, in common with Mutford Lock and Haddiscoe New Cut. Previously Oulton Dyke had been known as Lykeling Fleet.

The speed limit reduced to 5 mph. Oulton Broad is about two miles from the mouth of Oulton Dyke

O 1L & R   *Skeleton Reach.* (named after Old Skeleton Mill.) This first section has reed beds and whilst there is deep water, there is no landing or access. The marshes behind are known as Peto's Marsh, whilst wherrymen knew the corner as Horseshoe Point.

O 2L   The first piling cannot be recommended for mooring, but further up on the bend is a long stretch of piling with .96(3') - 1.25m (4') ALW alongside. Slutton's Dyke, which joins Oulton Dyke in two places, has been dredged for pumping mud onto the marshes. No mooring in the dykes or entrances. Carlton Marshes Nature Reserve lies behind this section.

O 2R   *Fishrow*, just around the bend there are good moorings.

O 3L   Reedy banks with shallows, to be avoided.

O 3R   No moorings. Piling below Waveney Hill is bad and private plots run all the way into Oulton Broad.

OULTON BROAD

O4 L& R Oulton Broad. Anglers often moor near the entrance and appreciate passing boats slowing down a little.

Oulton Broad is all navigable, with the exception of the shore around the Nicholas Everitt Park, which is marked. This broad has become notably shallower over recent years and boats with a draught in excess of 1.2m (4') can now expect to drag their keels, even in the centre of the Broad, on Low Water Spring tides. Average rise and fall of summer spring tides is .8m (2.75'). High Water at Oulton Broad is three hours after Yarmouth Yacht Station.

George Borrow, the Victorian author of "Lavengro" and "The Romany Rye" also credited with the expression " a fine city, Norwich", lived immediately on the left, on entering Oulton Broad. This bay is known as North Bay or previously Borrow's Ham.

Halfway down the Broad, on the right hand side are a number of boats moored to buoys in a bay known as Carlton Ham. Moorings are also now available at Broadland Holiday Village in Carlton Ham. The Holiday Village has not only moorings but self catering accommodation, including caravans, a bar open to the public, heated swimming pool and sauna, solarium and fitness studio. The smallest maltings on the north bank was once the home of A.D.Truman's boatyard. The maiden flight of the first hovercraft took place on the first floor.

The Nicholas Everitt Park covers almost 13 acres and was given to the Borough of Lowestoft by Howard Hollingsworth in January 1929. H.R."Nicholas" Everitt, notable local sportsman, author and solicitor was Britain's top spy in the First World War. He had lived in Broad House; now in the middle of the park, until moving to North Cove Hall, near Barnby. It was his intention to develop his property at Oulton Broad to provide sports and recreational facilities for local people, but he died before he could start his plans. Howard Hollingsworth stepped in, buying the estate for £10,500, which he duly presented to the town in memory of his friend. Broad House is now used by the Lowestoft Museum, which houses the town's collection of Lowestoft Ware. This porcelain was made locally for quite a short period at the beginning of the 19th century. The park now contains a wide range of sporting and recreational facilities, including an outdoor swimming pool and "Pets Corner" where children are invited to meet and feed the animals. The dyke through the park is known as *Landspring Dyke*.

At the western end of the Nicholas Everitt Park is the Waveney and Oulton Broad Yacht Club, who hold racing for dinghies and mainly local keelboats throughout the summer and also host a thriving winter series. W&OBYC. Secretary: J.Buckenham, 7 Cotmer Road, Oulton Broad, Lowestoft, NR33 9PN. Tel: (01502) - 581345.

Speedboat racing is organised on most Thursday evenings over the summer by the Lowestoft and Oulton Broad Motor Boat Club, who use the Waveney and Oulton Broad Yacht Club premises.

Facilities are available at the Yacht Station at the furthest end of the Broad, beside Mutford Lock and the Harbour Master (01502) - 574946, allocates moorings. There is a public telephone near the Yacht Station, whilst showers and other facilities are available to visitors. The Yacht Station also has a (shallow) public slipway available on request to the Harbour Master. The Free Quay, a public staithe given by the Great Eastern Railway in 1881 extends one hundred feet from the slipway towards the Wherry Hotel and includes the Everitt Jetty. Mooring arrangements can alternatively be made with the boatyards. The Wherry Hotel occupies a commanding position at the eastern end of the Broad but charges £5.00 for stern on mooring.

Oulton is the most urban of all the Broads and covers 130 acres. It is unique in its accessibility and boasts two railway stations, Oulton Broad North is on the Norwich to Lowestoft line, whilst Oulton Broad South is on the Lowestoft to Ipswich line.

The Dairy beside the Yacht Station carries a good range of provisions. It is a good man that resists one of their bacon rolls to ease the row back to the boat with the milk. Midland and National Westminster Banks are found in the village. There are several pubs, restaurants and takeaway food outlets around the eastern end of the Broad. There is a large Safeway to the south of Lowestoft and a large Tesco to the north. Rowing and day boats are available for hire beside the Yacht Station, whilst day trips on the Waveney depart from Mutford Lock.

Hamilton's Restaurant is the Parkhill Hotel in Oulton village for a special meal. A taxi will be required from the broad but the meal will be one of the best in the area served in a lovely small dining room.Booking, as usual is recommended. Credit cards are accepted.

Real ale buffs would be sorry to overlook the Green Jack Brewing Co. on Harbour Road, Oulton Broad.This microbrewery occupies an industrial premise just off Harbour Road. There are two bars, with decor in both distinctly industrial. It is not open at lunchtimes. Tel: (01502) - 587905. Just about next door to the brewery is the International Boat Building School that will prove irresistable to those who go misty eyed in the face of wooden boats. Further down Harbour Road is the Excelsior shipyard, home to a Lowestoft sailing trawler, now used as a sail training ship.

Pleasurewood Hills is an American Theme Park to the north of Lowestoft. It is open from mid May to Mid September from 1000 to 1800 and for reduced hours throughout the rest of the year. Tel: (01502) - 508200.
The Marina Theatre at Lowestoft regularly has international performers Tel: (01502) - 573318 or contact the Information Centre at the East Point Pavilion for details of the current programmes.

Taxis. Five One Taxis. Tel: (01502) - 515151.

Boatyards.
Hampton Boats Ltd., (Hoseasons) Caldecott Road, Tel: (01502) - 574896.
Newson Boats, Commodore Road, Tel: (01502) - 564598.
NJC Dayboats, 6 The Yacht Station. Tel: (01502) - 589556.
Pegasus Yachts, Caldecott Road, Oulton Broad, NR32 3PH. Tel/Fax: (01502) - 585631
Topcraft Cruisers (Hoseasons). Tel: (01502) - 563719.
Waveney River Tours, Bridge Road, Tel: (01502) - 574903.

Petrol is available from a filling station beside Oulton Broad North Station.
Chandlery. Jeckells Ltd., 128 Bridge Road, Oulton Broad - almost beside the Yacht Station. Tel: (01502) - 565007

LOWESTOFT. From the sea.

(Domesday Book, Lothu Wistoft)
Access to the Broads via Lowestoft is generally more satisfactory for private boats than through Gt. Yarmouth. Yachts with masts too tall to pass under Haddiscoe Bridge can enjoy far greater cruising on the Waveney. All the bridges between Lowestoft and Oulton Broad will open whilst Lowestoft harbour is open at all states of the tide.

Care should be taken to ensure that navigational charts to be used are updated prior to departure, as the channels are prone to change. Ness Point, just to the north of Lowestoft harbour is the most easterly point of the British Isles. The harbour is managed by Associated British Ports and the Harbour Master is Capt. J. Woolley, Port House, Lowestoft. NR32 1BG. Tel:- (01502) - 572286.

Rise Springs 2m (6.75'). Neaps 1.7m (14.75')
Depth at harbour mouth: Low Water Springs 5.19m (17')
Width of harbour entrance: 45m (150').
Width of passageway at bridge: 22.7m (75')
Depth MLWS at Bridge: 5.19m (17')

Lowestoft is a Standard Port and always found in the tide tables. High Water is one hour thirty three minutes before Dover. Those en route to the Broads with only Lowestoft tide tables may approximate the time of Low Water at Great Yarmouth Yacht Station by adding 25/30 minutes to the time of Low Water at Lowestoft. The harbour mouth has very characteristic shaped lights, marking the entrance on both the North and South Extensions. On the South Extension there are international port traffic signals.

Lowestoft harbour entrance.

When these are red outside the harbour, it is prohibited to enter; and similarly when the lights are red inside the harbour it is prohibited to leave. Usually this signal serves as a warning of the approach of commercial shipping and it is controlled from the Harbour or Bascule bridge. Approaching and departing vessels are requested to make every reasonable effort to contact the Bridge by VHF. Channel 14. Skippers may wish to bear in mind that the Port Control on the bridge have extremely limited vision. Any vessel without radio contact should pay particular attention to port traffic signals.

The Harbour or Bascule bridge has a clearance of 2.2m at Mean High Water Springs, with a reduction of .5m at the arch sides. The bridge will open for commercial shipping only, on demand. Pleasure craft may use a bridge opening for commercial shipping, provided that a prior arrangement has been made with Lowestoft Harbour Control - VHF Channel 14. Small craft may be given a bridge opening time, subject to 20 minutes prior notification at the following times:-

Monday to Friday, 0700, 0930,1100, 1600,1900, 2100 hours.
Saturday, Sunday and Bank Holidays, 0745, 0930, 1100, 1400, 1730, 1900, 2130 hours. Yachts in flotillas are requested to maintain close station to keep disruption to the road traffic to an absolute minimum.

Navigation in the Bridge Channel is controlled by VHF. with additional amber and green "traffic lights." The maximum permitted speed within the harbour is 4 knots. General Port details may be obtained from plans D and E on Admiralty Chart No. 1536, which is updated every year.

Yachts are permitted to moor against Associated British Ports property with permission or by the direction of the Harbourmaster. Experience shows that the cost involved is hugely in excess of mooring charges for the yacht basin and yachts not travelling straight through Lake Lothing are advised to make directly for the Royal Norfolk & Suffolk Yacht Club, on the south side of the harbour. Visitors moorings currently cost about £1.60 per metre per day (£10.00 per metre per week.) and arrangements can be made with the Club for longer periods. All vessels should contact Port Control VHF Ch. 14) before entering or leaving the yacht basin. There are no signal lights for vessels entering. A vessel with permission, may leave when three vertical green lights are displayed. Three red lights indicate vessels may not proceed.

The clubhouse, designed by Norwich architect George Skipper and completed in 1903 was built to entertain the Prince of Wales. It is an interesting eclectic example of British art nouveau. The facilities of the club are extended to visiting yachtsmen, including bars, showers, rubbish skip for waste disposal, car parking, bar snacks, etc.. The Club has a good, a la carte restaurant, where the tables are under the dissolute gaze of a full sized photograph of King Edward VII, the clubs first Royal patron.

Yacht basin depth at Low Water is now approximately 3.5m.(11'), although a bar is forming at the entrance to the yacht basin. The harbour provides berths for Lowestoft lifeboat, and from time to time the *Excelsior*, a Lowestoft sailing trawler, *Mincarlo*, a Lowestoft built trawler and occasionally *Lydia Eva*, a steam drifter hailing from over the border in Great Yarmouth.

Lowestoft Sailing Trawler *Excelsior* in the Yacht Basin

RN&SYC., Royal Plain, Marine Parade, Lowestoft. NR33 0AQ. Tel: (01502) - 566726. Fax: 01502 - 517981. Club secretary: Amanda Florence. Diesel, dinghy slipway and crane facilities to 2 tons are available. The Excelsior Trust (01502 - 585302), have two large slipways at their yard in Lake Lothing catering for just about anything up to 180 g.r.t.

Frithvale Chandlery lies a short walk north of the club on Battery Green Road. Tel: (01502) - 517992.
Lothing Marine, Commercial Road, Lowestoft. NR32 2TD. Tel: (01502) - 507545. Yamaha outboard motor sales and service.

Alan's Restaurant, just opposite the entrance to the yacht club on Marine Parade offers a good, cheap plateful for hungry yachtsmen.

Hamilton's Restaurant is an excellent Chinese next to the Post Office on Wellington Road, about half a mile south. The surroundings are unprepossessing but the food excellent.

Hamilton's pub is the Bluebell in Carlton Colville, a taxi ride from the yacht club. Nicely rebuilt old pub with good food and offering Green Jack Brewing Cos locally brewed real ales. Creditcards are accepted.

The Hollywood Theatre in Lowestoft is a four screen cinema complex on London Road South, hardly a couple of minutes walk south of the yacht basin. Tel: (01502) - 564567.

The large sandy beach beside the yacht basin has been recognised with a European Blue Flag, whilst nearer the pier, surfers are found on rough days at any time of year. The East Point Pavilion overlooks the beach and contains both a restaurant and a tourist information centre. To save duplication in a Broads orientated publication; Lowestoft's other attractions are listed under neighbouring Oulton Broad. Joseph Conrad, then a seaman lived at Lowestoft for a year as a new immigrant. His grasp of English had yet to be perfected and he was known in the town as "Polish Joe."

Passage through to the Broads involves travelling the length of Lake Lothing. Sailing boats are best advised to motor or arrange a tow. It may be possible to arrange a tow through the yacht club. There are no publicly available satisfactory moorings for pleasure craft in Lake Lothing, although there is a waiting pontoon on the south side of the lock. Lowestoft Cruising Club's moorings are on the north bank, quite close to Mutford Lock. Sec. Mrs. S.M. Bird, 12 Romany Road, Oulton Broad, Lowestoft. NR32 3PJ. Tel: (01502) - 531972.

Mutford Lock at the entrance to Oulton Broad has been recently rebuilt and reopened to enable access to Lowestoft from the Broads. This is the limit of navigation for Broads hire craft, which are not permitted through the lock to the "salt side". The maximum size of craft accommodated in the lock are length 22m (70') beam 6.5m (20.75') and draught 1.7m (5.5') at low water. There is a charge of currently £6.00 per vessel using the lock. It is recommended to book by telephoning (01502) - 531778. The lock monitors VHF channels 9 and 14 and is manned daily during BST from 0800 - 1100 and 1300 - 1600 BST. During the winter, manning hours are 0830 - 1130 GMT. The lock keepers are able to arrange the opening of Carlton Railway Swing Bridge and Mutford Road Bridge, if required. These bridges will not open at periods of peak traffic and 24 hours notice would be appreciated.

Mutford Lock was built in the late 1820's, as part of the ill fated Lowestoft to Norwich Navigation, which also included Haddiscoe New Cut. The lock is unique in Britain, having double gates at either end to enable passage at all states of the tide. International Collision Regulations apply up to Mutford Lock from the sea, thereafter the Broads Authority Bye Laws take over.

RIVER WAVENEY (contd. from page 63)

W 21L *St. Mary's Reach*. The speed limit is reduced to 5 mph for the village. No safe moorings. The banks and dyke by the Church are private. St. Mary's church at Burgh St. Peter is on a raised spit of land and has a distinctive tower of four steps; the nave and chancel are older and thatched. Everitt describes " one of the most extraordinary towers in England."

W 21R   No moorings.

W 22L   *Carlton Mill Reach*. The Waveney River Centre has a leisure centre, well stocked stores, fuel (including one of the few remaining petrol pumps beside the river), pump out, children's play area and is open 7 days a week. The two basins provide moorings for 170 craft to an average depth of 1.17m (3.75'). Waveney River Centre, Tel: (01502) - 677217/ 677343. The Waveney Inn, on the premises enjoys a splendid view over the valley but booking is advisable for the restaurant. If you are travelling by car, it may be as well to ask as many friends as possible to dine with you here. You can be secure in the knowledge that only a few of your guests will ever find the place by road.

The nearest Post Office is in the village of Burgh St. Peter, nearly two miles away.

W 22R   There is a stretch of piling in poor condition, moorings not recommended. Speed limit increased to 6 mph. Share Mill lies on this bank.

W 23 L & R   *Faithful Friend Reach.*   Low piling along both banks. Moorings are not recommended as the wash of a passing cruiser could easily leave your own boat on top of the piling.

W 24L   *Eight Mile Reach.* No moorings. Both sets of piling should be avoided as there is no depth at low water.

W 24R   Reeds and saltings.

W 25L   *Seven Mile Carr Reach.* No moorings, although there are two piled sections at the start of the reach.

W 25R *Castle Mill Reach* (once known as Barnby Mill.) Castle Mill Dyke mouths are bad moorings as the banks shelve into the river. The emergency mooring in this section is not one of the best, although there is access to Barnby 11/2 mile away. Barnby Broad is landlocked and lies some distance from the river.

W 26L   A reedy mooring exists with deep water 1.25m (4') on the main river at the dyke mouth. The dyke quickly gets shallower although the mouth may be good for shallow draught boats.

W 26R   Moorings must be chosen with care on reedy banks.

W 27L   No moorings on this bank. There is a footpath that leads to Burgh St. Peter via Eastend Farm.

W 27R *Six Mile Corner Short Reach.* Moorings are available at the Black Mill also known as Six Mile Corner. There is access by foot to Barnby; 11/2 miles to the Post Office and 3/4 mile to Barnby Siding.

W 28L *Cove Long Reach.* Banks in this section are rough and reedy with deep water.

W 28R   At Cove Staithe mooring is not encouraged nor is it good as the banks shelve. Upstream at Cove Mill moorings are better.

W 29 L & R   *Worlingham Mill Reach.* Moorings should be chosen with care. Approximately .78m (2.5') rise and fall of tide.

W 30L *Hanner's Yard Reach or Three Mile Reach*. No moorings.

W 30R Emergency moorings at Worlingham Mill. A marsh lane leads to the A 146 main Beccles to Lowestoft Road.

W 31L *Aldeby Short Reach*. An emergency mooring gives access to Aldeby (3/4 mile). A little further upstream at the staithe (emergency mooring) at the pumping house, with 1.25m (4') depth at ALW, has a footpath to Aldeby Hall. There is a Post Office and telephone, a public house, some ruins of an old priory and an ancient burial ground in the village. Moorings can be found with care.

W 31R The emergency mooring shown in this section should be approached with care, as shoals make the lower of these two dykes dangerous. Deep water and reedy banks elsewhere.

W 32L & R   *Aldeby Bridge Reach*. Rough moorings with deep water. There is a remaining central pier of an old railway bridge. Motor boats should leave this to port in either direction. Sailing craft should be mindful of the current flowing around the pier. Free 24 hour moorings

W 33L *Salt Fen Reach and Stanley's Reach* (downstream.) Just above the quay a long dyke runs NW. but it is very shallow and private. Not recommended for navigation or mooring. Day tickets for still water, coarse fishing are available in the village but be prepared for a long walk.

W 33R   No moorings. Shoals in places. Stanley Staithe, the remains of the Brickworks Cut was once known as Carpennter's Staithe.

W 34L   *Boathouse Reach and Lower Reach of the Mile*. Just around the bend where the reeds end there are good moorings with a firm grassy bank. The speed limit is reduced from 6 mph to 4 mph at Gillingham Marshes.

W 34R Rough Banks. No moorings.

W 35L *Betsy's Run* and *Middle of the Mile*. Piled moorings. The Beccles By Pass crosses at the end of this section. Clearance is 4.27m (14') at AHW. Width of this bridge is 28.9m (95').

W 35R Good deep moorings from Beccles Amateur Sailing Club to the bridge. B.A.S.C. Sec. R.Campling, 20 Darby Road, Beccles. NR34 9XX. Yacht racing takes place during most weekends in the stretches numbered

W34 and W35. Visiting yachts and powercraft are asked to take care through the racing fleets.

BECCLES. Chart B.

W 36L *Beccles Sluice and Town Reach*. At the lower end of this section the moorings are mainly private and many of the banks shoal badly. Aston Boats offer good moorings to all craft.

W 36R.   Beccles Yacht Station Tel: (01502) - 712225, comprises both banks of the dyke and part of the main river bank. There is a charge currently £4.00 for 24 hours mooring and good showers and toilets. Depth at ALW is .93m (3') to 1.25m (4').

The old bridge is low and has a clearance of only 1.98m (6.5') AHW in the centre. Width of the bridge is 12.6m (41.6'). There is quite a strong tide, so it is important to make sure your boat will fit underneath before approaching too closely. High Water at Beccles is approximately three hours after Yarmouth Yacht Station. The average range of summer spring tides is .6m (2'). Collectors of trivia will doubtless need to know that the time of High Water at Beccles Bridge is one hour earlier than London Bridge.

There are several "scores" along this bank of Beccles. These are effectively very small public staithes connected to Northgate by narrow passages. There is a public right of way and it is permitted to moor a dinghy for no more than two hours on every tide. Moving upstream the first is Tannery Score, Railway Score, Cambridge Score, Old Market Score, (The Score) and furthest upstream Puddingmoor Score.

W 37L   No moorings. Beyond the town of Beccles the speed limit is increased to 5 mph.

W 37R   There are public moorings beside the swimming pool, which is outdoor but heated. Water is on tap. There are no further public moorings on this section.

Beccles is an historic market town and without doubt the most attractive on the Broads. The name is thought to mean "pasture by the stream", whilst even Suffling describes it as "agreeably situated on rising ground." The church, built in 1369 is visible for miles and has a detached bell tower of some 28m (92'). Nelson's parents were married here in 1749, whilst Sir David Frost's father was a local man of the cloth.

Beccles has regular rail and bus services and there is a launderette in Blyburghgate. Just about every service the visitor could expect to find is present.

The Broads Authority Information Centre is close to the Yacht Station at The Quay, Fen Lane, and is open daily between Easter and October. Tel: (01502) - 713196

Beccles Museum is found on Ballygate and open from Easter to October, but closed on Mondays. Winter opening is restricted to a few hours on a Sunday. Tel: (01502) - 712941. This building was the Sir John Leman School and carries his arms on the North Gable. Sir John Leman was a successor to Dick Whittington as Lord Mayor of London.

Hamilton's pub is The White Swan, in the shadow of the Bell Tower. Hamilton's Restaurant is The Swan, Swan Lane, Barnby. Free House and Restaurant. Owned by a Lowestoft fish wholesaler; naturally fish is the speciality. It is advisable to phone in advance to book a table. Tel: (01502) - 476646. Credit Cards: Visa, Mastercard, Diners Club.

Boatyards.

Arrow Boats, House boats, chalet accommodation, dayboats. Puddingmoor. Tel: (01502) - 713524.
Aston Boats, (Hoseasons) Gillingham Dam, Tel: (01502) - 713960.
CC Marine, Dayboats and outboard/inboard repair. Breakdown service. Open 7 days. Tel: (01502) - 713703.
H.E.Hipperson, (Hoseasons) Gillingham Dam, Tel: (01502) - 712166
Waveney Valley Boats, Puddingmoor, slipway, craneage, brokers, engine sales and service. Tel: (01502) - 712538.

W 38L *The Narrows.* No good moorings, reedy without access.

W 38R No good moorings but some can be used with care.

W 39L Two small restricted moorings marked on the chart can be used. The small inlet just upstream should be avoided.

W 39R One good mooring beside the pumping station is well sheltered and has a footpath leading to Beccles, 1$1/2$ miles away.

W 40L   *Dunburgh Hill Reach.* In the lower reaches of this section a 100 metre section of quayheading will be found. With a depth of about 1m (3.25') ALW. The majority of the land in this section is private with no landing.

W 40R   Give this section a wide berth, trees overhang and there are some roots. No moorings.

GELDESTON (Chart B)

W 41L   *Geldeston Dyke Reach.* At the top of this section Geldeston Dyke joins the Waveney at a place known locally as Three Rivers. The speed limit is reduced to 3 mph. There are moorings on the dyke which has an average depth of 1m (3.25') The is a cut around the low concrete bridge that once carried a railway, to Messrs Rowancraft Tel: (01508) - 518208. Where there is a turning basin for craft up to 15.6m (50'). There is a village shop, telephone and Post Office. Hamilton's Pub is the Wherry at Geldeston.

A power cable crosses the river in this section at 11.9m(39'). This cable is low enough to require some of the larger broads sailing craft to lower their masts.

W 41R   No moorings, the banks have a distinct shelf along much of this section.

W 42L   *Barsham Reach and Lock Reach.* Much of the bank is piled high with dredging spoil. The right hand channel at the lock has good free 24hour moorings. This waterway is very old the Act of Parliament to improve the navigation was passed on 17th March 1670 and the earliest Act for this purpose. Geldeston Lock was last used in 1934 and its walls are now in serious disrepair. Historically it was known as Geldeston Lock in Norfolk but on the south, Suffolk bank of the Waveney, it was known as Shipmeadow (properly Sheepmeadow) Lock. This is now the limit of navigation of the River Waveney and is approximately 25 miles from Great Yarmouth. The Waveney rises in swampy ground about 1 1/2 miles south west of Diss at South Lopham. Not many yards away, just across the B 1113 road the Little Ouse rises and flows westwards. The source of the river is recorded as 58 3/4 miles from the sea.

There is a public house beside Geldeston Lock, called "The Locks", but still known to many with grey hairs as "Susan's", after the lady who ran it for probably fifty years. She worked without the aid of electricity or draught beer; the pub often flooded during the winter and she had dreadful arthritis. The bar was furnished with high backed pews and lit by Tilley lamps, whilst all transactions were religiously recorded by hand in a ledger. Susan was a powerful character and the youth that thought he was going to ply his young lady with strong drink had come to the wrong pub. Alas, Susan went the way of all flesh and the pub was extended, improved gaining a road and electricity. Nothing is for ever. The public house has subsequently closed but reopening is scheduled at the time of going to press.

Everitt notes with curiosity, very nearly a hundred years ago "the Puzzle Stone" just upstream of the Lock. He describes a square block of masonry on the river bank bearing the inscription: " This stone, is laid on the foundation of the old mill and over the piece of plank described by Mr. Thomas in his award, ten inches above the upper side of which plank is a watermark and three feet below, the bottom of this stone." He had no idea what the inscription meant and the editor's attempts to find it have proved fruitless. There has been a great deal of work over the years just upstream of the Lock, cutting new relief channels and removing the weir but it seems unlikely that a stone of such a size could have simply disappeared.

Wherries were able to trade up to Bungay, (both the town of Bungay and the river were formerly known as Avona, Waveney might be a corruption of this name.) through several locks, all now also fallen into disrepair. There is still a public staithe in Bungay, which is probably not overused. The Upper Waveney, when the locks were in use, was usually short of water, presumably due to the low amount of fall of the river. It would be splen-did to reopen this stretch of lovely river valley to navigation but the water shortage will not have been improved by an extraction plant about 500m upstream of Geldeston Lock, supplying South Lowestoft. Water extraction is causing great environmental concern for the whole of the River Waveney. A borehole has been sunk near the source of the river frequently abstracting large quantities of water . This has resulted in the drying out of both Redgrave and Lopham Fens, the springs that fed both the Waveney and the Little Ouse. The Otter Trust is at Earsham, on the banks of the River Waveney just upstream of Bungay and can provide a good outing. The Trust is open daily from 1 April to 31 October. Tel: (01986) - 893470. British otters are bred for release back into the wild and some have been released into the Broads. Whilst locals have seen signs of their presence in some areas, not many ever get the chance to see one in the flesh. The Otter Trust represents a unique opportunity to see the worlds' largest collection of these animals at close quarters. Also at Earsham are the small muntjac deer; no bigger than a small labrador (and just faster.) that are very common in Broadland but timid and rarely seen. The Otter Trust also has night heron and waterfowl; even the odd wallaby.

RIVER YARE.

This index describes the River Yare from the confluence of the Rivers Yare and Waveney, upstream of the Dickey Works groynes at the western end of Breydon Water. Notes for sea going craft entering via Yarmouth are found on page 49.

The River Yare is wide and deep and the reaches below Brundall are relatively free from trees. It offers some of the best river sailing to be found on the Broads.

The Yare can be used by coastal craft up as far as Norwich with an air draft of less than 10.67m (35'), although in practise, commercial shipping is rarely seen. Pleasure craft are required to keep clear of commercial traffic that will have severely restricted manoeuvrability. The coasters travel very slowly and will often be dragging through mud. If they hit silting on a bend, they can slew round dangerously, causing damage to any boats moored on that particular corner. Passing coasters first push the water level down in front of them, then as they pass, the water level quickly increases above its usual height, dropping to its former level when they are gone. This movement can impose an unexpected strain on mooring lines and rhond anchors.

The root of the Turntide Jetty at the end of Breydon Water is the end of Yarmouth Port Authority's jurisdiction and the beginning of the Broads Authority. The only implication to skippers is that Breydon is subject to International Collision Regulations and upstream of this jetty the Broads Authority's Navigation Byelaws come into force. The differences may only be of significance in the event of a serious collision at this point.

Y1L *Berney Arms Reach.* Good safe moorings between the Inn and Berney High Mill. Mooring should be single banked only to allow space for commercial traffic to turn. When travelling downstream this is the last safe mooring before Yarmouth. Hamilton's Tide Calculator will tell you when to expect low water at Yarmouth and how long you are obliged to wait in the pub. Not long ago the Berney Arms was not accessible from the land and all supplies had to be brought by water. It is a freehouse and is closed for the winter, which is advertised as the end of October to March. The onset of winter is apparently variable in these parts as the editor has called on the pub in mid October to wait for a tide, only to find it closed. When open, it provides pub food and is understood to charge £1 per night mooring fee.

Berney High Mill, built in the late 19th century, is the tallest working windmill in the country, with seven floors and a black protective tar covering. It was used for grinding flour and clinker for the cement works that were between the pub and the mill, as well as pumping the marshes. Now maintained by English Heritage (01493) - 700605, the mill is open to the public from Good Friday to the end of September and is one of the few Broads mills to be seen turning regularly. The Berney family had been landowners in Reedham since 1359 and were responsible for building Langley Hall.

The surrounding Berney Marshes are owned by the RSPB. Details of RSPB boat trips are available from the Warden, c/o Breydon Marine, Burgh Castle, Great Yarmouth. NR31 9PZ. Tel: (01493) - 700645.

Y 1R *Dickey Works.* The groynes are known locally as the "Dickey Works" at the river junction are a dangerous moorings, due to broken groynes and sea going traffic. There is a tidal rise and fall of just under 1m (3'). There is no channel between the signpost on Turntide Jetty and the shore. Stay inside the marked channel. Do not attempt a short cut as there are submerged piles.

Construction of the *Dickey* (old Norfolk term for a donkey.) *Works* groynes was blamed by the old time market gunners of Breydon for the decline in the wildfowl that just about provided them with a hard earned living. The groynes were built to cast the silt coming down with ebb from both rivers, straight onto the mud flats. Prior to its construction, the fresh water swept the flats clean at every ebb tide but built up a mud bar at the mouth of Yarmouth harbour. Haven Bridge was widened to permit vessels of 500 tons up the Yare and Breydon became subjected to much fiercer tides with salt water able to flood strongly up the Yare. Great Yarmouth survived as a port but the Breydon grasses and reed that needed freshwater died and much of the wildlife departed. Arthur Patterson always maintained that Breydon was the price paid for Yarmouth's harbour.

Y2 L *Five Mile Reach.* No moorings at all.

Y2 R. From the commencement of this section the bank has concrete reinforcement. Old submerged piles along this bank, barely visible at any time and as much as 6.25m (20') from the bank form a dangerous obstruction. Langley Detached Mill , which once had a red painted cap is in this section.

Y3 L&R. *Tile Kiln Reach.* Shelving banks. Shoals and submerged stakes. No moorings.

Y4 L. *Six Mile Rond Reach.* No moorings. A shallow shelf projects into the river at the dyke mouth opposite Six Mile House.

Y4 R No mooring on this bend. On this bank are the remains of Six Mile House Mill.

Y5 L Do not moor on piles as coastal traffic may swing here. Here is a group of three windmills. The two furthest upstream, Polkey's Mill with the remains of sails and Cadge's Mill with a flat top are awaiting restoration. The ruins of North Mill are furthest from the river and of course, lie to the north. The remains of a steam pump are also found nearby.

Y5 R Bank falling away, river bed shoals, keep clear.

Y6 L *Seven Mile House Reach.*

Emergency mooring at Seven Mile House. This is easily recognisable with the three mills and the steam pump just in section Y5L, just downriver from the house. There is a footpath to Wickhampton, some 2 miles away.

Y6 R It is dangerous to moor on this bend.

Y7 L&R *Bowling Alley Reach.*   No moorings.

Y8 L&R No moorings, reeds and saltings.

Y9 L & R *Eight Mile Trees Reach.* No moorings. Entrance to Haddiscoe New Cut.

CHANGE TO CHART D GOING UPSTREAM, CHART C GOING DOWNSTREAM.

REEDHAM.

Y 10L *Town Reach*. Good moorings at Pearson Marine Craft Ltd.,

Boatyard

Pearson Marine (Hoseasons.) Water, unleaded petrol, diesel, oil, Gas. Tel: 01493 - 700242.

Y 10 R. In this section Haddiscoe New Cut (about 2³/₄ miles long.) enters the Yare. It leads to the village of St. Olaves and on to Oulton Broad and Beccles via the River Waveney. Sea going craft are able to exit the Broads via Mutford Lock. (see page 71). There is a speed limit of 5mph for the whole length. Pylons cross the New Cut about midway with clearance at AHW of 28m (92') and there is a road bridge close to St. Olaves. Clearance on the road bridge is 7.5m(24'). All but the smallest sailing boats will have to lower their masts for this bridge which looks deceptively high. The New Cut narrows substantially to 12.1m (40') under the road bridge.

There are no good or safe moorings on the New Cut until south of Haddiscoe bridge. The banks have broken down piling, shoals or underwater obstructions. There is a small piece of quay heading north of the bridge on the east bank, for mast lowering with a depth at ALW of 1m (3.2'). The New Cut is getting increasingly shallow with an average depth of 1.25m (4') at ALW. See Chart A for the southern section and page 44.

Any moorings between the boatyard and the bridge are private. There are submerged stakes just above Holly Farm. The swing bridge has a clearance of 3.5m (11.25') at AHW. and a fast current running through it. Sailing boats are able to moor temporarily on the south bank whilst waiting for the bridge to open. The bridge opens on request but there may be a wait if a train is expected. The bridge will put out a sign giving an indication of the time to wait till opening. One red flag means the bridge is operational but two red flags mean that the bridge will not open. In the strong current, skippers should keep well clear until the bridge is fully open. Reedham Swing Bridge monitors VHF Channel 12, but has only a hand held VHF with a limited range.

Hathor clears Reedham Swing bridge under sail.   *Johnstone Bryden*

Reedham has a colourful past and was once a Roman station. Legend has it that Lodbrog, a Danish King was blown to England in a boat, having tried to rescue a favourite hawk. Lodbrog was taken to Edmund, King of the Angles, where he was murdered by Edmunds falconer who was jealous of his skills. The murderer was cast adrift without oars in Lodbrog's boat as a punishment. The wonderful vessel miraculously returned to Lodbrog's home in Denmark, where the offending falconer told the Danes that Edmund had killed Lodbrog. Lodbrog's sons, Ingnar and Hubba invaded with twenty thousand Danes, capturing Edmund at Hoxne in the Waveney Valley; where, tied to a tree they killed him with arrows. They cut off his head and threw it into a thicket. Edmund's friends searched for the head and found it in the paws of a wolf crying "Here, Here, Here" to the searchers. The wolf meekly gave up the head which promptly joined itself back on its body. Lo! two miracles. The remains of our royal saint were transferred to St. Edmundsbury (Bury St. Edmunds) where over the shrine, an Abbey was built. Despite divine intervention, Saxon rule was at an end.

For information on tides or towing across Breydon Water, telephone The Broads Authority Quay Attendant at Gt. Yarmouth Yacht Station (01493) - 332314.

Reedham has a tidal rise and fall at average spring tides of almost a metre (3') and high water is 1.5 hours later than Yarmouth Yacht Station. There are very good free 24 hour moorings along Town Quay which runs the length of the village. Double mooring is permissible but inadvisable close to the bridge in case of commercial traffic. Skippers should be careful to moor only whilst heading into the tide - even if this means going back under the bridge to safely manoeuvre into a mooring space. Attempts to turn near the bridge on an ebb tide can result in the boat being swept onto the piers of the bridge.

On the Green is a boat refuse skip, several shops including a Post Office, telephone and post boxes. There are public toilets behind the Ship P.H. There is a parish slipway on the Green, beside the River Commissioners mooring. The keys are held in the terraced houses behind. No doubt parishioners wish to reserve this for their own infrequent use but it may be worth a polite enquiry from an outsider. The slip is concrete and quite steep and would be best used on a flood tide as the diagonal cut across the green could cause boats being launched to be swept against the bank by the ebb.

The Lord Nelson, Tel: (01493) - 701239 and
The Ship, Tel: (01493) - 700287. The Ship is beside the Reedham Swing Bridge and its beer garden can provide hours of amusement, watching others negotiate the bridge.

Hamilton's pubs are: Reedham Ferry, a short distance upstream and

The Railway Tavern, well worth the short walk up to the station a must for real ale enthusiasts, or even those searching for the Holy Grail of the perfect malt

Pettitt's Animal Adventure Park, near the church, has displays of crafts, tame animals and birds to feed and handle. Tel: (01493) - 700094. They provide a "fun bus" with a pick up and return point outside the Lord Nelson P.H..

The railway station is ten minutes walk and has services running to Norwich, Lowestoft and Yarmouth.

Reedham Taxi Service Tel: (01493) - 700146.

Boatyard

Sanderson Marine Craft, (Blakes) Riverside, Reedham Norwich. NR13 3TE. Tel: (01493) 700242. Diesel, and gas.

Y11L *Taylor's Reach*. Sanderson's boatyard has five feet depth of water along the quay heading. Fuel and assistance of any kind is available but the quay should be left clear for fuel service.

Y 11R. Keep clear of large mooring pile which is reserved for trading vessels only. Chose moorings with care, mooring is not advisable during periods of high tides.

Y 12 L *Ferry Reach*. Good moorings, with .9 - 1.9m depth at ALW. at the Ferry Inn which are free to patrons.

Hamilton's pub is Reedham Ferry, one of the best pubs on the Broads, offering excellent food and facilities. Tel: (01493) - 700999) including camping, washing facilities, moorings and a slipway. Hot showers are available for a modest charge.

Reedham Ferry is operated by the inn and is a chain ferry. Skippers should take great care to allow the chain time to sink before crossing the path of the ferry.

The Red Mill is a capless mill which has been converted to a house immediately downstream of the ferry. Here was the original base of the Norwich Frostbites Sailing Club.

Y12 R. These are saltings with no moorings to be recommended at all.

Y13 L No moorings of any kind recommended.

Y13 R There is a quay heading running right up to Norton Mill, (built in 1863) below the entrance to the River Chet. Portions of this quay heading are not recommended for mooring. Beyond the Mill is the entrance to the River Chet.

HARDLEY CROSS is located on the river bank at the confluence of the Rivers Yare and Chet. Dating from 1676, it marks the historic limit of jurisdiction of the City of Norwich over the River Yare. The respective mayors of Norwich and Yarmouth met annually at Hardley Cross to discuss their differences. Yarmouth once tried to tax the goods and the citizens of Norwich that passed through their port.

RIVER CHET (or Ket).

C1 to C7. The River Chet is about 3.5 miles long and navigable for craft with a draft up to three feet. The river is narrow and has a speed limit of 4 mph over the whole length. Mooring on bends can obstruct navigation.

Hardley Flood Nature Reserve lies to the north of the river, just before the cable crossing. The height of this cable at AHW is 12.80 m (42'). Hardley Flood is an area of grazing marshes and alder carr that flooded in the 1920's. All subsequent attempts to redrain the area failed and it is now an area of lagoons and reedbed separated from the river by a small strip of land, which carries a public right of way. The bird life is wide and varied, although a purist may prefer the winter with the winter migrants present.

LODDON.

Loddon is a fine old 18th century market town, which since the Chet was dredged has become a favourite port of call for Broads holiday makers. There is a good turning basin at Loddon and free 24 hour stern on moorings at Loddon staithe and Chedgrave. Navigation ends at the bridge that marks their boundaries. Boat refuse compound, public toilets and recycling containers are found on the public car park alongside, whilst the various boatyards have their own facilities. Shorrocks Community Store is directly opposite beside the mill. There is a Broads Authority Information Centre at the Old Town Hall. Tel: (01508) - 521028. The centre is open from Easter to Oxtober, 1000 - 1200 hours, Monday to Friday and 1000 - 1500 hours over the weekends. A Post Office and other shops are just a short walk from the staithe into Loddon.

Tidal rise and fall at Loddon averages .76m (2.5')

Boatyards.

Aston Boats, (Hoseasons) (01508) - 520353. Slipway.
Gale Cruisers, (Hoseasons) (01508) - 520300. Caravan site.
Greenway Marine, (Blakes) Riverside, Loddon. NR14 6HA. (01508) - 520397.
Broadland Riverine Boatcraft. (01508) - 528735
Maffett Cruisers (Blakes) Riverside, Loddon. (01508) - 520344. Diving recovery.
Pacific Cruisers. (01508) - 520321.
Walklin Cruisers. (01508) - 520649.
RIVER YARE (contd.)   Chart D.

Y14 L *Cross Reach*. The bank before the pumping station is piled and has a depth of 1.9 - 2.5m (6' - 8') at ALW. A footpath from the pump from the emergency mooring near the pump leads to Limpenhoe.

Y14 R Reedy and no moorings except near Hardley Cross.

Y 15L *Little Head Reach.* Reedy. Limpenhoe Mill, an old disused windmill has a bad mooring.

Y15R Reedy with shoals to the entrance of Hardley Dyke. There is a good mooring at the mouth of the dyke, but with about .6m (2') at ALW depth.

Hardley Dyke is narrow and private moorings line each side. There is a public staithe at the end, signed "No mooring except for loading or unloading." This would make an emergency mooring, although turning will be difficult for larger craft. There is a 3mph speed limit for the length of this staithe and some submerged stakes, the remains of landing stages, close to the bank.

There was a Saxon village at Hardley Street and the staithe would have been dug to bring timber, bricks or fuel to the village by water. Between 1810 and 1840 the current, straight channel was dug to replace the original a few metres to the west. At the time there were three or four cottages and a pub at the end of the dyke; in 1854 a warehouse belonging to "Jas. Bellward coal & c. agent" and Staithe House, a pub managed by "Sarah Bellward vict." were   recorded. There are no longer buildings at Hardley Staithe and the nearest shops, telephones and Post Office are to be found at Langley 1.5 miles away.

Y16 L *Hardley Reach.* Chiefly reeds and no moorings.

Y 16R Marsh sides and no moorings.

Y17L *Devils House or Round House Reach.* Two sections of piling are marked on the chart that are not suitable for mooring as they have no suitable access. Reeds intervene between here and the site of a foot ferry (now apparently only used by British Sugar employees travelling to work at Cantley from the south bank.), followed by more reeds, submerged stakes and private boathouses. Walter Rye noted in 1901 that the Devil's House gained its name as no sooner had it been rebuilt, than it fell down again. Today we may be more inclined to blame the foundations.

Y17R Hardley Mill or the location of a steam pump upstream provide no mooring. The Round or Devils House at the ferry has a quay heading which is private.

Cantley Red House - pre 1912.

CANTLEY

Before the sugar beet factory, which dominates the skyline for miles, Cantley was a thriving centre of yachting. The Yare Sailing Club, which later became one of the constituent clubs founding the Norfolk Broads Yacht Club in 1939 was based here. It was said by Everitt to have become the largest sailing club in the world by 1897.

Y 18L *Limpenhoe Reach*. Moorings at Cantley Sugar Beet factory are reserved for commercial vessels serving the factory. If a commercial vessel is seen, take care to ensure they are not manoeuvring for the quay. The size of Cantley factory will have some effect on sailing boats, regardless of the wind direction. Round the bend is Cantley Red House Inn where there are good moorings for at least 100m on this bank. Tidal rise and fall averages .83m (2.75').

The Red House predates the sugar beet factory, which was Britain's first modern factory and built in 1912 with substantial Dutch investment. Everitt again cites the pub as "a remote inn, much used as a clearing house for contraband brought in by wherry" during the nineteenth century. The extent of contraband is surprising, given that the penalty for getting caught was transportation. Cantley railway station is only a couple of minute walk into the village and has a regular service to Norwich and Great Yarmouth.

Y18 R   Marshy and shelving banks up to the point where depth is only .6m (2') until exactly opposite the inn where the depth is 1.25m (4').

Y 19R   No moorings at quay heading, except in an emergency.

Y 20R   Submerged stakes on the bend are marked on the chart, followed by good moorings in places although these moorings are not recommended as they are on the bend. Depth varies from 2.5m (8') at the lower end to 1.8m (6') at the mouth of Langley Dyke.

LANGLEY DYKE

Langley Dyke has an average depth of .9m (3') ALW at the centre and there is a 3 mph speed limit over the whole length. Much of the dyke is lined with private moorings on both sides but there are free 24 hour moorings at a public staithe at the end. Originally cut to serve the Abbey, in the heady days of large regattas at Cantley, Langley Dyke was a significant centre for Victorian yachting.

The Wherry Inn (01508 - 528427) might be described as a good village pub serving real ales with a small restaurant. It lies at the end of Langley Dyke. There is a post box nearby.

The fragmentary ruins of Langley Abbey can be seen from the Inn and have been built into a farm.The Abbey was founded in 1195, when Richard the Lionheart was King, by Sir Roger Helke, then Sherriff of Norfolk and Suffolk. It housed an Abbot and sixteen canons of the Premonstratensian Order. The Abbey prospered and at one time owned nineteen Norfolk manors, as well as land in several towns in Norfolk and Suffolk. No less than sixty knights, barons and their ladies were buried at Langley and King Richard 2 lay in state at the Abbey after his mysterious death at Pontefract Castle. The ruins are not open to the public. In 1399, one John Skilley, a miller of Flixton was imprisoned at the Abbey for seven years " for his wickedness of eating flesh on Fridays."
Y 21 *Langley Middle Short Reach*. Reeds and no moorings.

Y21 R Old quay heading at further end of wood is marked bad. See chart. Above the wood, reeds and marsh provide no moorings. Just below the emergency mooring at the pumping station is a long patch of shelving bank.

Y22 L *Langley Upper Short Reach*. No moorings. At the clump of trees there is deep water and good fishing.

Y22 R   Emergency mooring with quay heading below the pumping station.

Y23 L *Hassingham Dyke Reach*. No moorings. The two floodgate outlets should be strictly avoided. Hassingham and Buckenham Broad lie some distance off the river on the nature reserve. They are of course closed to boats and were suction dredged in 1980. The bank here is known as Hassingham Hubbs. Hassingham Staithe was used by wherries until 1844 when the railway cut off access.

Y23 R Reeds, no moorings.

Y24 L *Ferry Reach*. Buckenham Mill is unsuitable for moorings as there are projecting stakes. It is possible to go to the mill from Buckenham Ferry. Upstream of the Ferry, the bank should be avoided owing to obstructions. Buckenham Marshes are owned by the RSPB.

BUCKENHAM and ROCKLAND(Rokelunda).

Robert Stevenson, the railway pioneer and builder of the "Rocket", constructed the first railway in Norfolk in 1844. It ran down the Yare valley from Norwich to Great Yarmouth with stations at Berney Arms, Reedham, Cantley, Buckenham Ferry and Brundall. There has been no ferry at Buckenham for over fifty years, but the name lives on, as does the rail service.

YL 24R At the Beauchamp Arms the moorings are excellent 1.25m (4') to 1.8m (6') at ALW. Fishing here is good. There is a 5mph speed limit enforced for .25 mile either side of the pub. The Beauchamp family lived at Langley Park, now a Public School.

Buckenham Sailing Club is based just downstream of the Beauchamp Arms. Sec: Jackie Howard, Oak House, The Street, Hockering, Norfolk. NR20 3HL. Tel: (01603) - 880224.

Y 25L *Buckenham Horseshoes Reach*. Emergency moorings with good quay heading 1.25m (4') at ALW, but the inlet is to be avoided as it is very shallow. The cottages just off this reach were once a public house called the Horseshoes.

Y 25R   Reeds and marshy banks extend beyond the bend where shelving banks spoil all the moorings. The public footpath from here runs along the track of a narrow gauge railway that brought sugar beet to be loaded onto wherries. The 15th century ruins of Claxton Castle, now built into Claxton Manor Farm are visible from the road, although the Castle is not open to the public.

Y 26L *Ashentree Reach and Rockland Reach.* From here to emergency mooring the bank is lined with old submerged piling. Footpath leads from emergency mooring to Brundall, about two miles distant across common land, but only half a mile to the nearest house. Further up this section the moorings are to be avoided owing to sunken piling.

Y 26R   At the beginning of this section the banks shelve. Short Dyke has been dredged to Rockland Broad.
There is a channel across the shallow broad marked by posts and buoys from both the Short Dyke and Fleet (or Deep) Dyke entrances. The Fleet has been dredged up to Rockland St. Mary Staithe where Rockland Beck flows in from Poringland, through Burnt Marsh beside the New Inn. There are good free moorings, a slipway and a public carpark towards the village.

A footpath runs along the wall of the Broad from the New Inn along Short Dyke and around Mill Corner out to the River Yare. There is an RSPB hide on Mill Corner. Rockland Broad was used as a graveyard for wherries and the remains of Myth, Tiger, Madge, Cambria, Providence, Chieftain, Diligence and the Star of Hope can be seen.

Tidal rise and fall is about a metre (3'.2").

A Floating Palace(1883) *George Christopher Davies*

Rockland Broad was home to one of the last of the Broadland characters to make a living from market gunning and eel catching. "Scientific" Fuller died in the late 1920's and was said to have had a remarkable feeling for movement of fish and duck and certainly for his own publicity. Styled by Christopher Davies the "King of Rockland", a title that apparently appealed to him, he is mentioned in just about every Broads book of that era and even had his portrait painted in his gun punt by Frank Southgate. There is a bus service to Norwich and a good off licence, shop, Post Office and telephone, open seven days a week in the village, which is about three quarters of a mile walk, west from the staithe. A pavement runs the whole distance.

The New Inn offers good pub food at the end of Rockland dyke.

Wheatfen Broad at Surlingham is closest to the river beside Rockland Broad and is part of what once was an extensive Yare valley swamp. It was extensively studied by Ted Ellis, an eminent Norfolk naturalist and local character, himself a protégé of Arthur Patterson. Patterson described Ellis as "having the eyes and ears of a hawk and the optimism of Sancho Panza." Touchingly, Ellis, who died in 1986, provided a foreword for a biography of Patterson, written by his granddaughter: "Fifty years after his death, it gives me great pleasure to contribute this brief foreword to a well researched account of his life, by one of his grand daughters, in whose eyes, from time to time, I catch a glimpse of my old hero." Norfolk is a place full of interconnecting circles.

Today, Wheatfen is managed by the Ted Ellis Trust, as a nature reserve of open fen, reed beds and the small broads of Wheatfen and Deep Waters. There is a nature trail of over three miles, with a shorter option for wheelchairs. The walk ends in Surlingham Wood. Ted Ellis bought the pleasure wherry *Liberty* and sank her across the entrance from Rockland Broad. *Liberty* was a small carvel wherry, built by Collins of Wroxham for their hire fleet, using oak from the Hoveton Estate.

Change to Chart E going upstream, Chart D going downstream.

Y 27L & R No moorings. Strumpshaw steam pump chimney is a landmark in section 27L and one of only two such chimneys surviving intact. Strumpshaw Fen and Surlingham Church Marsh lies to the North of the River. The reserve is 120 acres of meadow with a permanently based warden at Staithe Cottage, Low Road, Strumpshaw Norwich NR13 4HS. There are observation hides and an information centre. Strumpshaw Dyke, leading to Strumpshaw Broad, which is closed to boat traffic was suction dredged in 1983 to remove the enriched sediment. The bean goose is a visitor to these meadows come October.

Nearby, Strumpshaw Hall Steam Museum has a collection of steam engines including a steam wagon, working beam engines, fairground organ and a railway. Open from mid July to October 1 from 1100 to 1600 excluding Saturdays. Easter 1100 to 1600. Tel: (01603) - 712339.

Y 28L *Train Reach.* No mooring, marsh, reeds; further up the there is a private landing stage with a footpath to Brundall. Train Reach is the first part of the River Yare where sailing begins to be effected by riverside trees.

Y 28R No moorings. The bank is particularly shelving opposite the private moorings in Y28 L. At the end of this section is a dyke described as Brundall Bay Marina which has private moorings. At the end of this dyke is Brundall Motor Boat Club's clubhouse. Secretary: C.Coggs, Brundall Bay Marina, Brundall, Norwich. NR13 5TN. Tel: (01603) - 713399.

Y 29L *Coldham Hall Reach.* The banks of the river are mostly bungalows and private mooring plots. In Hobro's Dyke there are private moorings and a number of boatyards that offer good moorings and facilities. The Riverside Industrial Estate at Hobro's Dyke would push a point to describe itself as a scenic mooring.

Y 29R From the beginning of this section there are no public moorings as all the banks are privately owned. Moorings are good and free at the Coldham Hall Public House, which was built as a shooting lodge in the eighteenth century. There is a five mile an hour speed limit all the way through Brundall. The quay is particularly good with several interesting country walks in the vicinity. Surlingham Stores and Post Office with telephone and post boxes are in Surlingham Village beside the pond. Coldham Hall Sailing Club founded in 1951, is based just upstream of Coldham Hall Public House. Sec. Geoff. Pinder, The Hermitage, Chapel Loke, Surlingham, NR14 6HZ. Tel: (01508) - 538431.

Surlingham Broad. The South or Ice House entrance is just above Coldham Hall. It is owned by The Norfolk Wildlife Trust, but the navigation rights remain unaltered. Note; there is a three mile an hour speed limit. The channels have at least 1.4m (4.5') ALW depth as a result of extensive dredging. Surlingham Broad covers 253 acres and is a maze of dykes and waterways. *Bargate Water* is the navigable part of the broad. Above the South entrance there are no moorings.

Y 30L *Brundall Short Reach*. Private moorings.

Y 30R Private moorings only.
BRUNDALL, Chart E.

The average range of summer spring tides at Brundall is .3m (1'). High Water is approximately 3 hours later than Yarmouth Yacht Station. Salt water can penetrate as far upstream as Brundall.

Brundall has long been a major centre of yachting on the Yare and has in recent years been developed as a commuter suburb of Norwich. There is a frequent bus service to the city and the village has two railway stations. Brundall Station is next to the Yare Public House and Brooms Boatyard, whilst Brundall Gardens Station is closer to Norwich. There are services to Norwich, Yarmouth and Lowestoft.

Boatyards and moorings:

Alpha Craft, (Hoseasons), Riverside, (Hobro's Dyke) Tel: (01603) - 713266.
Alexander Cruisers, (Hoseasons), Riverside, (Hobro's Dyke). Tel: (01603) - 715048.
Bees Boats, (Hoseasons) Riverside, (Hobro's Dyke) Tel: (01603) - 713446.
Bell Boats/Bell's Marina.
Bounty Boats,
C.J. Broom & Sons, (Blakes), Riverside, Brundall. NR13 5PX   Tel: (01603) - 712334. Fax: (01603) - 714803. Brooms have one of the rare petrol pumps beside the river.
Buccaneer Boats, (Hoseasons) Riverside, (Hobro's Dyke) Brundall, Tel: (01603) - 712057.
Fen Craft, also day hire, (Hoseasons), Riverside, (Hobro's Dyke), Tel: (01603) - 715011.
Freshwater Cruisers, (Blakes), Riverside (Hobro's Dyke) Brundall. Tel: (01603) - 717355
Harbour Cruisers, (Blakes), Riverside (Hobro's Dyke), Brundall NR13 5PU. Tel/Fax: (01603) - 712146.
Lallagullis Sailing. Dinghy hire, RYA Recognised Sailing School. Riverside, (Hobro's Dyke) Tel: (01603) - 716317/410989.
Silverline Marine, (Hoseasons) Riverside, (Hobro's Dyke), Tel: - (01603) - 712247
Swancraft Cruisers, (Hoseasons), Riverside, (Hobro's Dyke) Tel: (01603) - 712362.
VIP Harvey Eastwood, dayboats, (Blakes), Riverside, (Hobro's Dyke) Brundall, NR13 5PT. Tel/Fax: (01603) - 713345.
Willow Cruisers, (Hoseasons), Riverside, (Hobro's Dyke). Tel: (01603) - 713952.

Fuel, oil and gas are available at most of these boatyards. Moorings are also available to boats of the same booking agency.

All local services are available in Brundall. The Yare Boatique and the Riverside Supermarket which sells clothing, chandlery and a wide range of fishing tackle is beside Broom's boatyard; one of the few locations where petrol is available on the riverfront. Taylor's Mace Convenience store (01603 - 713383) in Brundall Street (above the railway line.) is particularly good, includes a Post Office and is open seven days a week throughout the year. There are two repair garages also selling petrol; one at either end of Brundall Street.

There are three pubs in Brundall, The Ram at the Norwich end of Brundall Street, The Yare, a freehouse down by the boatyards at Riverside, next to Brundall Station; whilst up the hill from Brundall Station, the White Lion has a fish and chip shop in its car park.

Restaurants. Old Beams. Brundall Street, Tel: (01603) - 712215

Y 31L *Brundall Long Reach.* The dyke is privately owned.

Y 31R Old piling and submerged stakes make the banks of this section unsuitable for mooring. Surlingham Broad and Dyke are now navigable. See section Y 29R.

Y 32L *Back of the Fen Reach or Surlingham Short Reach.* Brundall Gardens Railway station is about 200 yards distant. Private bungalows are situated higher up the river. Brundall Broads (not navigable) lie off this section. Brundall Outer Broad was suction dredged in 1980 whilst the Inner Broad is thought to have been enlarged as part of Brundall Gardens. At Brundall Gardens are the archaeological remains of slipways used for repair and building of Roman galleys. There is a new, free 24 hour mooring at Church marsh with access to Brundall Street - but mind the level crossing.

Y 32R Reeds and no moorings.

Y 33L *Greasehouse Reach.* Marsh and reeds extend up to and beyond Surlingham ferry.

Y 33R Reeds up to within 150 yards of the Ferry Inn. There are submerged stakes and bad moorings up to the pub. At Surlingham Ferry the moorings are good, 1.5 - 1.8m (5 - 6') at ALW. The ferry is no longer in operation although its docking space remains as a mooring. There is a footpath along the bank for the Ferry Inn to both the Strumpshaw Church Marsh Nature Reserve and about a fifty minute walk to Bramerton Woods End P.H.

Y 34L *Surlingham Ferry Reach* and *Horseshoe Reach.* Reeds and marsh up to the corner. Mooring in the bend is dangerous owing to large craft swinging. Beyond are some old stakes and stumps.

Y 34R Marsh and submerged stakes in the corner of the bends. There is a footpath along much of this bank forming part of the RSPB Surlingham Church Marsh Nature Reserve. The marshes dry out at low tide and there are a couple of hides available. Local naturalist Ted Ellis is buried beside the ruins of St. Saviours Church nearby. There is limited space for car parking beside St. Mary's Church, Surlingham.

Y 35L *Brick Kiln Reach*. Emergency moorings only with gravel bottom. 1.25m (4') ALW. Path leads to Postwick 3/4 mile away. Reeds followed by sunken stakes and wherry wrecks.

Y 35R Marsh in the corner of the bends. No mooring on the bend; avoid submerged stakes and stones.

Y 36L. *Underhill* or *Norton's Reach*. Reeds or marsh. The wide dyke has submerged stakes and no useful depth of water.

Y 36R   Good moorings at the village common. There is a 5mph speed limit past the common and Bramerton Woods End P.H. The older Broads pubs are usually found on bends in the river. It is said that this was to ensure that when the wherries came to a bend and faced a head wind, they had somewhere to wait for wind or tide. Certainly all the pubs on the Yare are found on bends in the river.

Y 36L *Bramerton Woods Reach*. Moorings on the opposite bank are good so there should be no need to look for any here. Sunken stakes are shown on the chart.

Y 37R Excepting the Bramerton Woods End quay, no attempt should be made to tie up or even approach this bank - hard shoals and obstruction are everywhere. Bramerton Woods End PH. is picturesque and about 6 miles out of Norwich. There is a slipway, although this does end rather suddenly at the quayheading. Excellent free moorings with 2.5m (8') depth at ALW. Immediately upstream of Woods End P.H. is a long dyke leading to Kirby Bedon staithe, now almost completely silted.

Hathor at Bramerton Woods End.   *Photo - Johnstone Bryden*

Y 38L *Postwick Grove Reach*. Moorings cannot be recommended as the shelving banks are a menace on a falling tide and in the wash of passing motor boats. A five mile an hour speed limit is imposed upstream from this reach, till Carrow Bridge in Norwich.

Y 38R No good moorings.

Y 39 L *Postwick Bridge* carries the Norwich southern bypass. Clearance at AHW is 10.67m (35') In places marked on the chart there are stakes. Close to the wood there are sunken stones which project into the stream. The bend opposite the discharge is very shallow with a gravel bottom.

Y 39R No moorings in this section as the banks and dykes are those of Whitlingham Sewage Works.

Y 40L *Thorpe Short Reach.* A shallow shelf extends all the way up to the boat sheds.

Boatyards:
Maidencraft, (Hoseasons) Tel: (01603) - 435173.
Kingfisher Cruisers, (Blakes), Bungalow Lane, Thorpe St. Andrew, Norwich, NR7 0SH. Tel: (01603) - 437682.
The above two boatyards are located on the river.
Highcraft, day boats, (Blakes) Griffin Lane, Thorpe St. Andrew, Norwich. NR7 0SL.Tel: (01603) - 701701.
Griffin Marine, Griffin Lane,

At the end of Griffin Lane is the Griffin Public House and very close by on Pound Lane, is a large Sainsbury's supermarket with a petrol filling station.

Y 40R The shore here has a shelving bank. Do not moor or get too close on a falling tide.

Whitlingham Marsh is just upstream of Postwick Bridge. This is a small wildlife reserve, with one of its paths actually under the bridge. There is adequate car parking with access either from Trowse or through the sewage works, but none from the Southern Bypass. There is a hide and a screen overlooking two small ponds and both viewing areas may be accessible by wheelchair; although to a mercifully inexperienced eye it would seem wise to ensure adequate motive power. The noise from the Norwich Southern Bypass close by is considerable and constant.

Y 41L *Whitlingham Reach.* Private quays and bungalows up to the reeds. Just beyond the reeds is an outlet that should definitely be avoided with submerged stakes even at low tide. The shelving bank continues to the corner. The rise and fall of the tide is approximately .6 - .91m (2 - 3'). There are three rowing clubs on the River Yare just before Norwich. It is not at all uncommon to see skiffs and sculls with their attendant launches on these reaches. Skippers should remember that i) a rowing eight travels very quickly indeed. ii) they are not the most manoeuvrable of craft iii) they take up quite a lot of the width of the river and iv) they have very little freeboard and it is surprisingly easy to sink them with excessive wash from a motor boat. Hamilton's advise a reduction in speed of motor boats when passing rowing skiffs, as eight, very large and fit young men may take exception to a ducking. Local rowing clubs welcome visiting spectators and are pleased to welcome visiting rowing men at their boathouses.

Y 41R   Very pronounced shelving up to the quay and opposite the reeds and dyke mouth in section 41 L. The piling is broken and sunk and can extend as far out into the channel as 1.8m (6'). Mooring is not advisable within 100m of the corner due to the swing of commercial shipping.

 Whitlingham Country Park lies behind this reach, which has good car parking, public toilets and a trail suitable for wheelchairs. It is hoped that a ferry will shortly be established between the Country Park and Thorpe Green.

Y 42L   *Thorpe Short Reach, Hobrough's Dock*. Hobrough's was sold to May Gurney over half a century ago. The first dyke is *Commissioners Cut* where there are free 24 hour moorings in the dyke for no more than four boats. Depth at the end of the Cut is no more than .5m (approx. 18") at ALW. There is an area kept mown and seating provided, but the quayheading upstream of the Cut provides no mooring as it is very shallow. The next small dyke leads to and some private moorings and a boatyard. The remainder of this reach consists of private moorings. Here are the homes of the Norwich Frostbites Sailing Club and the Norwich Union Rowing Club. The Frostbites are one of the Broads winter sailing clubs and there will usually be a fleet of dinghies racing on winter Sunday mornings. The club has a large fleet of Norfolk Dinghies (a local one design). Secretary: C.E. Gilbert, 4 Furze Avenue, 4 Grange Close, Thorpe St. Andrew, Norwich NR7 0AX. Tel: (01603) - 434846. Access to these clubs is from Lane, Yarmouth Road, Thorpe. An unmanned railway crossing which may require use of the telephone provided, must be braved.

Thorpe Marsh behind this reach will be excavated for gravel when the Whitlingham side of the river is completed. The whole area will eventually be managed as a 43 acre nature reserve. There is access to Thorpe Marsh and the Station Marsh walk down Whitlingham Lane from Yarmouth Road, Thorpe at the Thunder Lane junction where there is a footbridge over the railway line.

Y 42R   *Whitlingham Reach, Cave Reach*. No moorings. Mooring can be dangerous due to the remains of piling dating from 1900, sometimes as far as 1.8m (6') out into the river and only just visible at low water. The dyke entering the river here was cut to serve the chalk diggings and is known as *Colman's Dyke* or the *Flushing Channel*. Large quantities of chalk were moved by wherry to cement works that were at Burgh Castle and the Berney Arms. These diggings are now overgrown and used as a picnic area. The dyke is no longer suitable for navigation and contains many posts and other obstructions.

Above the woods behind was the Colman family residence, Crown Point. A huge example of Victorian opulence with a particularly lovely, massive conservatory that would do credit to Kew. The mustard dynasty had the house virtually doubled in size by Edward Boardman, later to become Russell Colmans brother in law. More recently Crown Point has seen service as Whitlingham Hospital. Crown Point enjoys quite the best vantage point over Norwich and on a clear day the Britannia Pier at Yarmouth is visible from the roof.

White Lodge, a substantial house beside Colman's Dyke predates Crown Point but was used as the gamekeepers residence during Victorian times.

THORPE.

Thorpe railway bridges have a clearance of 1.83m (6') and are very deceptive. Both bridges have headroom gauges. Skippers should take these very low bridges as slowly as possible, making sure to not only lower canopies, flagstaffs and windscreens, but also to ensure that no member of the crew is standing on deck. This is an old course of the River Yare which leads to Thorpe Green. In 1844, the current course of the river was dug out, so that commercial river traffic could avoid having to pass under two low railway bridges. Whilst the road at Thorpe Green is still busy, it is a great deal quieter now the main A47 does not pass through Norwich. There are shops, newsagents and off licences next to the Green. Hearts Cruisers (01603) - 433922 are located on Hart Island formed between the old and current course of the River. Mr. Hart once kept the Thorpe Gardens Inn, now renamed the Rushcutters by Scottish and Newcastle Breweries. They are apparently oblivious that rushcutting is not a local activity. The pub does have good moorings and offers food and accepts credit cards. Tel: (01603) - 435403

Hamilton's pub at Thorpe Green is The Buck, Tel: (01603) - 34682, just opposite the moorings on Thorpe Green; bar meals are available.

Petrol is available from a filling station towards Norwich and just visible from the Green.

The River Garden, recently renamed has moorings for patrons and provides bar meals (01603) - 433540, whilst the Town House Hotel (01603) - 700600, is a Beefeater pub and restaurant, just upstream.

The dyke that was once in the grounds of nearby Thorpe Old Hall, was cut to enable wherries to load chalk from the nearby chalk diggings.

There is another and similar railway bridge at the upstream end of Hart Island.

Y 43R. *The New Cut.* The left hand channel avoids both Thorpe village and the two low bridges for craft heading direct to Norwich. Mooring is not advisable along this bank due to submerged piles and the wash of trading vessels. Whitlingham Country Park is planned to extend along this reach. The flooded gravel diggings here were created to provide materials for building the Norwich Southern Bypass. They are not connected to the river and are to be rehabilitated for leisure use. They are described as Whitlingham "Broad" and Whitlingham Little "Broad".

Y 44R & L *Aldecar Reach,* No moorings until the port of Norwich is passed.

RIVER WENSUM.
There were substantial Saxon settlements in this area and many churches remain. Wensum is Saxon for "winding" whilst Hythe is a Saxon word meaning quay.

Trowse Eye (or Hythe.) The River Yare joins the Wensum from the south; upstream of the confluence, the Yare is narrow, shallow and closed to hired craft. There is a sluice immediately past the Trowse road bridge. The River Wensum flows through Norwich and these sections bear the prefix WM. There are three bridges up to Norwich Yacht Station, two opening and one fixed. An open bridge probably indicates commercial traffic, so care should be maintained. Norwich Rowing Club are based at Trowse Eye.

Boatyard.

Kingsley Farrington, The Boatyard, Whitlingham Lane, Trowse, NR14 8TR. Boat builder and transporter. Tel: (01603) - 666545.

NORWICH. Chart E. (Saxon - Northwic)

WM 1L. *Swing Bridge Reach*. The power station is redundant.

WM 1R. Carrow Works, for many years the home of Jeremiah Colman's mustard empire and all built on what we left on the side of our plates. Moorings are private and factory wharves continue. Trowse Railway Bridge has a clearance of 3.05m (10') at AHW and 9.1m (30') width. The railway bridge opens on request and there is a mooring if you have to wait. There may well be some delay, as the bridge carries the main Intercity line to London. The bridge monitors VHF Channel 12.

WM 2L. *Carrow Bridge Reach*. Wharves continue and Carrow Bridge, clearance 4.27m (14') AHW. Width is 9.1m (30'). Depth is 3.75m (12') ALW. Carrow Bridge will lift, but now requires an engineer to do so. Contact is on VHF Channel 12 or by telephone. The River Inspectors are based at Carrow Bridge Tel: (01603) - 625091. If you must misbehave on the water, this might not be the best place to do so. On the right is Norwich City Football Club's ground and the Boom Towers that form part of Norwich's 2 miles of intact city walls. Dating from 1334, these towers were once joined by two massive chains of Spanish iron. The southern tower was later used as a coke oven to supply the local maltings. Fishing is good from Carrow Bridge right through the centre of Norwich. Through the Boom Towers, Norwich Cathedral is straight ahead, deliberately set to dominate and inspire the major route into the city.

WM 2R *King Street Reach. Queen Anne's Staithe* (now known as the *Turning Basin.*) The Port of Norwich lies in this section, most of which has fallen into disuse and commercial traffic is now exceptional. It is unfortunate that some of the river frontage has been adopted by a form of waterborne New Age Traveller, camping in a selection of extremely tatty boats, nearly all long since discarded by local hire fleets. The Ferry Inn has moorings outside at £5.00 per night. King Street is one of Norwich's most historic streets where several wealthy mediaeval merchants houses have survived the developers. The best known is the Dragon Hall, which is open to the public. Robert Toppes, a rich cloth merchant, born in 1405 adapted the building as his showroom. Toppes died in 1467 and the wool trade declined. The building was divided and subdivided many times until the great Wool Hall was completely forgotten. In the 1980's the build-ing was carefully restored and a wonderful carved wooden dragon in a roof spandrel gives the building its name. It may be a timely warning to all and possibly those who wish to walk, that King Street is located in Norwich's surprisingly thriving red light district. This is neither threatening nor dangerous, but it's usually as well to know where you're headed.

WM 3L These are very public moorings close to Norwich Thorpe Station, although a notice prohibits hire craft. The commercial vessels which may have caused them damage whilst turning, have not been seen in Norwich for years. A large new development on this bank will provide a footbridge across the river to Old Barge Yard off King Street, just behind the Dragon Hall. Opposite the Hotel Nelson is an old lightship, moored next to the Floating Restaurant. It has been repainted blue, with its light removed and is now the Training Ship Lord Nelson for Sea Cadets.

Southern River Steamers Tel: (01603) - 624051 run day trips immediately downstream of Foundry Bridge.

WM 3R The Swallow Nelson Hotel (01603) - 760260, is beside Foundry Bridge. This hotel has its own leisure club with heated swimming pool, sauna, steam room, jacuzzi, solarium and gym. Moorings are at Norwich Yacht Station.

Foundry Bridge has a clearance at AHW of 3.05m (10') and a width of 16.4m (54'). Ferry Reach is downstream of Foundry Bridge. The bridge was built in 1886 with iron from the foundry on the site of the Hotel Nelson.

Norwich Yacht Station Tel: (01603) - 622024, lies immediately upstream of Foundry Bridge, beside Riverside Road. It was built out the towpath in 1934 and is owned and operated by Norwich City Council. The Station Ranger mans the office for most of the day. Mooring fees are currently £7.00 for 24 hours. Facilities available are: Toilets (incl. disabled) showers, shaving point, hairdryer, tumbledrier (there is a small charge), fresh water, bins, barbecue and picnic area. Pump out facilities are also available for a charge, together with a strange request not to forget to lower a mudweight whilst moored alongside. The City Council gives the tidal rise and fall as 1.2m (4'), although it is unlikely to be more than .6m (2') at average summer spring tides.

Diesel and petrol is available at a 24hr filling station on Rose Lane, a short walk and just off Prince of Wales Road.

Pulls Ferry on the opposite side of the Wensum to the Yacht Station, is an old watergate, once an inn and beloved of generations of painters. The watergate was built to span a dyke the monks dug to bring stone for building the cathedral closer to the building site. From Riverside Road, just beyond Pull's Ferry, is a splendid view of Norwich cathedral, looking over the Norwich School playing fields.

If you need bread whilst moored at Norwich Yacht Station, a stroll to the bottom of Kett's Hill to Kett's Hill Bakery, where it is baked on the premises will be worth the effort. There is an Off Licence in a row of shops on Riverside Road, just before Kett's Hill roundabout. The energetic may wish to continue a little way up Kett's Hill and take some steps off to the right. This leads up to a small park known as Kett's Heights. Access is not suitable for wheelchairs or the less able. Whilst this would not qualify as Norwich City Council's best kept park; the view over the whole of Norwich is quite outstanding. (The entry to this park from Gas Hill is currently locked.) From beside the 12th century ruins of St. Michael's Chapel, which were used as Kett's headquarters in 1549; it is easy to see how his artillery could have been credited with the condition of the top of the Cow Tower, a free standing, mediaeval artillery tower on the opposing bank of the Wensum below.

Norwich has everything expected of an historic provincial capital and repays a little time spent exploring.

Suggested walk through historic Norwich from Norwich Yacht Station.

Cross Foundry bridge at the bottom of Prince of Wales Road, opposite Norwich Thorpe railway station, turn immediately right along the riverside walk. When you reach Pull's Ferry turn left towards Cathedral Close. Norwich School is within the grounds. The school's most famous product is probably Lord Nelson.

The Dutch had a significant influence on the area. In 1565, thirty households of religious refugees were brought from Holland to settle in Norwich and teach the locals how to make different types of cloth. Norwich is thought to have lost forty percent of its population during the Black Death and it was not long before the Dutch "strangers" outnumbered the English. Their impact is witnessed everywhere. The worsted industry may have gone, but the fore and aft rig of a wherry and the windmills bear witness to the Strangers; they even brought their canaries to Norwich for company.

Norwich Cathedral was founded by Herbert de Losinga in 1096. He failed in his bid to obtain Bury St Edmunds as his share of the spoils of the Norman conquest, so Norwich became his prize. His cathedral was built from Caen stone and not consecrated until 1278. It falls to us mere mortals to wonder, both how so much stone was brought from Normandy without proper navigational aids and once delivered, how ever a 96m spire, second only to Salisbury, was built without the aid of modern cranes and scaffolding. Visitors are welcome at services whilst Hamilton's more faithless navigators may wish to simply look around inside the cathedral, before exiting through the Erpingham Gate. The gate dates from 1420 and was given by Sir Thomas Erpingham, who lead the English archers at Agincourt.

If the morning's exercise has proved too strenuous, refreshments are recommended in the old back bar of the Maid's Head, where one of the nicest pints of Adnams is to be found in the city. There is a good second hand book shop opposite for those who, like the Editor, are unable to resist such places. Be warned; your crew will have to pass a silver shop and an antique centre on the way which may prove expensive. Tombland, the open area nearby was the original market in Norwich. Walk just a few paces down Magdalen St. (pronounced Magdalen; without Oxford affectation.) and take the first turning left up Elm Hill. This is a mediaeval cobbled street that somehow escaped the developers. There are several shops to interest visitors; art galleries, one dedicated to teddy bears and an extraordinarily hospitable off licence. The Briton's Arms, once an inn, but now a coffee shop, might provide refreshment. Just opposite the Briton's Arms, Hamilton's suggest that a visitor may wish to wander through St. Andrew's and Blackfriars Hall, now used for concerts and other public events; exiting onto St. Andrews Street Plain. Cross St. Andrews St. by the pelican crossing.

Briefly turn right and walk up Bridewell Alley to the left, which is both narrow and pedestrianised. On the right hand is a fishing tackle shop for those in need and on the left is Bridewell Museum. The museum was built of squared flints in 1325, as a home for a wealthy merchant, but later became a prison for tramps and beggars and briefly a factory, before conversion to a museum for local industry in 1925. It is open from 1000 - 1700 for six days a week between April and the end of September. At the top of Bridewell Alley is Hovells, claiming to be the largest basket shop in the UK., in a shop where basket ware has been sold for over a hundred years. Turn right and immediately left and carry on straight up Swan Lane. Turn right into the bottom of London St. (the first pedestrianised street in England in 1967 and one of the prime shopping streets in the city.). You will find yourself walking towards Norwich Market. As you see the market, on your right is Jarrolds department store, whilst a keen eye may spot a rare Victorian hexagonal post box to the left. Norwich Market is the largest covered market in Europe and if you have failed to find anything en route that suits your pocket; then you will surely find something there. The market is overlooked by Norwich City Hall (1938), and flanked by St. Peter Mancroft Church and the Guildhall, which currently houses a Tourist Information Centre. Tel: (01603) - 666071. Beyond St. Peter Mancroft are the Assembly Rooms, recently almost entirely rebuilt after a disastrous fire.

From the market, we suggest you walk through Royal Arcade, an art nouveau fantasy, designed by a local architect, George Skipper and built in 1899. Those who have sailed to the Broads through Lowestoft, will already have seen an example of Skipper's work, in the clubhouse of the Royal Norfolk and Suffolk Yacht Club. Skipper is considered to rate nationally amongst the very best of Victorian architects and also designed the Norwich Union Head Office in Surrey Street, Norwich; a monumental stone building with many different types of marble in its sumptuous interior. The Mustard Shop, a successful public relations operation of Colman's Mustard is found in the Royal Arcade.

From the end of Royal Arcade (it's worth a look back at the exit.) you will be able to see the mound of Norwich Castle, which dominates the centre of the city and its traffic system. In 1067 the Normans built a wooden castle, which was replaced by Caen stone and flint in the early twelfth century. The Castle was used as a prison for many years and fell into disrepair. It was extensively rebuilt and re-clad in Bath stone in 1830. In 1887, the Castle was acquired by Norwich City Council and converted to a museum and art gallery. Your closest access to the castle is directly opposite on Castle Meadow and follows steps up the Castle mound. The museum is open Monday to Saturday from 1000 - 1700 and from 1400 - 1700 on Sundays. Tel: (01603) - 223624. Guided tours of the dungeons are sometimes available.

Norwich Castle was besieged several times in the Middle Ages. Robert Kett was hanged from the battlements in 1549 and forty eight of his followers were executed after their unsuccessful uprising. Kett was 57 years of age; many local people felt sympathy for their modest enough demands and it required two Royal armies to suppress the insurgence. Beside the Castle is Castle Mall, a mainly underground shopping mall, opened in 1993.

Walk around Castle Meadow at the foot of the Castle. The large church like building of brick and stone on your left, immediately before Bank Plain, calls itself Barclays Bank. This is something of an undersell, as it was the first branch of Gurneys Bank, the family of Norfolk Quakers that founded Barclays. Just further down the hill is red brick building, once the Royal Hotel. It was designed in eccentric French Baronial style, complete with turrets, by Edward Boardman; Hamilton's Navigators may already have seen his home at How Hill on the River Ant. Prince of Wales Road was built as an impressive sweep from the city down to Thorpe Station and coincidentally returns you to your boat.

Hamilton's have pleasure in including for the first time, details of the two miles of River Wensum above Bishop bridge in the hope of encouraging greater use. Whilst this part of the river is beyond bounds for hire craft there is no reason why the short distance cannot be explored by dinghy or the Riverside Walk. To help turn and propel the wherries beside the buildings in the city, posts were driven into the river alongside the bank at about 12.5m (40') intervals between Trowse Eye and New Mills. Many of these have been removed for no good reason, but some remain.

WM 4L *Bishop Bridge Reach.* Bishop Bridge is the limit of navigation for hire craft. Built in about 1340 it is the oldest of ten Norwich crossing points of the River Wensum. Now closed to road traffic, in the distant past it sported a small tower which was home to a hermit, who was fed from passing boats. Opposite (under the old gas works) was the Lollards Pit where the bodies of heretic Protestants were thrown to burn in quicklime.

Bishop Bridge has a clearance at AHW of 3.2m (10.5') in its central arch. The size Byelaws regulating the size of vessels forbid a greater beam than 12'6" upstream of this bridge.

Zaks Waterside Restaurant is recommended on Petch's Corner opposite the Cow Tower, for the type of burger not found at drive thru's. It is possible to go up by dinghy and moor outside their old boathouse.

William Murrell Petch had a wherry yard on this corner, known to the wherrymen as Petch's Dock. There is a famous painting of a wherry being repaired here by John Thirtle of the Norwich School in 1812. On the bank is a wherry mast, regrettably without it's Jenny Morgan or fathom of scarlet.

This bank is mainly industrialised to Whitefriars Bridge. The six storey building, now occupied by Jarrolds, was built as a factory for the Norwich Yarn Company in 1836, on the site of Whitefriars monastery. Only a doorway remains to show where the priory stood.

Whitefriars Bridge. 1925. Clearance 3.6m (12'). Just north of Whitefriars Bridge, is the redundant church of St. James, Whitefriars, which is now occupied by Norwich Puppet Theatre. Tel: (01603) - 629921. Just upstream is a small jetty which was once a collection point for the City's rubbish; tipped into dismasted wherries and towed downstream to be dumped

WM 4R *Hospital Reach, Dead Walls, St. Helen's Wharf.* Norwich School playing fields, The Great Hospital. The banks shelve badly at *Petch's Corner* downstream of the Cow Tower. The Cow Tower was rebuilt in 1399 as tollhouse by the Priory and later used as a prison by them, before it was sold to the Great Hospital. Later the tower was converted to a medieval artillery tower. Just upstream, there is a small wooden bridge where a narrow channel leads into a brick basin, known as the Swan Pit. Built in the 18th century, young swans were kept here to fatten for the table. The Riverside Walk runs along this bank. Just beyond the Swan Pit is the Adam and Eve P.H., first built in 1249 as a brewhouse for those building the cathedral. It is the oldest pub both in the city and on the Broads and a pleasant evenings stroll from the Yacht Station. The walk closes at dusk but the return journey takes no longer past the Great Hospital, founded in 1249 by Walter de Suffield, Bishop of Norwich and William de Dunwich who provided the site between them for as a "shelter for poor and decrepit chaplains."

The Great Hospital was always closely associated with the cathedral and enjoyed substantial influence. Not only the object of a large number of substantial bequests, it also achieved a substantial income through the sale of indulgences in the middle ages. Miraculously surviving both the dissolution and indiscriminate German bombing, The Great Hospital continues to this day as an old peoples home.
The new Law Courts just are downstream of Whitefriars Bridge.

Quayside, just upstream of Whitefriars Bridge was the busiest landing place for keels and wherries with warehouses and stalls beside. Gossips, prostitutes and other women of ill repute were marched along Wensum St. (formerly Cook St.), preceded by a bell ringer to the ducking stool at Quayside.

WM 5L Fye Bridge. 1932. Clearance 2.9m (9.5'). Magdalen St. crosses above whilst the bridge is flanked by the Mischief Tavern and the Ribs of Beef PH. Opposite Elm Hill Gardens and the monastery car park is Friars Quay. This was a European Heritage Award winning "Flemish" style housing development from the 1970's designed to encourage housing back into the city centre. The Riverside Walk has been closed in some areas of this section for repairs to old quayheading. The Riverside Walk crosses St George's Bridge and regains the river at Dukes Palace Bridge. The large red brick building on the corner was once the largest shoe factory in Britain and it became Norvic Shoes. Until comparatively recently this block was almost entirely boot and shoe factories.

WM 5R The Riverside Walk leads up through Elm Hill Gardens behind Elm Hill, through a quadrangle known as The Garth. This leads to St. George's St., where the walk turns right past Norwich Art School to St. George's Bridge. Clearance 3.1m (10.1') and behind is Norwich Art School. Now much altered, St. George's Bridge, was originally designed by Sir John Soane and built in 1783.

River bus service from Elm Hill.

Duke St. Bridge or Dukes Palace Bridge. This bridge was built in the 1972 and the earlier steel bridge dating from 1822 has been incorporated with the Castle Mall shopping development in the centre of Norwich. Clearance 3.1m (10.1').
St. Miles' Bridge. Clearance 2.9m (9.8'). This cast iron bridge is now pedestrianised and was built in 1804. At pavement level there is a hole and a spout which looks as if it were for drainage but in fact was to enable fire engines to draw water direct from the river.

On a sunny day, enjoying lunch sitting outside at the wine bar at *Anchor Quay*, a largely pedestrianised development in what was once Bullards Brewery, might help prepare the strength for the row back to Norwich Yacht Station. The fermenting block of the brewery that had stabling for sixty or seventy dray horses can still be seen.

New Mills is the Victorian, water powered air compressor that blocks the Wensum and stops migratory fish from making greater use of the river. The original "new" mill was a corn mill dating from the fifteenth century. The current installation was built in 1899 and extended in 1936, to be used as a sewage pumping station. The plant was closed in 1972 and is now maintained by a charitable trust. Coupled with the work being done to clean up the rivers, just a little imagination and a small investment on behalf Norwich City Council could see leaping salmon and sea trout, once again running through the centre of Norwich and up the Wensum to spawn. It is not uncommon to see sea trout up as far as New Mills in August, where they are unable to travel further. The Editor has seen kingfishers at New Mills, right in the former industrial heart of the city.

New Mills is 29 miles from Great Yarmouth. Further upstream the River Wensum rises in Whissonsett and becomes one of only two Norfolk chalk streams in its upper reaches. The Riverside Walk continues upstream for three miles beyond New Mills where it becomes much more rural in character and links with Marriotts Way, a long distance footpath.

New Mills. The head of navigation on the River Wensum

Norwich Thorpe Railway Station is within sight of Norwich Yacht Station. Inter City and local services run from the station.

Norwich Airport has scheduled UK and continental services. The flight to Amsterdam (Schipol) is only 45 minutes. Tel: (01603) - 411923.

Taxis are available at 70a Prince of Wales Road from Beeline and Dolphin Taxis, Tel: (01603) - 767676 / 623333.

The Bus Station is on Surrey St., a little distance away from the Yacht Station; although there is a bus stop on Riverside Road.
Hamilton's Pubs.

As late as the 1960's, Norwich was said to have a church for every week of the year and a pub for every day of the year. The redundant churches have found alternative uses but despite concerted efforts by many of the locals, several of the pubs have closed. There are still a very large number of good pubs to choose from, but we have deliberately selected a small number, close to Norwich Yacht Station.

Maids Head, Tombland. Tel: (01603) - 761111. We suggest a pint of Adnams in the small, original back bar. Credit Cards: Visa, Mastercard.

The Adam & Eve, 17 Bishopsgate. The Howes family were landlords in the 19th century and they also traded a wherry of the same name from nearby St. Helen's Wharf. The wherry took chalk from Norwich to the cement works at Burgh Castle near Yarmouth and brought back sand to be spread on the floors of Norwich. Under the sand travelled the contraband; the Adam and Eve was another wherryman's pub. This is a small pub, but children are welcome in the snug. It is mercilessly open all day from 1100 to 2300. Tel: (01603) - 667423.

Hamilton's Restaurants. As expected of a provincial capital, the choice of restaurants is the widest in the area and can prove the most expensive.

Floating Restaurant. Tel: (01603) - 611129. This is located on a 100 year old, converted Dutch barge called The Vagabond, moored at the exotically described *Corporation Wharf*, beside Norwich Thorpe Station. It is only the shortest of strolls from the yacht station and immediately downstream of Foundry Bridge. Despite the rather dour exterior, the restaurant is reasonably priced, welcomes children and has a bright interior with good service. Customers are mainly local and most credit cards seem to be accepted.

China City Restaurant, 81 Prince of Wales Road. Tel: (01603) - 768688. Good Chinese restaurant that Hamilton's have no hesitation in recommending and just a few paces up the hill from the Yacht Station. Booking is advisable on Friday or Saturday nights. Visa, Mastercard and Amex cards accepted.

Adlard's. 79 Upper St. Giles St., Norwich. Tel: (01603) - 633522. A taxi ride from the yacht station but probably the best restaurant for miles around; Adlard's holds a Michelin star. A suitable location for a really memorable meal - both the quality and the price will be comparable to Central London. Credit cards: Mastercard, Visa, Amex.

Marco's, 17 Pottergate, Norwich. Tel: (01603) - 624044. Good Italian restaurant and a suitable outing for somebody else's credit card. Marco threatens retirement but his crespolinis are the best for miles. Behind some glass in the kitchen is a piece of the old City Wall in the kitchen. Credit cards: Mastercard, Visa.

Hamilton's Navigators may be excused attendance at Norwich's nightclubs. The city has a thriving nightlife till well into the small hours and within easy walking distance of the Yacht Station. Those who say they know about these things, recommend Ritzy's in Tombland (opposite the Erpingham Gate to the Cathedral) Tel: (01603) - 621541.

If the boat really does get too much, the Theatre Royal in Norwich is a short taxi ride away and rates as one of the UK's foremost provincial theatres. Tel: (01603) - 630000. Hamilton might suggest a meal after the show at either Adlards, or just opposite, Greens Seafood Restaurant, 82 Upper St. Giles St. Tel: (01603) - 623733.

RIVER BURE. Chart C and F.

B 1L & R. If required, between Breydon Bridge and the Bure there are a couple of white capped, green navigation posts fitted with "jug handle" brackets for mooring in emergency or whilst raising or lowering a mast. The shore to the north of the yellow dolphin dries out at low water to reveal a hard bank known as the *Knowle*. It is essential to round the dolphin to port (left) before turning north into the Bure from the Yare. There may be commercial traffic moored on the starboard bank at the mouth of the Bure on Bowling Green wharf. Try to occupy the centre right, if other craft permit. The riverbanks on this reach are shallow and strewn with obstructions. (See aerial photograph on page 44)

Bowling Green Wharf occupies the site of the Bowling Green P.H. that gave the Breydon market gunners a view down their water, whilst they sat and supped or enjoyed a game of bowls.

If you have used your *Hamilton's Slack Water Calculator* to time your tides to perfection, there will be a very small amount of ebb from the Bure to stem. This will give you more steerageway, enable you to stop if required and make mooring a great deal easier if required. *Vauxhall Bridge* now seems to serve no useful purpose, except as a hazard to navigation. It has a theoretical clearance .3m (1') higher than the road bridge but the difference in the timing of the ebb on both rivers causes water to back up into the first part of the Bure effectively reducing the clearance for both bridges to 2.18m (7') at AHW during the summer. The road bridge has a width of 21.3m (70'), whilst Vauxhall Bridge has a width of 30.4m (100'). Both bridges have clearance gauges on their approaches to advise the height available above the water. Southbound traffic on the Bure should note three vertical red lights on the A47 road bridge. These are ususally only iluminated when a very high water allows insufficient clearance under the bridges or commercial traffic is manouevring downatream of Vauxhall Bridge. When they are illuminated further navigation is obviously prohibited.

Once north of the bridges skippers should to bear in mind that there are there are no safe moorings after Yarmouth till the Stracey Arms, nearly eight miles upstream.

The Broads Authority operate free 24 hour moorings (Tel: 01493 - 332314) below the North West Tower, which now contains one of their Information Centres. The centre is open during school summer holidays 1000 - 1600 hours.

Upstream on the east bank is Yarmouth Yacht Station (01493 - 842794) Mooring fees have been increased to £11 per 24-hour stay with non-stayers being charged £3.00 for water. These must be the most expensive moorings on the Broads. Shore side facilities are open for restricted hours.

Hirers or owners of craft much over 11m or 35' who wish to moor at Yarmouth Yacht Station would do well to phone in advance. Skippers are advised to always moor facing upstream given the strong tides. If the river is blocked or the manoeuvre misjudged, turn towards the West Bank and away from the moored boats. It is better to hit the bank than the other boats. Skippers travelling downstream should be prepared to go through both bridges to obtain space to turn if required. Double mooring is sometimes necessary, with some moving of boats to keep the largest nearest the bank. Facilities offered are basic, the outlook less than scenic, including harsh concrete quayheading. Nevertheless, the delights of Yarmouth are irresistible to some. Should you decide to moor, ensure you have left sufficient slack in your mooring lines to allow for the rise and fall of the tide. The average range of summer spring tides is 1.7m (5.5') although tides with a range as great as 2.2m (7') are not uncommon.

Great Yarmouth (Chart C.) Yare - mouth. The "Great" was added in by Royal Charter 1272.

Troll Cart

Arthur Patterson on an "obsolete troll cart " outside the Tolhouse. This was the last example and had been used by Yarmouth brewers, Lacons to deliver beer to Nelson's fleet. Patterson had obtained the troll cart in 1902 for the museum and insisted that he was photographed on it. Troll carts were specially designed with a narrow wheel base to enable them to pass through the Rows fully laden with herring. A replica is found on the Market Place. The Tolhouse, in common with other Yarmouth Museums is open over Easter and from the second May Bank Holiday to October. Patterson would have cried if he had seen what the heavy German bombing did to his town, but at least he was spared the rebuilding. Post war clamour to rebuild has destroyed nearly all of the "Rows"; a grid system of 145 narrow alleys between houses; quite unlike anything else seen in England. They were aligned to the sea for circulation of a breeze. Presumably space was at a premium in a walled town built on land reclaimed from the sea; particularly when a quarter of the area available was taken up by religious institutions. The narrowest row rejoices in the name of Kitty Witches Row. Many writers, Charles Dickens and Daniel Defoe included, thought the rows gave the town a mediaeval feel.

A Yarmouth Row.   *P.H.Emerson*

Historic Yarmouth is present and most interesting but a little direction helps an initial exploration. The barons of the Kentish Cinque Ports, whose boats used to follow the herring to this part of the coast during the autumn, originally controlled the sandbank that became Great Yarmouth. It was a no mans land; used for drying nets and packing fish and not till the 17th century did the Cinque Ports power officially cease. Great Yarmouth's prosperity must have been considerable. The town was controlled from the Tolhouse; also known as the "Heigning Chamber", as the Yarmouth officials used the building to meet when they "heightened" or raised the prices of all the herrings brought into Yarmouth. The Tolhouse is now a museum and underneath are dungeons.

By King John's reign, Great Yarmouth was required to provide 57 ships, as often as required, in time of war. By comparison, the famous Cinque Ports were only required to provide 57 between them. The town owed its prosperity to the sea and much of it to the herring. There have been many attempts at keeping and preserving a deep water harbour. One attempt was ruined by Kett, who failed to take the town but demanded supplies for his revolution. When they could gain neither supplies, nor access to the town, his men ruined the work on a new harbour. The current harbour is the work of Joyce Johnson, a famous Dutch engineer. He strengthened the river banks and built two harbour piers. In essence, his work is to be seen today at the harbour mouth, but it did cost £250,000 in 1770.

A short walk over Caister Road from the moorings will take you to St. Nicholas' church, claiming to be the largest parish church in England. Herbert de Losinga, Bishop of Norwich and Lord High Chancellor of England, took pity on the people of this new town and founded the Church of St. Nicholas for their use. The church contains a shrine to Sir John Fastolf, who built Caister Castle with the ransom he obtained for capturing the Duke of Alencon at Agincourt. The building was considerably extended in the fourteenth century, but work was ceased largely as a result of the Black Death that hit Yarmouth at the end of 1348. It is recorded that 7,052 persons died out of a population of 10,000. The church was rebuilt between 1957 and 1960, after near total destruction by bombing. The spire was not replaced on the tower which sometimes helps to date photographs or paintings.

Beside St. Nicholas' Church was Anna Sewells birthplace in 1820, now a restaurant. Noted in Pevsner as sixteenth or seventeenth century, it is in fact a reconstruction erected in 1932 by Harry Johnson, a local builder and J.Ecclestone, Lacons Brewery architect from materials rescued from houses in demolished rows. Just across Market Street are some alms houses quaintly described on their outside as "an hospital for decayed fishermen." Great Yarmouth was one of Oliver Cromwell's strongholds and the next house was owned by Miles Corbett, the last signatory of King Charles' death warrant, who was tried for regicide and hung, drawn and quartered. The resident chip stalls on the market place were a famous local delicacy well before kiss me quick hats.

Hamilton suggests wandering along Market Row from the Market Place towards Hall Quay beside Haven Bridge. On the left hand side in Howard Street South is a first rate, second hand book shop.

Once onto Hall Quay, The Town Hall, built in the Baltic style contains a Tourist Information Office and has a display of the Towns regalia on the ground floor. The Star Hotel nearby was the home of one Bradshaw, President of the Commissioners who pronounced death on Charles 1. The current fascia is Edwardian but traces can be found of the original knapped flint walls. Lord Nelson used this building as his headquarters. He had strong connections with the town and when visiting injured sailors, Nelson is said to have remarked to one, indicating his own armless sleeve, "There Jack, you and I are spoiled for fishermen." After his death at Trafalgar, the lofty monument seen on South Denes, was raised to his memory in 1819, 24 years before the column in Trafalgar Square.

Much of South Quay survived the bombing, although currently overrun by one way traffic,car parking and the activities of a commercial port.

26 South Quay is the proposed location for new Norfolk Nelson Museum to contain a permanent exhibition to Norfolk's most favoured son. It is planned that the museum which will contain several hither to private collections.

Marina Leisure Centre., just opposite on Marine Parade, which contains amongst other attractions a large indoor swimming pool complete with wave making machine is open daily, all year round. Tel: (01493) - 851521.

Great Yarmouth Pleasure Beach is open from for early summer Bank Holidays and weekends and continuously from the end of May to September. Tel: (01493) - 844585.
Sea Life Centre, Marine Parade, Gt. Yarmouth. Tel: (01493) - 330631.
Britannia Pier Theatre, Marine Parade, Gt. Yarmouth. Tel: (01493) - 842209.

Wellington Theatre, Marine Parade, Gt. Yarmouth. Tel: (01493) - 842244.

Taxis, Drifter Taxis, 1 Yarmouth Road, Ormesby. Tel: (01493) - 730350.
Hamilton's Restaurants are:

The Seafood Restaurant, 85 North Quay, Gt. Yarmouth. Tel: (01493) - 856009. This restaurant is unpromisingly located on North Quay, very close to the River in-between the two Bure bridges. Whilst the outside appearance betrays a previous incarnation as a public house, it is one of Hamilton's personal favourites. The inside decor too, does little to impress; but the fish is wonderful. Credit cards Visa, Mastercard, Amex and Diners. A location for a special meal out.

The Italian Restaurant, 136 King Street, Great Yarmouth. Good Italian in the centre of Yarmouth. Reservations recommended at weekends. Tel: (01493) - 331141

Lazzarella, No3, Row 75, Howard Street South, Great Yarmouth, Tel: (01493) - 33062. Good, very small, Italian restaurant. No credit cards

Lower Bure. Boats with deep draught and sailing boats should keep well away from the banks of the lower Bure.

B 2L *Cinder Oven Reach*. Once the site of a railway bridge, much feared by local yachtsmen, this is now a continuation of the Yacht Station.

B 2R No moorings on this shore. At the bend are private moorings mainly used by fishing boats. All are held away from the shore due to the shelving bank. Keep clear of posts.

B 3L&R *Mile House Reach*. Mud rocks and debris. Very unsafe moorings.

B 4L Port of Yarmouth Marina moorings. These have about 1.09m (about 3.5') at ALW which will be insufficient for some boats. Mooring fees are currently £7.00 per night and there have been recent efforts to improve the facilities. There are showers, lavatories, a small shop and takeaway food kiosk. Pumpouts are available but no fuel. There is a filling station immediately behind these moorings with access from the river.

B 4R *Two Mile Steam Mill Reach*. No moorings, mud shoals. The steam pump was on the east bank and has long since disappeared. The land beside the west bank was an area called Nowhere. In the eleventh century it is thought to have had salt pans and was officially annexed to the parish of Acle by 1862. The name was changed by the Bailey family to White House Farm in the early part of the 20th century. Folklore has Mr. Bailey celebrating after a successful visit to Yarmouth market. The local constabulary had reason to speak to him and asked where he lived. His reply of Nowhere only placed him in deeper trouble.

B 5L The end of Port of Yarmouth Marina Moorings. Upstream of these moorings control of the River passes back to the Broads Authority and a 6 mph speed limit is imposed.

B 5R *Black Mill Reach*. No moorings, mud shoals. Black Mill is no more.

B 6L *Frog's Hall Reach and Three Mile House Reach*. No recommended moorings. Three Mile House is the first (or last) remaining of a series of land marks that were traditionally used to indicate the distance from the confluence with Yare. It is slightly incorrectly named, as it a little short of three miles to Yarmouth. There was once a Two Mile House and a One Mile House, whilst the ferry at Three Mile House was discontinued some years ago.

B 6R *Ashtree Farm Mill* is just a downstream of a collection of piles. It is dangerous to moor opposite Three Mile House. Further upstream at Ashtree Farm there is a path that connects with the A 47 Acle to Yarmouth Road. Yarmouth by road is approximately 1.75 miles. Emergency only mooring marked on Chart C. Rise and fall of tide is approximately 1.56m (5'). Ashtree Mill was the last Broads drainage mill to be worked regularly and was in use until caught aback by a gale in 1953.

Change to Chart F going upstream, Chart C going downstream.

B 7L *Scare Gap* No moorings are recommended. Shoals up to 3.75m (12') out from the bank are marked by posts.

B 7R No moorings.

B 8L *No Man's Friend Reach*. No moorings. The shore is bad as the banks fall in and create shelves. The posts marking the channel start or finish here. Odd numbers are on this bank.

B 8R In this sections there are pilings which are dangerous moorings; at the foot of these pilings there is no water.

B 9L *Mautby Swim.* Mautby Swim was a cattle crossing. Mautby Marsh Farm, no moorings recommended due to shelving whilst some are marked as dangerous near the outfall. Mautby Mill has been recently rebuilt and is converted to a private house. Its sails are tied.

B 9R Emergency mooring only opposite the farm which has access via footpath to the A47 Acle New Road. From the piling to further around the bend opposite Mautby Swim the banks have fallen in. At the dyke opposite Mautby Marsh Farm, old piling, submerged at AHW is dangerous. The next dyke is very shallow, .46m (1.5'). Tidal rise and fall up to 1.56m (5').

B 10L *Bowling Alley Reach.* No moorings recommended.

B 10R No moorings recommended. The banks overhang and are flooded at AHW. Five Mile House Mill is in this section and helps marks the distance from the River Yare.

B 11L *Runham Swim and Howe's Short Reach.* No moorings. There is a footpath to Runham village a mile away. Runham Mill is enjoying some restoration work.

B 11R   *Five Mile House* is now demolished but some potentially dangerous remains of some quay heading, visible at low water marks the site. No moorings. There is a footpath to the main A47 Acle straight. Runham Swim Mill.

B 12L *Martha's Reach*. No moorings.

B 12R No mooring. Banks shelve. Six Mile House Mill, (also known as Lakes Mill) is at the end of this section. The sails of Broadland mills were often used to send messages between the mills. Sails would be left in a certain position to signal, for example to another miller to send the millwright over; whilst they almost certainly carried warnings of enforcement officers to those involved in contraband.

B 13L   Reeds all the way, no mooring.

B 13R *Six Mile House*. The banks have only .46m (1.5') at ALW. Deeper water is found beside the reeds at 1.25m (4') but increased difficulty in mooring.

B 14L *Building New Staithe Reach*. There is a short stretch of quay headed mooring with approx. 1.25m (4') at ALW. Rise and fall of tide is still in the order of 1.56m (5'). Herringby Hall is visible from the river.

B 14R No moorings.

B 15L *Duffers Reach*. No moorings; all reeds. Here was once Duffers Mill and its successor, a steam pump.

B 15R No moorings, a dangerous point is marked with submerged piling sticking out into the reeds.

B 16L *Slut's Haven*. No moorings. Try as we can, we have found no explanation for this name. Once, the Bure flowed into the sea at Caister through a channel known as Grub's Haven and Slut's Haven might be a corruption; or it might just have been out of the way.

B 16R The bank by the Stracey Arms Mill is piled and is safe to moor. Allow for .94m (3') rise and fall. This mill was turned into a fortified post during the Second World War. The tower bears the scars of gun ports and cannon scars from attacking German aircraft. The mill has been restored by Norfolk Windmills Trust and is open to the public from Easter to the end of September. It contains an exhibition of photographs and a history of Broads wind pumps. Admission tickets are available from a small shop beside the mill, where there is a "Pets Corner."

The speed limit is reduced from 6 to 5 mph past the Public house and mill.

B 17L No moorings, reedy throughout. Here are the remains of Old Hall Mill and Bure Cottage beside.

B 17R *Stracey Arms Reach*. The piled bank offers the first safe moorings west of Yarmouth. Depth by the quay heading is 2.8m(9') to 4.38m (14'). At particularly high tides the water can flood over the bank and it is prudent to ensure that the bilge of a motor boat has not been left on the quay by a falling tide. Piling for bank preservation has been carried out some distance upstream.

The Stracey Arms at Tunstall (01493 - 750263), was once a small, brick wherryman's pub, but suffered a dreadful rebuild in the 1960's. It has recently changed hands and been considerably refurbished. A restaurant has been provided and the inn renamed the Three Feathers. Quite how long it will take river users to get used to a new name remains to be seen but the improvements are considerable. Food might be described as "value for money" or "family." The main A47 adjoins the pub and mill. Tunstall Dyke is now little more than a ditch and known to most only as a hump in the Acle straight. Navigation rights are preserved, although records show that the last wherry to use it was the *Albert and Alexandra* in 1897.

B 18L *Tunstall Mill Reach*. Tunstall Mill has been replaced with a mechanical pump. No moorings Recommended. Speed limit once again 6 mph.

B18R No moorings recommended.

B 19L *Ferry Reach* and *Trett's Mill Reach*. Moorings can be found on the bend at the piled section after the reeds with approx. 1m (3.25') There is a speed limit of 5 mph through Stokesby. The tide flows quite quickly through the village and there is a rise and fall of .6m (2'). The village no longer has a ferry and lies nine miles upstream of Yarmouth. There is usually a patch of disturbed water by the Ferry Inn which is caused by the remnants of a Roman ford. The bank between the shed and the quay should be avoided. Care should be taken whilst mooring in front of the pub as the current swirls around the small bay in an eddy. The rest of the inn's moorings provides 1.24m (4') ALW. Trett's Mill is in the village.

The Candlemaker and Model Centre is at Stokesby. (01493) - 750242. The workshops are open daily through the season. There is free parking and mooring by the village green.

B 19R   There is deep water 2.18m (7') opposite the Ferry. For approximately 100 yards mooring is possible with an average of .9m (3') ALW but the bank is soft.

B 20L   *Two Mills Reach and Muck Fleet Reach*. No mooring up to the Muck Fleet Dyke mouth. Commission Mill has had some restoration work on the tower only. The Muck Fleet is the outlet of Ormesby, Rollesby and Filby Broads; also known as the Trinity Broads. With the exception of this dyke, these Broads are not joined to the main Rivers. The Muck Fleet itself is very much overgrown and there is a dam across the mouth to ensure it is unnavigable. Ormesby Broad is a major source of water for Gt. Yarmouth.

B 20R   Emergency mooring opposite the *Muck Fleet*, .93m (3') ALW. From the above to Marsh Farm there are no moorings. At the farm there is a depth of .93m (3'). This can be used in case of need as there is a footpath leading from the farm to the main road 3/4 mile distant and 13/4 miles from Acle.

B 21L   *Horseshoes Reach*. No moorings. A deep scour hole which may be of interest to anglers is found here at about 4m (13') deep.

B 21R   Some moored private boats and modern steel quay heading.

B 22L   *Hermitage Reach* or *Acle Dyke Reach*. No moorings on this bank. The speed limit is reduced from 6 mph to 5 mph just before Hermitage Dyke.

B 22R The dyke itself is narrow but there is a public staithe at the end. This can provide closer access to the village of Acle or a hundred yards from the end of the dyke lies the Riverside Inn. (01493) - 750310. Previously known as The Hermitage, Claud Hamilton could often be found supping within. Today, the inn could be described as a good village pub; unspoilt and offering decent ales and food at reasonable prices. It is only a short walk to and from Acle Bridge along the newly created footpath. Just upstream of Hermitage Dyke lies Hermitage Marsh and the location of St. Mary's Priory.

There are some moored boats further up this stretch outside Marsh House and beside is the stump of Hermitage Mill (once known as Charlie Waters Mill).

ACLE (Chart C)

Passage makers through Yarmouth or those requiring a tow through Yarmouth and Breydon Bridges may wish to call the Broads Authority Quay Attendant at Great Yarmouth from Acle (01493) - 332314. Tides at Acle are 2.5 hours later than Yarmouth Yacht Station. Average rise and fall is .38 - .53m (1.24 - 1.75')

There are moorings downstream of the bridge either at the Bridge Inn (01493 - 750288, good moorings, if the concrete seems a little unforgiving.). or on the opposite side of the river, downstream of the boatyard.

Acle Bridge is also known as Acle Weybridge. The new structure was built during 1997. The first recorded bridge had three arches. Sometimes used for public executions, it was said to be haunted. Yachts without auxiliary power should be advised that the depth of water in the centre of Acle Bridge is too great to effectively quant.

B 23L *Bridge Reach*. Quayheading has 1.25m (4') - 1.5m (5') ALW. to the boatyard. Above the bridge are the Bridge Stores(01493) - 750355, a well stocked riverside facility open from 1 May to 30 September. Cycle hire is also available. Moorings are charged at £3.00 for 24 hours. The indentation in the riverbank outside Acle Bridge Stores, causes eddies in the current that can create difficulties in controlling a yacht being quanted through the bridge.

There are public lavatories and a small car park behind the Bridge Stores. Upstream of the moorings, the speed limit once again becomes 6 mph.

Acle Taxi service can be contacted on (01493) - 750455.

St. Margaret's Mill, Acle Bridge, Tel: (01493) - 750182., has been converted into a restaurant and is a short walk from Acle Bridge. This mill was built on wooden foundations.

Boatyards.

Anchorcraft, (Blakes) Acle Bridge, Norwich NR13 3AS. Tel: (01493) - 750500.
Bridgecraft.(Hoseasons) dayboats. Tel: (01493) - 750378
Horizon Craft Cruisers, (Hoseasons) Tel: (01493) - 750283
Norfolk Broads Holidays. Tel: (01493) - 751651.

Upstream of Acle Weybridge there are many miles of good river sailing. There is an absence of trees and the river is wide and deep. The largest cruisers can sail with only very occasional problems with depth and then usually whilst pushing their luck on the bends. Past Anchorcraft and Bridgecraft the moorings are all excellent with between .6m(2') and 1.56m(5'). A charge is made for these moorings.

B 24L Moorings fair for depth, poor landing.

B 24R *Fishley Mill Reach.* Moorings are good with ample water. A small mooring fee is charged. There are two bungalows on this reach; one of which belongs to the Northern Rivers Sailing Club. Sec. John Roper, Blackrow House, Shortthorn Road, Felthorpe, Norfolk. NR10 4DE. Tel: (01603) - 754695. Fishley Mill was a steam pump. The chimney is now demolished.

B 25L *Lower Daveys Reach.* Depth along this bank fair.

B 25R From practically the beginning of this section to Upton Dyke, the bank is all reeds. The small stages are for anglers to sit in comfort and not for mooring.

B 26L *Upper Daveys Mill Reach.* The first set of piling has a bad shelf alongside .3m (1') ALW. The second set has 1.25m (4') AWL. There are emergency moorings at the top of this section with 2.18m (7') The moorings are not good as they are corrugated iron sheeting.

Davey's Mill is also known as Clippesby Mill. Mills were usually known by the area (level) they drained, the name of the owner, parish or the marshmen that operated them or sometimes all four.
UPTON.

B 26R Upton Dyke off this section has an average depth of about 1.25m (4'). The dyke has good moorings and access to Upton village; it is quite narrow and large boats may experience difficulty in turning. There is a slight bar across the mouth of the dyke and larger sailing cruisers tacking up the Bure should keep clear. There is a free slipway for small boats and dinghies at the end of Upton Dyke, beside a small car park and bottle bank. Palmer's Hollow Post Mill is near the end of the dyke, it is the sole surviving example of a hollow post, plunger pump, drainage mill in existence and has been relocated from its original site near Acle.

The village of Upton is about a mile walk from Upton Dyke and has a Post Office, shop and one of Hamilton's Pubs, The White Horse. (01493 - 750430). The pub sells a wide variety of real ales and is open all day. Hot and cold food are available and the fish and chips, straight from Lowestoft are excellent when available. The pub has a garden and children are welcome. On no account should Hamilton's Navigators ask over the bar about local taxis. The landlord is likely to provide 10p, a phone number and gesture in the direction of the public phone box. When the unfortunate returns to the pub, he learns (eventually) that he has telephoned back to the pub, who also operate the local taxi service.

Boatyard.

Eastwood Whelpton Ltd., (Blakes) Yacht Station, Upton, NR13 6BN. Tel: (01493) - 750430. Fax: (01493) - 750902. Craneage available.
Half a mile away from Upton village to the north west, lies Upton Broad which is spring fed and not connected to the main river. Next to Upton Broad is Upton Fen, a nature reserve

From the mouth of Upton Dyke upstream, the banks are reeds and no moorings are available.

B 27L *Oby Short Reach*. At the beginning of this section above Wisemans Mill or Oby Mill, the quay affords good mooring in places, but the depth at ALW varies considerably between 2.18 (7') and .65 (2') so soundings are necessary before making fast. This is the oldest mill of known age in the region, dating from 1753. The corrugated iron building nearby contained a saw bench that was driven by a shaft from the mill. South Oby Dyke lies upstream of mill and is private.
B 27R   At the draining pump beside Tall Mill, there is an outlet with a mud shoal jutting out into the river for a distance of 1.8m (6'). Careful observation will show that Tall Mill, like many other mills has been "heigned" - a Norfolk corruption of heightened. The additional height is quite clearly visible.

B 28R   Much of this bank is shallow and should be avoided. There has been considerable erosion close to Thurne Mouth.

B 28L   Moorings against the quay heading are safe, but the wash of passing cruisers may be a disturbance. Oby Dyke is private. The tidal rise and fall here is about a foot (.31m).

B 29L   *Thurne Reach.*   From above the dyke to Thurne Mouth there are moorings all along the quayheading with a depth up to 2.5m (8'). Here is the confluence of the River Thurne with the Bure. The Thurne flows down from Potter Heigham, Ludham, Hickling and Horsey Mere. (For River Thurne see page 162).

B 29R   The Bure takes a sharp bend at Thurne Mouth. Do not cut the bend as the apex is very shallow. Moorings are good on piled sections.

B30L   *Mile Bars Reach.*   There are several short stretches of quay heading with .96m (3') ALW. In this reach the speed limit drops to a maximum of 5 mph. This is the maximum speed permitted on the whole of the Upper Bure.

B 30R   Moorings to be found with care.

B 31L   *South Walsham Southerly Reach* or *South Walsham Mill Reach*. No moorings, shoals and flints from St. Benets quayheading some distance out into the stream. Keep inside navigation posts.

B 31R   Four more sets of pilings depth around 1.56m (5'0) ALW. The overflow dyke near the drainage pump is shallow. The river deepens to 2.5m (8') and from here to the mouth of Fleet Dyke, leading to South Walsham Broad (1 mile) the banks are reeds and marsh. Craft are asked to avoid this stretch of river before 0900 on Sunday mornings to enable early morning fishing matches to take place.

Change to Chart G going upstream, Chart F going downstream.

BF 1 *South Walsham Fleet Dyke.* The dyke has recently been dredged and there is a good depth of water and good moorings against the pilings. When travelling from the Bure to South Walsham Broad, the channel divides and skippers should keep to the left hand channel. The right hand channel is the old course of the River Bure which once re-emerged opposite Ant Mouth. It is both private and impassable.

BF 2 Good moorings can be found along the piling. There is a spit which juts out into the stream at the end of the piling. From here to the entrance of the Outer Broad is private.

BF 3 South Walsham Broads are considered by many to be the prettiest of all the Broads. There is a good depth of water 1.25m (4') to 1.56m (5') at ALW, although an easterly gale can reduce this depth. In the south east corner is a staithe with a slipway, signed as being for the use of parishioners; but check the depth before mooring. Near the slipway is a small public carpark. Although the inner broad is private, it is open but mooring, landing and fishing are prohibited. There are two small islands in the Broad, the first island is man made; whilst west of the second is too shallow for navigation. There is no exit to the west. The average depth over South Walsham Inner Broad is .9m (3') to 1.25 (4'). The water between the two Broads is called The Weirs, it has a gravely bottom as a relic of attempts by a previous owner to close off public access.

Beside R. & J. Russell's boatyard are both public toilets and a boat refuse skip.

SOUTH WALSHAM.

Fairhaven Garden Trust runs water trips every half hour during the summer though the gardens in a vintage style launch. Closed on Mondays. Tel: (01603) 270449.

South Walsham Hall. Hotel and Country Club. Sports facilities and swimming pool. The Fairhaven Restaurant. Tel: (01603) - 270378.

The village is a walk of 1.25 miles from the Broad. There is a shop and a Post Office and Hamilton's pub. The Ship, which offers a good range of beers and wholesome food. Tel: (01603) - 270553. On the way to the village you will pass Pratt's " Old Curiosity Shop", itself probably an antique, but filled with smaller antiques, which may be worth a pause. Tel: (01603) - 270204.
Boatyard.

R.& J. Russell, (Hoseasons) moorings, repair work, diesel, pump out, gas. Tel: (01603) - 270262.

River Bure (contd.)

B 32L The greater part of this section includes the foreshore of St.

BENETS ABBEY. Flint buildings and quay headings once lined the river but over the centuries these have fallen into the river. The flints are now extremely dangerous and it is important not to moor or get too close to this bank. The channel is marked by posts. Just above the Abbey is a piled section, which provides good moorings to a depth of 1.25m (4'). A century ago Davies notes that wherrymen believed that they were scraping their keels on the top of a tunnel from St. Benets to Ranworth. It does seem more probable that these were the remains of an ancient building.

On the first Sunday of August the Bishop of Norwich (as Abbot of St. Benets) visits the ruins, usually by wherry, to take a church service. The Bishop is the only remaining Episcopal Lord Abbot (Mitred Abbot) in the country and therefore had two claims to a seat in the House of Lords.

It is possible to walk to or from the remains of the Abbey to Ludham Bridge. The site of the Bishops Palace is near Ludham Hall.

SAINT BENETS ABBEY.

A small number of Saxon monks founded a monastery at St. Benets at Holm, on a natural hill known as Cowholm, in the midst of the surrounding fens during the ninth century. The original monastery was destroyed by Viking invaders in 870 AD., and the current Abbey was founded by King Canute as a Benedictine Order early in 1020.

Monastic houses wielded considerable authority prior to the dissolution. There were monasteries not only at St Benets, but also at Acle, St Olaves, Aldeby, Bungay, Langley, Hickling and Ingham, but St. Benets was one of the wealthiest in the area, second only to Walsingham. Canute endowed the black friars of St Benets with the manors of Horning, Ludham and Neatishead. Edward 1 gave the Abbot the rights of fishing between Wroxham and Acle bridges. By Henry VIII's reign the Abbey is recorded as enjoying an income of £677:9s:8d per annum. South Walsham and Horning had close connections with St. Benets. Richard de South Walsham was a fifteenth century Abbot and St. Benets Court was held at Hare Hill.

Sir John Fastolf, a knight of the Garter, built Caister Castle and fought at Agincourt. He failed to fill those walls with English dead and was buried instead by the north wall of St Benets Abbey, where his wife built a chapel over the grave to his memory. Learned opinions vary as to whether he was the subject of Shakespeare's lampooning as Jack Falstaff; the "bombard of sack". In any event, he was very wealthy; his inventory records three thousand ounces of silver plate in safe keeping at St. Benets.

Naturally, the abbey has a ghost. A monk called Ethelwald is said to have betrayed his colleagues to invading Normans, on the condition that they made him Abbot. He let them into the Abbey; they duly invested him and immediately hung him from the gateway he had opened. This is likely to be more folklore than factual, although the Abbot at the time of the Norman invasion was called Ethelwald. Enthusiasts of the supernatural should keep the date of May 25th clear.

St Benets was unique in escaping the dissolution of the monasteries in 1536. The Abbot was also Bishop of Norwich and gave the King the bishopric and a great deal of the abbeys income, whilst retaining the abbey for himself. Deprived of their income, the monks left shortly afterwards and the abbey's stones were used in many local villages for building. In the 1920's, Charles Carrodus, yachting correspondent of the Eastern Daily

Norfolk Museums Service

Such a small amount of the abbey remains above ground that it is difficult now to envisage its form in the middle ages. Built like a castle, it covered 38 walled acres; a vast area considering it was only rarely home to more than twenty five monks.

The surviving single arch and the remains of a Georgian windmill built into it, were not part of the main abbey but the main gate house in the fortified walls. The area of reed next to the mill and beside the river was a dock that the monks dug out to safely unload their requirements. So important was this considered, that they even diverted the course of the River Bure around Ward marsh to improve access and defence. From the gate house to the bottom left hand side of the photograph is a clearly visable causeway across the marshes that lead to St. Johns Hospice, then controlled by the Almoner of St. Benets and now in the grounds of Horning Hall. In those days the Ant flowed down the Hundred Dyke into the River Thurne; the river was later artificially joined to the Bure, probably as a drainage measure, cutting through this causeway. The large feature above and to the left of the main gate and still a boggy area, was the site of stew ponds where fish were kept to for the table. Carp was a particular delicacy.

The side of the abbey facing the River Bure was largely a line of buildings, including a brewery and a bakery and a visible swan pit, where cygnets were fattened for the table. The flint foundations of some buildings can be seen today. A large wooden cross, erected in 1987 is on the site of the main altar. On the river bank, the abbot's lodgings became the Chequers Inn.

The Chequers Inn.1880 *G. Christopher Davies*

In 1883 Christopher Davies wrote of two massive parallel walls two hundred yards to the east of the gate; also there are arched doorways and strong walls in the house by the riverside, whose cool recesses speak of ancient days. This house was once a public house - the Chequers Inn shown in the photograph.

The Chequers Inn was a wherryman's inn and the last inhabited part of St. Benets. It was a notable centre for smuggling in the nineteenth century. The landlord operated a steam tug to pull wherries through this difficult reach. Latterly the building was used as a house by the farmer that rented the grazing, before being divided into several farm workers cottages and finally burning down in 1886.

B 32R *St. Benets Reach, South Walsham Dyke Reach* and *Ward Reach.* The bank from Fleet Dyke over this section has deep water near the bank, but no good moorings.

B 33L *Old Jays Short Reach*. Ant Mouth. (for River Ant see page 110). A private dyke leads to Horning Hall. The grounds contain the ruins of St. James' Hospice, which served St. Benets. Ebb and Flow Marshes or Church Fen contained in this bend in the river is a Norfolk Wildlife Trust nature reserve. This is believed to be the last breeding ground of the Bittern on the Bure and is home to a thriving colony of Swallowtail butterflies. There is 1.25m (4') to 1.8m (6') of water on the quay heading upstream of Horning Hall's private dyke.

B 33R Marshy and reedy with a good depth of water available.

B 34L *Beggars Oak Reach*. Piling and concrete wall continues to the mid point of this section, followed by reeds. It is not advisable to moor along the concrete sections. This reach is said by A.J.Rudd to have been named after a tramp, who "many years ago, hung himself on an oak tree here. The oak like the beggar is now defunct."

B 35R Upstream of the sharp bend opposite the concrete pilings, a shelf juts out into the river and mooring is dangerous. There are many small dykes running into Ranworth Marshes but these all are very shallow. Moorings without access can be found with care on the main river.

B 35L 'Ranner' Dam or *Staithe Reach*. Moorings can be chosen with care but it is better to carry on to the broad. Sailing on the Bure begins to deteriorate upstream of this reach, as a result of encroaching trees.

RANWORTH & MALTHOUSE BROADS.

BM 1 *Ranworth Dam* is the name of the tree lined dyke that leads from the River Bure, down to Ranworth and Malthouse Broads, some 17.5 miles from Yarmouth. The entry to Ranworth Broad which is a large, but quite shallow broad, is barred. The Broadland Conservation Centre (Tel: 01603 - 270479). located over the remains of several wherries, sunk to keep the banks in place. The Centre shows the Broads, past and present and there is a short walkway through the aldercarr. It is open from April till October and admission is free.
BM 2 *Malthouse Broad*.

24 hour free moorings, without access, are found on your port hand as you enter the Malthouse Broad. There are also free 24 hour, stern on moorings on the staithe. The moorings on your starboard hand as you approach the staithe are private.

There is a Broads Authority / Blakes Holidays Information Centre at the Staithe. Tel: (01603) - 270453. and a children's playground beside the public moorings on the staithe. A boat refuse skip is hidden in the trees opposite the Maltsters P.H., whilst the pub car park includes public lavatories and receptacles for recycling bottles, paper and cans. A public telephone box is just up the hill from the Malsters PH.

The Granary Stores includes an off licence, a Post Office and there is a Licensed Restaurant (Tel: 01603 - 270432) next to the Information Centre. Electric launches are offered for hire. The Maltsters P.H. is just across the road.

A trip up Ranworth church tower, braving the iron ladders is obligatory for the best view in Broadland, but certainly not for the infirm or fainthearted. It is easy to see from the top, how local church towers were used for signalling in the Middle Ages. The 15th century, delicately painted rood screen is delightful and managed to survive black paint during the reformation. Ranworth church has a mediaeval illustrated manuscript known as the Sarum Antiphoner; 285 sheepskin pages drawn by the monks of Langley Abbey. Like Langley, Ranworth belonged to the Premonstatensian order of white canons. The book is on public view contained in a glass topped safe. It has many lovely illustrations containing fine illustrations, including Jonah and the whale and the seven services in mediaeval Latin. The Antiphoner was bequeathed to Ranworth church in 1479 by William Cobbe. After dropping from sight for 300 years, it reappeared in a private collection in 1852. Another sixty years passed and it was put up for sale in London, purchased anonymously and returned to Ranworth. The misericords (hinged choir seats) have the every appearance of starting their life on the other side of the river Bure. The underside of one of the seats does carry the coat of arms of St. Benets, but since it also carries a carving of the gate house complete with windmill, is unlikely to be original.

St. Helens Church, Ranworth can offer guided tours for ten or more people. There is no charge for this, as the guides are volunteer members of the congregation, but a donation to the visitors centre would be appreciated. Contact Mrs. Margaret Bunn, Tel: (01603) - 720511, giving as much notice as possible.

Christopher Davies in his "Handbook to the Norfolk Broads and Rivers" mentions a tunnel from St. Benets Abbey to Ranworth, presumably an escape route for the monks and cites a large subterranean space found under Ranworth school yard with a seven foot high tunnel leading towards St. Benets. Local folklore has a tunnel emerging into the well supplying three Ranworth cottages. This well was filled in some years ago and the cottages converted into one house, now appropriately renamed Benets.

Should a Hamilton's Navigator find himself on the broads in the depths of winter, then Malthouse Broad is usually the first to freeze and offers excellent skating.

River Bure (contd.)

B 36L *Old Staithe Reach, No Spitting Reach* and *Horning Church Reach* or *Storeys Reach.*

About 400 yards up this reach, the river bends to the west and on the bend is a water extraction installation for Great Yarmouth's water supply. This installation has hardly been used since 1979, as the water company prefer to abstract from Belaugh. Further upstream there is a lower amount of phytoplankton making the water less costly to treat. Signs beside the installation caused this to be known as the No Spitting Reach. The dyke downstream of the extraction works is private.

Upstream, there is a public staithe below Horning church which of late has been in poor repair. There is access to St. Benedicts Church, Horning where there are stall ends bearing the oldest arms of St. Benets Abbey.

Next to Horning Vicarage is Storeys Reach. This large house once belonged to a Mr. Storey and used to have immaculate grounds; now apparently abandoned to large numbers of geese. The bridges, weeping cherries and garden houses were laid out in the style of willow pattern china. Keen observers may spot that the remains of the quay heading (which is private but now a danger to be avoided) still has the letter S on metal tie bars. There are some unusual animals that live in the grounds understood to be shoats. Local folklore has them as a cross between a sheep and a goat.Whilst unlikely, this makes a good tale.

B 36R No moorings on this bank.

B 37L No moorings, banks overgrown with trees.

B 37R At the bend there are moorings with 1.25m (4') ALW. A shallow shelf calls for care.

B 38L *Cockshoot Dyke* and *Horning Ferry Reach*. At Cockshoot Dyke the speed limit is reduced to 4 mph for Horning village. Hobb's Mill is an open framed wind pump driving a "scoopwheel" and is located upstream and opposite Cockshoot Dyke. This mill is currently without sails. There are two dykes off to starboard, travelling upstream. Wild's Dyke, just before the first of the houses leads to Horning Pleasure Craft, whilst the next leads down to King Line Cruisers, Wood's Dyke leads to Woods Dyke Boatyard and the Ferry Boatyard is just beyond.

B 38R   There are free 24 hr. moorings in Cockshoot Dyke. There is no access to Cockshoot Broad and the dyke is dammed. Cockshoot Broad is a Norfolk Wildlife Trust Reserve and was suction dredged in 1982. It has been deliberately cut off from the main river to prevent the reaccess of contaminated silts. It is open everyday of the year and there is a walkway along the bank from Horning Ferry (Woodbastwick bank) to Cockshoot Broad and a bird hide. Breaks between the trees along this reach are usually filled with angling positions, which often come as a surprise to a sailing boat struggling to creep around the bend. Horning Ferry is a pedestrian ferry, in use during the summer only. There is road access to this side of the ferry from Woodbastwick village and limited car parking.

B 39L *Ferry Reach.* There are good moorings for patrons with an average depth of 1.25m (4') to 1.5m (5')., at Horning Ferry Inn. A boat rubbish compound and a small shop are in the grounds. Tel: (01692) - 630259. Beer, food and gaming machines are available. The Helska Leisure Centre (01692) - 630392 lies between the Ferry Inn and Wood's Dyke. Facilities available are sauna, sunbed, pool, gymnasium, snack and wine bar. Horning Ferry Marina alongside charges for moorings. Horning Ferry Mill lies in this section, which might unkindly be described as a parody of a Broads mill. Its foundations or "cants" are original and apparently intact, but otherwise the mill has been converted and considerably altered. Originally a brick tower, it has been rebuilt as a smock mill with a Dutch style flare.

B 40L *Horning Town Reach.* The New Inn and the Swan Hotel both have moorings for patrons. Behind the Swan Pavilion there are public lavatories and boat refuse disposal facilities. Beside the Swan Hotel on Horning parish staithe is the permanent mooring of "Southern Comfort" which runs daytrips. The boat is a charicature of a Mississippi paddle boat and for many years has been a familiar, if incongruous sight on the Broads. Mississippi River Boats, Tel: (01692) - 630262. There is a slipway beside the Swan. The key is held by Ralph's Newsagents and there may be a small charge.

The nearest station is Wroxham, but the bus service runs to Norwich and Gt. Yarmouth. The are a selection of shops and a Post Office on Lower Street. At the end of this reach is the clubhouse of Horning Sailing Club. Sec. P. E. Ollier, Breeze Barn, South Reepham Road, Bawdeswell, Dereham, Norfolk. NR 20 4RU. Tel: (01362) - 688727. During the winter, the premises serve as a clubhouse for the Snowflakes Sailing Club. Sec. Phil. Ellery, 7 Watkin Road, Norwich. NR4 6LH Tel: (01603) - 478915.

B 40R.   There are moorings in this section, but most are private. Moorings for hire craft may be arranged with one of the boatyards. Lower Street, with its shops and pubs are of course across the river.

HORNING.

There is a steady current at Horning; strong enough to effect a sailing boat, but the rise and fall of the tide is very small.

Boatyards.

Burehaven, (Hoseasons) Cottages, Houseboats. Tel: (01692) - 630842.
Ferry Boatyard Ltd., (Blakes), Ferry Road, Horning. NR12 8PS. Tel: (01692) - 630392. Ferry Boatyard has both petrol and diesel pumps beside the river.
Horning Pleasurecraft, (Hoseasons)
King Line Cruisers, (Blakes), Ferry View Estate,
Norfolk Broads Yachting Company, (Blakes), Lower Street, Horning NR12 8PF. Tel: (01692) - 631330.
Woods Dyke Boatyard (Blakes), School Road, Horning, NR12 8PS. Tel/Fax.: (01692) - 630461.
Horning stretches along the Bure for about a mile; by water it is 4 miles downstream of Wroxham and some 20.5 miles upstream of Yarmouth. Telephones, car parking and public lavatories are found by the Swan Inn where moorings are available free to patrons.

Mr. Chan, a Chinese restaurant is in Lower St. Horning. Takeaways are available. Tel: (01692) - 630091.
Hamilton's pub/restaurant is the Petersfield House Hotel. It has moorings available for patrons and is open to non residents. Tel: (01692) - 630741.

B 41L *Cinder Oven Reach.* This bank consists of a line of private houses and chalets until the entrance to Black Horse or Hoveton Little Broad. This broad is open for Easter Week and from the late May Bank Holiday until the end of October, when the gates are locked. The Broad was suction dredged in 1990 and mooring is prohibited around the edges of the broad. Horning Sailing Club run some of their regattas on Blackhorse Broad. There is no access to the shallow western section which is a nature reserve.

The speed limit on the river is increased to 5 mph, upstream of Black Horse Broad.

B 41R No mooring, all the banks are private.

B 42L *Dydlers Mill Reach* or *Hoveton Long Reach.* There are several moorings along this reach. Dydlers Mill has been converted to a private dwelling. Encroaching trees make sailing further upstream progressively more difficult. Unless you have a very tall mast or topsail to pick up a breeze over the trees, yachtsman are best advised to motor, seek a tow or resign themselves to quanting to Wroxham.

B 42R   Reed banks and scrub are found in this section. No good moorings.

B 43L *Dydles.* Scrub and reeds, no recommended mooring.

B 43R *Parsons Dyke* which gives access to *Decoy Broad* is chained, but the mouth of the dyke provides a mooring. Beside the entrance to Decoy Broad are the remains of the wherry *Ella.* Built in Wroxham in 1912, she carried 24 tons and was the last trading wherry built. Nat Bircham was her final owner; he also skippered the *Albion* in the early days of the Norfolk Wherry Trust. *Devil's Hole* is private as are the other dykes and the large wet boatshed.

B 44L *Blackcurrant Reach* and *Salhouse Broad Reach.* The Dam, one of the entrances to Hoveton Great Broad has an ALW depth of 1.56m (5') but the dyke is closed. At the end of this section lies *Foxburrow Dyke*, another closed entrance to Hoveton Great Broad opposite the entrance to Salhouse Broad. Both provide a frustrating glimpse of one of the largest of all broads, closed to navigation. These broads were once the major public highway for the area. There were no trees and wherries faced with a head wind were able to sail from Wroxham to Horning without using the river. Local feeling on rights of navigation and fishing is deeply ingrained. One of Robert Kett's demands 1549 was "... ryvers may be ffre and common to all men for fyshing and passage".

B 44R   There is an entrance to *Woodbastwick Old Hall Broad* almost opposite the Dam. This is very shallow, small and private.

The small inlet by the eastern entrance to Salhouse Broad is shallow and care should be taken to stay inside the navigation posts. The island formed between the entrances of Salhouse Broad provides good quayheaded moorings on the on the river side.
SALHOUSE BROAD. (Sallowes)

Salhouse is an attractive Broad, with grassy slopes and sandy hills running down to the water. The wood that runs down the hill, nearly to the water is full of bluebells in the spring.

For depths at ALW see chart; the bottom is mostly gravel. There is a speed restriction of 4 mph. A mooring fee is charged.. There are some quay headed moorings at the southern end or it is possible to nose a boat into one of the "beaches" that are formed along the southern shore, where the grass runs down to the water. Nudge the bow in gently keeping a sharp lookout for tree stumps and tie either to one of the trees or a rhond anchor.

The wreck at the entrance to Salhouse Dyke should not be used for mooring. The dyke is shallow and narrow and can only be entered by rowing boats; it is all that remains of the parish staithe that supplied Salhouse village. There is a good footpath (which is suitable for wheelchairs) from Salhouse Broad to the road where there is a small carpark and public toilets.

Payne Jennings

Wherry at Salhouse Parish Staithe. The use of the reclining model is rather more typical of Payne Jennings than wherrymen of the period. The wooden ducks in the foreground are entirely entirely typical of his work.

Hamilton's Navigators may care to take a decent stroll and visit one of Hamilton's pubs. Turn left at the road and walk up the hill towards the village of Woodbastwick. The Fur and Feather Public House is about half a mile on the left hand side. It is semidetached to Woodforde's Brewery, a small, local brewery producing prize winning, real ales. These come through the wall in perfect condition and enable a choice of wonderful ales that most have never stumbled away from. The pub serves wholesome meals.

There are two more public houses in the village, the Bell and the Lodge, both of which are quite a long walk from Salhouse Broad. The Bell and the village shop and Post Office are on Lower Street which is reached by turning right out of the car park for the Broad. Salhouse Equestrian Centre (Tel: 01603 - 720921) is just before the Bell; whilst between the Equestrian Centre and the Bell is a small cottage with an inscription over one of the first floor windows "God's providence is mine inheritance". This was the only house in the village to survive the Black Death. This plague had a huge effect on the locality. Forty per cent of Norwich's population are believed to have perished, whilst seventy per cent of Yarmouth's souls were lost.

Salhouse Station is several miles away from the Broad and it would be better to take a train from Wroxham. The Post Office and stores are about 3/4of a mile from the broad. Salhouse Church, which is thatched and inevitably on high ground, is removed from the village and also some considerable distance from the broad. Several other Broadland churches are visible from Salhouse church tower.

Boatyards.

Marinepower Engineering, Outboard motor specialists, The Mill, Wood Green, (off Station Road) Salhouse, Norwich NR13 6NS.Tel; (01603) - 720001.

B 45L *Gravel Dyke Reach.* Midway through this section is some quayheading which provides moorings for the Hoveton Great Broad Nature Trail. This is free and the half mile trail is open during the season from 10.30 am. to 5.30 p.m. weekdays, 2.00 till 5.30 on Sundays but closed on Saturdays. The third entrance to Hoveton Great Broad is *Gravel Dyke*, which is also blocked.

B 45R There are quayheaded free 24 hour moorings on the neck of land separating Salhouse Broad from the river. The water varies form 1.56m (5') to .93m (3'). Salhouse Little Broad lies just beyond Salhouse Broad. It has also been closed to the public.

Compare Gravel Dyke Reach today with G. C. Davies' photo taken in 1883

B 46L *Old Woman's Pulk* is the name of the next small water which is closed off to the river. There is a small wherry decomposing in a dyke along this stretch. Care is required to find moorings.

B 46R   No moorings recommended.

B 47L   *Willow Tree Reach.* No moorings in this section. There are two entrances to Hudson's Bay in this section; a small, very shallow piece of water which is close to the northern end of Hoveton Great Broad and also closed to the public.

B 47R   On this stretch is the lower entrance to Wroxham Broad. Moorings can be found with care on the neck of river bank next to Wroxham Broad.

WROXHAM BROAD. Chart G.

Wroxham Broad is one of the largest and best known of all the Broads. It about a mile long, covers 120 acres and is the home of the Norfolk Broads Yacht Club. Secretary is Mr. K.A.D. Izatt, Wroxham Broad, Norwich. NR12 8TS. Tel/Fax:- (01603) - 782808. The Club was formally established at a meeting on October 27th 1937 to take over the lease of the Broad. It was an amalgamation of the Yare and Bure Sailing Club, the Broads Sailing & Motor Club, the Horning Town Sailing Club (who considered Horning too crowded for racing even in those days; not every one agreed and Horning Sailing Club was established the next day.), and the Great Yarmouth Yacht Club. The Norfolk Broads Yacht Club is numerically the largest yacht club on the Broads.

It is best to moor to a mudweight as the banks on the west side and the buoys are private. There are some places close to the east bank that are dangerously shallow but are both buoyed and marked on the chart. Visitors may care to watch the yacht racing which takes place during most weekends over the summer and is often quite a spectacle. Care should be taken to moor off the racing course; that is if you do not wish to be asked to move. Windsurfers are unwelcome over weekends or when racing is taking place.

There is public access to the broad by car, to a small area once known as Collinson's Meadow; in effect a "beach" beside the broad. A modest charge is made for both launching (there is a rudimentary slipway, only deep enough for dinghies.) and parking.

Wroxham Broad is fed by springs and is on average 2m (6.25') deep. The bottom is largely featureless (and it has to be said lifeless), although there is a slightly deeper trough at 2.8m (about 9') about 12.5m (40') off the island, by the downstream entrance. There is a slight current off this bank, flowing downstream, which may be the result of the springs, or it might be caused by suction from the current flowing down the main river.

John Nudd caught a British record pike from the banks beside Hospital Farm on the South shore of the Broad, in 1901. The fish itself was set up by J. Bullock of Swaffham and for many years resided in the bar of the New Inn at Horning. It is now in the clubhouse of the Hemsworth Blue Bell Angling Club in Yorkshire. The Club visited the Broads every year and Gillie Tallowin, then landlord of the New Inn at Horning, gave them the fish, which was no longer in it's first flush of youth.

B 48L *Hillpiece Reach.* Sailing from Wroxham Broad to Wroxham is hampered by the large trees on each side. Downstream of the entrance to Wroxham Broad is an entrance to Hudson's Bay, the northern most extremity of Hoveton Great Broad. There are no moorings. From here to

Wroxham Bridge is found some of the best winter pike fishing the Bure has to offer. When the river has no flow, it seems the boatyards and dykes fish better than the river itself.

B 48R   At the lower end of this section the speed limit is reduced to 4 mph for Wroxham at the upper or north entrance to Wroxham Broad. The trees make it difficult to see craft using this entrance and a sound signal is advisable. Sailing craft are unable to give an audible warning. Just around the bend, is the beginning of the private houses and quayheading that runs all the way into Wroxham.

B 49L *Snapes Reach*. Snapes Water is behind the trees covering the lower part of this section. It is private and unnavigable but sometimes visible through the trees during the winter. From here on, moorings become increasingly difficult to find up as far as Wroxham Bridge. Most are private, although some are available by arrangement with one of the boatyards. On Saturdays the boatyards are very busy and permission to moor is unlikely. The Hotel Wroxham (01603) - 782061) beside the bridge has moorings for patrons but suggests telephoning for a reservation.

B 49R Moorings are private all along this bank. You may see a wherry or two on this reach as their base is at Barton House opposite the boatyards. Moores of Wroxham's Marina, opposite the Hotel Wroxham has a leisure centre, including a sauna and pool which is open to the public. Next to the Bridge is the Wherryman's Galley which provides a good quality, average priced family meal and has a bar. Tel: (01603) - 784041. The narrow bridge has caused a considerable amount of local scour and just downstream the depth increases to a maximum of 4.6m (14.75') which will be of interest to fishermen and those having to quant. Wroxham Bridge is very old and attractive, but its downstream view has been hidden for several decades by a Bailey bridge slung over the top for commercial vehicles and a footpath hung alongside. There is a suspicion that clearance is reducing as the old bridge slowly sinks under the weight of traffic. The traffic congestion the bridge causes can be considerable on a summer Saturday morning. There is a quay beside Wroxham Bridge which is usually available for temporary moorings whilst lowering a yacht's mast. The Bure at this point is not tidal but care should be taken with boats that are close to tolerance in passing through Wroxham Bridge, as a heavy rainfall may leave them stranded upstream of the bridge.

B 50L *Bridge Reach.* Wroxham Bridge is small and low having a AHW clearance of 2.34m (7.75') with a width of 8m (26.5'). The curved arch means that its practical clearance is much lower. This bridge does not cross the River Bure at right angles, visibility is very limited and a sound signal will warn other boats of your presence.

Wroxham Bridge viewed from upstream.

Moorings are available through the bridge for patrons of the King's Head for which they charge £3. The King's Head is a Chef and Brewer pub with a carvery and bar snacks. Visa and Mastercard are accepted. Tel: (01603) - 782429. Next to the King's Head are free 24 hour moorings, which back on to the Broads Authority Information Centre on Station Road, Hoveton. The Centre is open mornings and afternoons from Easter until October. Tel: (01603) - 782281. A public lavatory and boat refuse compound are located nearby.

The railway bridge is located at the end of this section. This has a clearance of 4.74m (15') AHW. Width is 14.3m (47'). There are overhead lines each side of the railway bridge, both power and telephone. The clearance of both is much greater than the railway bridge. Just upstream of the railway bridge is a long distance of free 24 hour moorings running well into the next section.

B 50R This section is entirely holiday homes and boatyards. Halfway between the road and rail bridges is an access to the downstream half of Bridge Broad; this part of the Broad is entirely covered with motor boat moorings (a bridge over the entrance effectively restricts access) and of little interest. It has an average depth of 1.7m (5.75') in the channel and may be used as temporary moorings by arrangement with Connoisseur

Cruisers. The small but attractive upstream portion of Bridge Broad is entirely separated from the other half of the Broad by the railway embankment. This Broad has a 3 mph speed limit. There are two entrances (one in this section, just beyond the bridge and one further upstream). This little broad would make a quiet overnight mooring, lying to a mudweight, for a boat without too much draught.

Hamilton's cannot recommend trying to sail upstream of Wroxham Bridge, as the river is flanked by such a heavy growth of trees. The low bridge does serve to keep out a large proportion of river traffic so the delightful scenery can be appreciated, far from the madding crowd.

WROXHAM VILLAGE.

What is often known as Wroxham Village is actually two villages. The east side of the river is properly called Hoveton, whilst Wroxham applies to the west bank. The broads boat hire business effectively started here, when John Loynes, moved his boat hiring business from Elm Hill in Norwich to Wroxham in 1878.

The first boat yard in Wroxham, just beside the bridge. The yacht in the photograph was the Caister Maid, described as a "wherry barge".

The view of the village from the river has changed greatly over recent years, with the replacement of most of the boat sheds with holiday housing. Whilst these may not be traditional, they are a great deal more attractive than many of the old sheds; although the villages would still be unlikely to win an award for architecture.

All holiday makers requirements are catered for in Wroxham, where there is a wide range of shops and the four major clearing banks all have branches. Suffling's guide to the Broads published in the 19th century warns visitors "that fresh meat cannot be relied upon... cigars which are smokable cannot be had at all"; whilst he remarks that "Norfolk is noted for bad cheese." Nowadays the area is as well supplied with supermarkets as any other part of the UK; Hamilton's feel sure that Mr. Roy would wish to assure his customers that his cheeses are at least as good as elsewhere. Roys of Wroxham will deliver groceries to boatyards in Wroxham to await hirers or to private yachts. They request, if possible a couple of weeks notice either by telephone (01603) - 782131 fax: (01603) - 784256. or letter to the Store Manager, Roys of Wroxham Ltd., Norwich. NR12 8DB.

Hamilton's Restaurant is La Carozza disguised as part of the railway station with an interior decor evocative of the Orient Exprtess. Good Italian food personally prepared by Nando. Most credit cards accepted. Tel (01603) - 783939.

Wroxham has a tourist narrow gauge railway which runs from near Wroxham mainline station to Aylsham. The Bure Valley Steam Railway runs a regular service from Easter to the end of September. Tel: (01263) 733858. The main line station is close by and has a regular service for an excursion to either Sheringham or Cromer on the coast, or Norwich.

A launderette is situated a few yards to the west of Wroxham Bridge. There is a good fishing tackle shop, nearly opposite the Broads Authority Information Centre. Petrol can be obtained at Broadland Service Station, probably a couple of miles towards Norwich.

Boatyards.

Barnes Brinkcraft. (Blakes), Dayboats, Riverside Road, NR12 8UD. Tel: (01603) - 782625. Fax: (01603) - 784072.
Brister Craft, (Hoseasons) Tel: (01603) - 783783.
Broadland Passenger Craft & G. Smith & Sons Boat Hire, boat trips from Riverside Road, Wroxham. Tel: (01603) - 782527.
Broads Boats Ltd., boat trips, Wroxham road bridge, adjacent King's Head

p.h. Tel: (01603) - 783043.

Broads Tours Ltd. (Office, south of the bridge). Faircraft Loynes boatyard. Electric dayboats available. Tel: (01603) - 782207.Educational discovery cruises, Santa Cruises at Christmas.

Camelot Craft (Blakes) , The Rhond, Wroxham. NR12 8UE. Tel: (01603) - 783096. Bicycle hire. Yachts and sailing craft with auxiliary electric motors.

Connoisseur Craft. (Hoseasons). Tel: (01603) - 782472.

Faircraft Loynes. (Blakes), Wroxham. R12 8RX. Tel: (01603) - 782207. Fax: (01603) - 784272.

Fineway Cruisers. (Blakes), Riverside Rd. Wroxham. NR12 8UD. Tel: (01603) - 782309. Fax: (01603) - 784838.

E.C. Landamore & Co. Wroxham. Tel: (01603) - 782212.

Moore & Co. (Blakes) Staitheway Road, Wroxham. NR12 8RX. Tel: (01603) - 783311. Fax: (01603) - 784295.

Royall & Sons. Dayboats, (Hoseasons), Riverside Road, Wroxham. Tel: (01603) - 783743.

Sabena Marine. (Hoseasons) Tel: (01603) - 782552.

Summercraft. (Hoseasons), Tel: (01603) - 782809.

Wherry Yacht Charter. Barton House, Hartwell Road, Wroxham. Tel: (01603) - 782470.

Yacht Chandlers.

Norfolk Marine, Church Road (01603) 783150. Fax: 782471 Open seven days a week.

Jeckells of Wroxham, sailmakers, Station Road. Tel: (01603) - 782223. Fax: (01603) - 784023.

B 51L *Millcarr Reach, Turnpudding Hole* and *Hagen's Folly.* Free 24 hour moorings between the railway bridge and the bend in the river. Hagen's Folly is said to refer to a Mr. Hagen's unsuccessful marl digging nearby.

B 51R   No moorings. This section contains the furthest upstream entrance to Bridge Broad.

B 52R & L *Cockle Fen* and *Two Acre Reach*. The banks are private and there are no moorings. The outflow in B 52L is Anglian Water's Belaugh Sewage Treatment Works. Between the river and the Old Hall is Belaugh Old Hall Mill.

B 53L *Cranes Yard Reach.*

B 53R *Caen Meadow.* This reach provides a splendid view of Wroxham Church across Caen Meadow which runs down to the river. The meadow is common land and its slopes provides wonderful sledging in the winter. Much of this bank is marked as shallow but there are quayheaded, free 24 hour moorings for three or four boats only.

B 54L *Belaugh Broad Reach.* Belaugh Broad is a small private broad with access closed from the river. It was suction dredged by the Broads Authority in 1987.

B 54R The chart shows a good depth of water along these sections, Norton's Broad is private and about midway up the section. A gas main crosses under the river and there is no mooring to the associated quayheading.

B 55L *Avenue Sheep Wash Reach.* This reach carries permanent Broads Authority signs prohibiting mooring due to bank restoration.

B 55R

B 56L *Doctors Cut Reach.* Do not moor on the bends.

B 56R The dyke running into this section is private and wired off. It runs through Boat Dyke Carr to a complex series of waterways once serving marl diggings known as Little Switzerland.

B 56R *Grovesend,* Grovesend Dyke runs into this section.

BELAUGH. (Chart G)

Belaugh is an attractive village and untypical of the area. The village church of St. Peter sits up on the hill, overlooking the whole of the river valley. The speed limit reduces from 4 mph to 3 mph for the village. The public staithe gives a free 24 hour mooring for two boats (check depth before mooring) and there is a small mooring for visitors to the church. The village has a public telephone and post box but no shop or public house.

Boatyard

Belaugh Boats, (Hoseasons). (01603) - 782802.

B 57L The public staithe lies in this section, much of the rest of this bank is shoal.

B 57R No recommended moorings in this section.

B 58L   *Cooks Carr Reach.* With care, a few moorings can be found. Suffolk Water Company extracts water from here, which is pumped to Ormesby for eventual use in Great Yarmouth.

B 58R   No moorings in this section.

B 59L   *Coltsheds* and *Boatwrights Reach.* At the northern end of this section, Coltishall begins, though the village proper is a mile further upstream. The speed limit is again reduced to 3 mph. On the bend is the site of Clifford Allen's Boatyard, now private houses and moorings. This bend is very sharp and craft should travel as slowly as feasible. Anchor Moorings on the bend charge £5.00 per night with an additional charge for water. Recommended moorings are on Coltishall Common.

B 59R The river bottom is hard over this section but there are no moorings.

B 60L   *Coltishall Hall Reach.* A beautiful spot with a large number of free 24 hour moorings on Coltishall Common. The common is about five minutes walk from the village shops and Post Office. The boat house in the middle of the moorings is private and there is a small shallow section, marked by a surface water outflow just beyond the downstream end of the quayheading.

B 60R   No moorings.

COLTISHALL.

There are two pubs on Coltishall Common, which share a carpark; the Kings Head (01603) - 737426, nearest to the river and the Rising Sun (01603) - 737440. Further pubs along the village are the Red Lion, (01603) - 737426, favoured by villagers and the Recruiting Sergeant, (01603) - 737077 which is just over the bridge in Horstead. There are several antique shops by the road bridge upstream from the lock and other shops are no more than five minutes walk from the Common.

Hamilton's Pub and restaurant is the King's Head on Coltishall Common.

B 61L *Manor House Reach.* 3 mph speed limit. Good free moorings but without quayheading are available for patrons of the Norfolk Mead Hotel c1700. Tel: (01603) - 737531. Some of the banks contain submerged piling and need to be approached with care.

B 61R Soundings along this bank give an average of 1.25m (4').

B 62 L The northern section of the river goes up to what is still described as Coltishall lock. The lock has been unused since 1912 and there is now a sluice for use in flood prevention. This is the limit of navigation of the River Bure and there is tuning space for craft up to 12.7m (42'). There are slipways beside the old lock to enable portage of very light boats and access for them further upstream.

B 62R The southern branch of the river goes only as far as the remains of Horstead Mill, burnt out in 1963 and never rebuilt. This branch of the river has become very shallow, overgrown and only suitable for dinghies. The mill pool proves irresistable to anglers.

The navigable Bure ends at Coltishall Lock, 31.5 miles upstream from Gt. Yarmouth. The Bure rises near Melton Constable and absorbs a large number of smaller rivers and streams on the way. The upper reaches and some of its tributaries are stocked with trout. Wherries were once able to trade for a further nine miles through five locks to the picturesque market town of Aylsham.

Walter Rye, antiquary, genealogist and the last Mayor of Norwich (prior to Lord Mayors) lived at Lamas. Rye lived to the ripe old age of 85 and died in 1929. He spent months on the Broads during all seasons and wrote that he saw two otters on Wroxham Broad one Christmas Day. A prolific writer and noted eccentric, he was famed for receiving Edward VII in a Norfolk jacket, reasoning that old clothes, old books and old friends were best. He may have been right but the discourtesy was said to have cost him a knighthood. Anna Sewell, author of Black Beauty is buried in Lamas where many of her family lived and farmed.

RIVER ANT

The Ant is a tributary of the Bure and approximately eight miles are navigable. It is narrow and very largely unspoilt; whilst it is possible to have a nice gentle reach all the way down the Ant, the river is largely unsuitable for sailing until Barton Broad. It is too narrow to tack a large boat and can be quite heavily trafficked, particularly on changeover days for the large hire fleets at Stalham. Of all the rivers of the broads the Ant has been moved by man furthest from its original course.

The prefix A is used for the River Ant. AB is used for Lime Kiln Dyke which runs between Barton Broad and Neatishead. The prefix AS is used for the sections between Barton Broad, Sutton and Stalham and AD for Dilham Dyke.

The River Ant joins the River Bure at Ant Mouth; section B 33L on page 132. A four mile an hour speed limit is in force as far as Barton Broad.

A 1L *Mill Brig Reach* or *Little Duffers Reach*. At Ant Mouth there is an ALW depth of 2.18m (7') but about 150m up the River there is a shoal with an ALW of 1.56m (5') which crosses the river. This is the remains of the old causeway which once joined St. Benets Abbey with St. James Hospice, now in the grounds of Horning Hall Farm. At this point the bank is made up with stones and rocks. Before the causeway was dug out to create the confluence with the Bure, the River Ant flowed along the Hundred Dyke. This dyke joined the River Thurne which flowed the other way to the sea near Horsey. Beyond the shoal the bottom is soft - 1.56m (5') ALW. No moorings are recommended in this stretch, the river is too narrow and there is submerged piling along the banks.

A 1R. The river is really too narrow to recommend moorings. Watch out for a concreted disused sluice, a little too far out into the channel for comfort.

A 2L *Mussel Corner.* The Hundred Dyke runs off to the east and is thought to be an old course of the River Ant in the Anglo Saxon period, flowing into the River Thurne. At the time the River Thurne flowed in the opposite direction and emptied into the sea beyond Martham Broad. The remains of Ludham Mill are in this section which was used as a gun emplacement during the Second World War. This is the only remnant of three mills once located beside Ludham Bridge.

Ludham Bridge crosses the Ant carrying the A1062 Horning to Ludham road. The river makes a sharp S bend just downstream of the bridge. Visibility is restricted and all craft should slow down as far as feasible. The bridge has a clearance of 2.6m (8.5') AHW. The quays are 5.4m (18') apart, whilst the top of the quay is 2.18m (7') above the river bed. There are plenty of good, free moorings on either side. Riverside fuel, provisions and public telephone are available. Bridge Stores is a General Store, Off

Licence, Café, etc. Just beyond are public toilets. The Dog P.H., a freehouse is three minutes walk, due east.

Just beyond the Dog P.H. is a lane leading to Ludham Hall which was built into the remains of the Bishops Palace. These are not open to the public. Down a farm track from the Hall is the only access by vehicle to St. Benets Abbey. Almost opposite the turning off the Ludham Road is a house suspiciously clad in beautifully napped flints.

Boatyard.

Ludham Bridge Boat Services, electric dayboats, diesel, petrol, gas, fishing tackle, temporary boat licences, cycle hire. Tel: (01692) - 630486.

A 2R Good moorings can be found in this section but there are some protruding bolts and stakes in the quayheading.

A 3L *Horseshoe Reach*. Once past the Bridge Stores quay, the piling is in a dangerous condition and mooring cannot be recommended.

A 3R There are occasional places recently piled giving safe moorings.

A 4L *Neave's Reach*. No good moorings. Neave's Mill, although derelict, still has much of its original machinery.

A 4R No moorings at the old pump. Around the bend a recently piled section gives safe moorings with 1.25m (4') AWL.

A 5L *Spuntey's Mill Reach*. Moorings are not recommended as the piling is bad. At the end of the section is an emergency mooring with access to Ludham (1.5miles) by a lane.

A 5R No Moorings. There is sunken piling at the end of this section.

A 6L *How Hill Reach* (High Hill). How Hill is an imposing house built by the Boardman family in 1904. Before the house was built, the hill was topped by a windmill, which is still in the grounds. How Hill is now a 353 acre Nature Reserve and Environmental Centre, managed in the traditional manner by the Broads Authority.

Norfolk County Council sell day tickets for bank fishing along this stretch.

Just before Boardman's Trestle Mill, close to the boat shed lies an area of gravelly shoal which has only 1.25M (4') at AWL. Clayrack Mill was moved from it's original location at Ranworth in 1987 to its current position just upstream of Boardman's Mill.

Toad Hole Cottage Museum, a former marshmans cottage, is furnished just as it would have been a hundred years ago. It is also open as a Broads Information Centre from Easter to October. Trips may be booked from here on the "*Electric Eel*" a silent, electric powered launch, through the How Hill Nature Reserve. Tel: (01692) - 678763.

A 6R No good moorings, Turf Fen Wind Pump, lies on this stretch which was restored in 1987. Behind the mill lies Reedham Water and what were once some of the finest flight ponds on the Broads.

A 7L There are good moorings at Cromes Broad Dyke, but no access to Cromes Broad, which forms part of the How Hill nature reserve. Cromes Broad appears to have been dug as a turbary around 1380.

A 7R Moorings should be chosen with care.

A 8L *Skeleton Reach.* There are several moorings on this bank with 1.3m (4') ALW.

A 8R There are no moorings to be recommended. Quay headings in this section are overgrown and in some cases sunken. Keep clear.

A 9L *Icehouse Reach.* No recommended moorings.

A 9R *Irstead Shoals.* There is a public staithe and private moorings are marked. Overhanging trees interfere with navigation and can require sailing boats take to the centre of the river. There is sufficient depth throughout but if the water is low, yachts with a draught in excess of four feet may find they bottom briefly in midstream on what is probably the trunk of a fallen tree. Behind the green lies St. Mary's Church, partly thatched with a square tower. William of Wykeham was Rector of Irstead 600 years ago, although he was a noted pluralist and probably never came to Norfolk. Towards the entrance of Barton Broad there are several moorings but none have access.

BARTON BROAD and NEATISHEAD. Chart G.

At some point in history the river Ant has been diverted to run through Barton Broad, The original course of the river is now only marked by a sinuous dyke along the Barton/Catfield parsh boundary. Barton Broad covers an area of about 170 acres. It is a nature reserve, claimed by Norfolk Wildlife Trust although there is a body of local opinion that the area was once common. Speed limit on the broad is 5mph. The tidal rise and fall is only .15m (.5') For safety, boats should navigate between the posts and skippers are asked to remember that these are not intended for mooring.

The Broads Authority have undertaken a major, five year restoration programme of Barton Broad, begun in 1995. Suction dredging was been sponsored by the soap and detergent industries and aided by a £1.15m National Lottery grant. Accumulating over the last fifty years, the silt had reduced the area available for sailing and the murky water caused by phosphate and nitrate enrichment created a super abundance of algae, with consequent deterioration of aquatic life. Disposal of an estimated 250,000 cubic metres of mud has been a major exercise in nearby fields.

All of the broads but particularly the upper Ant have suffered from the uncontrolled growth of riverside trees. This has entirely changed the character of the area and spoilt many upper reaches for sailing. Before the trees grew up, the Victorians were able to see Barton Turf, Stalham and Irstead Churches from Barton Broad.

For Sutton, Stalham, Wayford and Honing, keep to the right hand channel and leave Pleasure Hill Island to port. Pleasure Hill is very shallow with underwater obstructions outside the navigation posts. It was left when Barton Broad was dug out for turf and forms the boundary between Barton and Neatishead parishes.

Wood End Staithe is a public staithe just beyond Pleasure Hill Island, but this is now overgrown and there are submerged tree stumps.

Catfield Staithe to the north of Woods End Staithe, is accessible in a dinghy is somewhat over grown and has regrettably been blocked about half way down. Catfield had staithes leading to both Hickling and Barton Broads.Barton Broad is the home of the Norfolk Punt Club (Sec. Mrs. K. Mason, 146 Trafford Road, Norwich. NR1 2QS Tel: (01603) - 662804. whose pontoons can be seen moored in the middle of the Broad. The

Norfolk Punt is descended from the local gun punts. They are still very low boats but carry large rigs, often two trapezes and have a good turn of speed. They are another example of a local class developed specifically for sailing on inland waters.

AB 1   For Neatishead take the port hand channel. The Nancy Oldfield Trust's (provides sailing for the disabled. Warden: R. Slater, Tel: 01692 - 630572.) pontoon lies to the North of this channel.   About a quarter mile up this channel there is a marked and navigable channel to the west of Pleasure Hill Island to the northern part of Barton Broad. Turkey Broad, the area of open water to the south has only a few centimetres of water.

AB 2   *Lime Kiln Dyke* leads down to Neatishead. The dyke is tree lined and becomes very narrow, so there is no point in trying to sail. A dyke leads off to the right to private houses and Carrow Green Staithe. It was in a boathouse on this staithe that the most famous of all broads lateeners, the *Maria* was found during the 1970's. She was built in 1834 by Brown of Great Yarmouth from "heart of oak" and owned for many years by Sir Jacob Preston of Beeston Hall. She was considered for many years to be the fastest thing on the Broads and can now be seen (by request.) intact at the Yarmouth Maritime Museum. Lateen rigs are usually associated with Arab dhows. No one has been able to explain how this rig came to be transplanted to a small number of sailing boats on the Norfolk Broads in the early 19th century.

Maria on Barton Broad.   *Broadland Sport.*

Gay's Staithe leads off Lime Kiln Dyke to the left and the speed limit is further reduced to 3mph. There are free 24 hr. moorings and a path leads to one of Hamilton's Pubs and Restaurants, The Barton Angler, Irstead Road, Neatishead, Tel: (01692) - 630740, offers good bar food and real ale. Weather permitting, there is a barbecue on summer Saturday evenings. The Barton Angler has both an a la carte restaurant and accommodation, but bookings are advised for both. Visa, Mastercard, American Express are accepted. Rowing and motor dinghies are available for fishing or simply access to Barton Broad. The Inn also offers cycle hire.

The house was once a vicarage and the public bar contains several pieces of masonry presumably at some time removed from a dissolved religious establishment; possibly St. Benets. They were found in the garden by a previous landlord and fixed to the walls. A previous encumbent was Lord Nelson's uncle, which is Barton Broad's claim, in company with several other local waters, to be where Nelson learned to sail.

Do not attempt to take a boat up the next dyke upstream of Gay's Staithe, it is very shallow, private and ends in a house built as an arch over the river. This was a part of Grove Farm and built as a granary for loading wherries. There are no moorings in Lime Kiln Dyke, which has a depth of 1.25m (4') ALW until Neatishead Staithe where there are free 24 hour moorings, although somewhat limited but with just about enough turning space. The village is just about two hundred yards from the landing. The White Horse Stores on Irstead Road is a general store and newsagent, who also sells fishing tackle.

Another of Hamilton's pubs is found at The White Horse P.H. (01692) - 630828, on the road junction. Very friendly, village pub welcoming yachtsmen. Bar snacks are available together with a children's room and dining room. The bars are lined with photographs of local yachts and with just a little good fortune you may even be served by a bishops daughter.

A 11 L&R. A continuation of Barton Broad. At the Northern end of this section is a dyke leading down to Barton Turf. The name of the village betrays its origins. The speed limit is reduced to 4 mph at the end of the Broad. On the public quay can be seen the old coal shed where trading wherries would unload, and the remains of several wherries lay in nearby dykes, including the wherry Victory. There are boat refuse compounds at the public staithe. Free 24 hour moorings can be found at either the public staithe or on Paddy's Lane. Barton Turf Church has a rood screen to rival Ranworth. The village shop is a short walk into the village.

There is a dyke that leads back from Barton Turf, further upstream on the River Ant; forming a triangular island, now covered in trees, between the river and Paddy's Lane with Barton Broad at its apex. This island is known as The Heater. The river upstream of Barton is narrow and usually heavily wooded. Sailing is difficult.

Boatyard.

Cox's Boatyard, Barton Turf; moorings and maintenance on private boats. Tel: (01692) - 536206.

A 12L *Willow Tree Reach*. There are no recommended moorings as trees badly hang over the river. Closer to Barton Broad the banks are piled high with dredging spoil which destroys both the wind and the view.

A 12R There is a mooring in the downstream part of this section. Further upstream bank erosion makes mooring unsafe.

A 13L About half way down this section craft bound for Sutton or Stalham swing east. The junction is signposted.

SUTTON BROAD. (Chart G.)

AS 1 Turning into Sutton Broad, a few bad moorings might be available in the trees.

AS 3   Reeds on both sides, no moorings. Sutton Broad has 1.4m (4.5') of water throughout. There is a very shallow and private dyke on the starboard hand leading to Longmoor. This remote house was built by the Gurney family in 1903 as a freshwater research centre.

AS 5   Sutton Staithe is about 1.25 mile from the River Ant. Speed should be reduced towards Sutton Staithe as manoeuvring and turning space is limited.   There are free 24 hour moorings on the northern bank. Recent tree felling has left stumps on the south bank which could prove a hazard. There is access to the main (A149) which runs from Wroxham to Gt. Yarmouth, via Stalham and Potter Heigham. Sutton Staithe Boatyard (Hoseasons) Tel: (01692) - 581653. lies at the end of the dyke.

The Broad had largely grown over with reeds with just a channel maintained to the farm which Basil Hitchin opened as the Sutton Staithe Hotel in 1928. A nice, old red brick building with an unfortunate restaurant extension added during the 1960's. Credit Cards are accepted.

Sutton Mill is signposted from Sutton Staithe and lies about a mile to the east. This mill was built in the 1789 and with nine stories, is the tallest in England. It last worked in 1940, when lightning struck and destroyed the sails. These have not been replaced but the basic machinery is still intact. The mill houses a collection of agricultural machinery and bygones but its real attraction is the view from the fanstage which includes some twenty churches, two lighthouses, twelve other mills, Horsey Mere, Hickling Broad and part of the coast. Sutton Mill is open to the public daily April and September. Tel: (01692) - 581195.

AS 2   No moorings. *Chapelfield Dyke* (private moorings) and Broads Edge Marina lies off the west bank.

STALHAM. (Chart G)

AS 4   *Stalham Dyke*. This section comprises the last quarter of a mile of Stalham Dyke. Go dead slow approaching the boatyards, as the end of the dyke is masked by buildings. Cook's Staithe lies to the right and at the end is a granary built in 1880 over the dyke to enable wherries to load underneath. This was converted to a house in 1977. There are free moorings on the right at the public staithe at the end of Stalham Dyke with an average depth of 1.25m (4') ALW. Next to the staithe is a boat refuse disposal compound.

Stalham is a large village lying across the A 149 from the moorings and boatyards. It is well catered for in terms of groceries, chemists, garages, hardware, banks, a dentist and launderette. Early closing at Stalham is on Wednesday and some shops still close for the afternoon.

The Museum of the Broads has a new home on Stalham Staithe. It is open from Easter to October on Mondays to Fridays from 1100 hrs - 1700 hrs. The same times apply at weekends over school holidays. Parking and moorings are available at Richardson's boatyard. Tourist Information, gift shop and picnic area are available. There is access for the disabled and admission charges are currently: Adult £2; Children and concessions £1. Family ticket £5. Tel: (01692) - 581681.

Stalham Taxis. (01692) - 581666.

Boatyards.

Broadsedge Marina, David Will and Son. Tel: (01692) -651420
Broads Holidays (Hoseasons) Tel: (01692) - 580748.
Stalham Pleasure Craft. (Hoseasons), Tel: (01692) - 582986.
Richardsons Cruisers, (Hoseasons), Tel: (01692) - 581081
Stalham Water Tours, Tel: (01692) - 670530.
The four businesses above, all operate from the same basin.
Stalham Yacht Services, (Blakes) The Staithe, Stalham, NR12 9DA. Tel: (01692) - 580288. Fax: (01692) - 582636. Motor cruiser, dayboat and canoe hire, Houseboat and cottage rental.
John Williams Boats, Cookes Staithe, Stalham, NR12 9DA. Electric boat recharging, Tel: (01692) - 580953.

River Ant continued upstream from the Stalham/Sutton junction.

A 13L & R Broken quayheading at A13L could prove dangerous moorings.

A 14L & R *Hunsett Mill Reach.* The mill, now a private residence, was built in 1860 and has double scoop wheels. Motor boats proceed slowly. The outside of the bend is shallow with a hard bottom and the bend itself an awkward turn for larger craft.

A 15L

A 15R The remains of Moys Mill lie off this stretch.

A 16L & R   24 hour free moorings by the bridge. Depth of 1.25m (4')
to 1.56m (4.9') ALW all along to Wayford Bridge. Tidal rise and fall can be
ignored.

WAYFORD BRIDGE. (Chart G and Insert).

Once the site of a ford, the current Wayford Bridge was built in the 1960's
and has a clearance at AHW is 2.12m (7'). The width of the bridge is 6.1m
(20') but at ALW the depth of water available under the bridge is only
.93m (3') deep and the bottom hard; this renders Wayford Bridge the end
of navigation on the River Ant for many boats.

Fairview Garage and filling station is a short walk from the river. The
Wayford Bridge Hotel lies immediately upstream of the bridge. Tel:
(01692) - 582414.

Boatyards.

Bank Boats. Repairs, moorings, Tel: (01692) - 582457.
Manor Houseboats. Tel: (01692) - 618140
Neatishead Boatyard, (Blakes), Wayford Bridge, Stalham. NR12 9LL. Tel:
(01692) - 582465.
Urwins Boats. Holiday Accommodation, moorings, Tel: (01692) -
582071.
Wayford Bridge Marina, Tel: (01692) - 582555.

AD 1 *Dilham Dyke* or *Tyler's Cut.* 200m upstream of Wayford Bridge the
river forks to Dilham beside Dilham Dyke Mill. Originally dug to allow
access for smaller "market" wherries, Dilham Dyke is now owned by the
East Anglian Waterways Association. Dredged in 1970, the dyke is once
again navigable by small boats. Relatively free from boat traffic, the dyke
provides excellent winter pike fishing. There is a three mile an hour speed
limit and 1.25m (4') of water. No moorings are recommended until the
free 24 hour moorings at the public staithe at Dilham. Dilham Dyke ends
quite suddenly at Brick Kiln Bridge, just after quite a sharp bend; although
there is a turning basin. There is a public telephone outside the Cross Keys
Inn.

Hamilton's pub is the Crown at Smallburgh, a short distance away.

North Walsham and Dilham Canal.

A 18/19/ 20/21 L&R.

The North Walsham canal is no longer navigable and a large sign proclaims "Private, No Power Craft." The Inland Waterways Association has maintained that a right of navigation exists but no right to moor. The first few yards of the canal has overhanging trees but once past these, the west bank has been dredged and completely cleared of trees. The first stretch is quite usable but the canal can be weedy in summer. There is a right of way along the west bank and a track from Tonnage Bridge to East Ruston to the East. Tonnage Bridge, newly rebuilt, has a clearance of 2.18m (7'). Two sets of power cables cross the canal further upstream although the clearance is far greater than Tonnage Bridge. It is possible to get as far as the cut leading to East Ruston with ease, where there is still a couple of feet of water. It may still be possible to go up to the first lock at Honing in a dinghy, but the overhanging trees hinder progress.

Tonnage Bridge

Constructed in 1825, the canal originally ran for 8½ miles (some of the milestones are still on the banks), through six locks which were large enough to take a fifty foot wherry to the source of the River Ant at Antingham Pond. The canal was built to enable the market town of North Walsham to trade with Yarmouth, but the railways and improved roads that were built soon after the canal, soon saw a decline its use. The upper section above Swafield Bridge fell in to disuse in 1893 and was closed by the Ministry of Transport in 1927. The three locks in the four mile section below Swafield were last used in 1935. Today the length between Honing Lock and Swafield still holds water. Upstream of Tonnage Bridge is Honing Lock, Honing Bridge, Briggate Lock and Bridge, Ebridge Lock, Bacton Wood Lock and Swafield Lock.

RIVER THURNE.

The River Thurne runs into the River Bure at section B 29L (page 126). Sections of the Thurne carry the prefix T. From the junction of Candle Dyke, the prefix TH is used for the sections leading to Hickling and Horsey.

There is a 5 mph speed limit in force from Thurne Mouth.

T 1L *Short Thurne Reach.* Half a mile from Thurne Mouth is Thurne Dyke with Thurne Mill a distinctively white painted mill at the mouth. Thurne Mill and St. Benets Level Mill opposite were built at the same time and are sometimes known as Jack and Jill. The free 24 hour and longer term moorings are very popular on both sides of Thurne Dyke. The Lion Inn (01692 - 670796) is at the head of the dyke as are Post and Telephone boxes. There is a small shop and a gift shop at the staithe. Thurne is the headquarters of the East Anglian Cruising Club. Sec: A.Wiggins, 7 Review Drive, Upton, Norwich, NR13 6BH. Tel: (01493) - 750828.

T 1R Moorings can be found in this section but without access. St. Benets Level Mill.

T 2L *Coldharbour Reach.* No moorings the banks are reserved for fishermen.

T 2R Moorings can be found at piled sections of bank.

T 3L *Ludham Dyke Reach.* Good moorings and a good depth of water.

LUDHAM

T 3R An emergency mooring is found with access by footpath to Ludham one mile away. Depth at AWL is less than 1m (3.25').

The painter Edward Seago lived at Ludham. He was a well known figure about the Broads and several of his paintings were on board the former Royal Yacht Britannia.

On the starboard hand is a the base of the Norfolk Heritage Fleet. Originally built as Percy Hunter's hire fleet, the sixty year old mahogany sailing boats have been kept together as a fleet of engineless boats for hire. In days of yore, some of these yachts were hired and raced in local regattas.

Womack Water, near Ludham. The speed limit is reduced to 4 mph. Womack has been dredged in the main channels but the maze of tiny waterways are badly silted. Good stern on moorings are available at the parish staithe, where moorings are free for 24 hours and there are public toilets, boat refuse facilities and bottle banks. Benita's Maritime Shop is beside Ludham Marine Ltd. Ludham Village is a short walk from Womack where there is a Post Office, garages, several shops and a public house, the King's Arms. (01692) - 678386.

Planet Codwood, a fish and chip shop is immediately beside the Kings Arms.

Boatyards.
Colin Buttifant, Swallowtail Boatyard, Horsefen Rd. Ludham. NR29 5QG. Tel: (01692) - 678066.
Ludham Marine, (Blakes), Womack Staithe, Ludham, Gt. Yarmouth. NR29 5QG. Tel: (01692) - 678322.
Ludham Ferry Marina, Outboard Motor Specialists. School Road, Ludham. Tel: (01692) - 678406. Fax: (01692) - 678303.
Norfolk Heritage Fleet, Hunter's Yard, Horsefen Rd., Ludham, NR29 5QG. Tel: (01692) - 678263. email:huntersyard@btinternet.com

T 4L & 4R *Owle's Reach*. Ludham Marshes National Nature Reserve are on Horse Fen together with the remains of Womack Mill at T 4R. The speed limit is reduced in this reach 4 mph.

POTTER HEIGHAM.

T 5L *Repps Dyke Reach*. Free 24 hour moorings at Repps Staithe. Repps Mill is capless and currently painted red.

T 5R Private Bungalows, no mooring. The mill like structure on this bank started its life as a helter-skelter on the pleasure beach at Great Yarmouth.

T 6L *Johnson's Reach*. Opposite Maycraft there are good moorings on a piled section of bank with access to the village, along a path behind the bungalows. Moorings are available opposite Messrs. Herbert Woods. Potter Heigham's mediaeval road bridge lies in this section. Approach this bridge very carefully as visibility and clearance are strictly limited. Clearance at AHW is 2.03m (6.7') width 6.4m (21'). Like so many old bridges, it does not lie square to the river. If the boats is a marginal "fit" skippers should be advised to keep an eye on the weather forecast, or at least be aware of the possibility of becoming trapped upstream of the bridge.

Please bear in mind that sailing craft with their masts down, have restricted manoeuvrability; many lowered masts hang a long way over the transom and will sweep around as they turn. Reversing is almost impossible.

Hire craft are recommended to seek the services of a Pilot for this bridge. The service is free to Blakes and Hoseasons customers and currently costs others £3.00 per passage. The Pilots are located at the Phoenix Fleet boatyard beside the old bridge Tel: (01692) - 670460. Service is available every day between 8.30 am and 5.30 pm from the week before Easter to 31 October and 10 am to 4 pm weekdays for the rest of the year. However good the pilot; some boats will be unable to pass under the bridge.

Try to arrive at Potter Heigham two hours before low water, easily calculated with the aid of Hamilton's Tide Calculator. When the wind is at any point between South West and North there is a "funnelling" effect caused by the bridge. Craft going through the bridge can seem quite under control until hit by a gust.

T 6R   Mainly private moorings and Herbert Woods boatyard. Herbert Woods have all facilities including those for recharging electric boats. There is a Public Staithe just before the old road bridge and beside a Broads Authority Information Centre. The area between the staithe and the bridge once housed George Applegate's Boatyard; the first yard to be established in Potter Heigham in 1895.

River cruiser *Zingara* clears Potter Heigham bridge.

T 7L & R   *Heigham Bridge Reach*. Moorings on T7R. The new bypass bridge at Potter Heigham, upstream of the old bridge has a clearance of 2.36m (7.75') and a width of 2.4m (73.5'). There are moorings on both sides upstream of the new bridge with those closest to the bridge reserved for yachts to lower their masts.

The village of Potter Heigham (locally pronounced "Ham") lies some distance from the river although there are all facilities within a close distance. Shops are close by, notably Latham's Stores who have a large fishing tackle department. Public telephones and Post Box are beside the bridge, as is the Post Office, a fish and chip shop. A Broads Authority Information Centre is beside the public staithe, downstream of the bridge.

Boatyards.

Herbert Woods, (Blakes), Dayboats, day cruisers, chandlery, repairs, Broads Haven, Potter Heigham, Gt. Yarmouth, NR29 5JD. Tel: (01692) - 670711. Fax: (01692) - 670734.
Phoenix Fleet, Electric Dayboats, Repps Staithe Boatyard, Potter Heigham. Tel: (01692) - 670460.
Maycraft Ltd., (Hoseasons). Tel: (01692) - 670241.

T 8L   *Shannon Wall Reach*. Moorings are private in the first part of this section but some are available at the upstream end, although much of the quayheading looks to be broken down.

T 8R   Numerous private bungalows and no public moorings. Behind the bungalows is High's Mill, which, assisted by its steam pump, once drained a thousand acres.

T 9L   *Martham Steam Mill Reach.* Martham Developments offer free moorings. Fuel, water, telephone etc. are all available.

T 9R   Moorings are to be found without access, those upstream belong to the boatyard.

T 10L *Martham Ferry Reach.* Private bungalows and no moorings till the Ferry. The ferry, which is more of a hinged bridge, is now only in private use for farm vehicles. The ferry does constrict the river but there is just room for two cruisers to pass. Permission can be obtained to moor in the dyke from Martham Ferry Boatyard. Martham village is about a mile away and there are several shops around the village green. Martham Level Mill has been converted to a residence.

Boatyards

Martham Ferry Boatyard. Tel: (01493) - 740303.
Martham Boat Building and Development Company. Tel: (01493) - 740249.

T 10R *Candle Dyke* enters the River Thurne in this section and leads to Hickling Broad and Horsey. (for Hickling Broad and Horsey Mere see pages 168 and 170.) Upstream of Candle Dyke towards West Somerton the speed limit is reduced to 4 mph and boats are asked to steer clear of this stretch of river before 0900 on Sundays to allow anglers some undisturbed time.

T 11L & R   *Martham River Reach.* There is a depth of 1.2m (4') all along this reach and moorings can be found but there are several angling stages along this bank which should not be used for mooring.

T 12L   The depth of water in this channel is 1.2m (4'). In this section are the entrances to Martham Broad which is managed by Norfolk Wildlife Trust. Not far from here, Derrick Amies caught a 42lb 2 oz.British record pike at the end of August in 1985, whilst a thirty five pounder was caught on Martham Broad (private) by Reg Pownall on a large plug in 1961. Keep between the navigation posts.

T 12R   *Dungeon Corner.* There are no moorings in this section. Sock Drain or the Hundred Stream is a straight continuation of the river, blanked off by posts, just downstream of Martham Broad. This is unnavigable but is of interest as the old course of the River Thurne, when it flowed directly into the sea, through Horsey Gap. Over centuries there have been many courses of these rivers flowing out into the North Sea, although none are now visible. From time to time, and the last serious occurrence was in 1953, the sea breaches man's coastal defences, causing serious flooding. When this happens, the sea, somehow, always finds a previous course of one of the rivers. Heigham Holmes Mill lies in this section.

T 13 L   Having passed through Martham Broad and into West Somerton Dyke, moorings are good.

T 13 R   West Somerton is the end of navigation and Winterton beach is only two miles away. West Somerton Mill is in the section. Its last three sails were removed in 1959. You can clearly see the modern wind farm at Winterton, consisting of ten, large, modern windmills, with a still larger addition planned. Some mediaeval wall paintings have been uncovered in Somerton Church and the Norfolk giant, Robert Hales is buried here. Hales died in 1863. In his prime, he stood 7'8" tall and weighed 452 lbs. He had a sister, a mere shadow of her brother at 7'2", who died at the early age of twenty. Sadly but typically of the age, both spent time as fairground exhibits.

Hamilton's pub is The Fisherman's Return in Winterton which is a couple of miles away, but well worth the walk or a short taxi ride. Good food. Tel: (01493) - 393305. Eggs, milk etc. are available from the farm.

CANDLE (or Kendal) DYKE TO HICKLING BROAD.

Returning to the junction of Candle Dyke and the River Thurne in section T 10R the route to Horsey Mere and Hickling Broad is now taken. These sections bear the prefix TH and finally Hickling Broad carries the suffix R whilst Horsey is shown with the suffix L.

Immediately north of the eel set in Candle Dyke is the beginning of Hickling Broad National Nature Reserve which includes Heigham Sound, Hickling Broad and much of the surrounding land. Norfolk Wildlife Trust administer and own most of the land. Posts and buoys mark the channel.

TH 1 L&R   There are intermittent quayheaded moorings on both sides. Candle Dyke has a depth of 1.2m (4') ALW. TH 1R has warnings of eel setts immediately before a house called "The Holt".

TH 2L   Heigham Sound is weedy and shallow with a channel left for navigation which is marked by posts and buoys as is Hickling Broad. Duck Broad lies to the east on entering Heigham Sound. Continuing upstream the water has a depth of .9m (3') with 1.2m (4') in the channel.

TH 2R   Reeds along this section and no moorings.

TH 3R   Hickling Broad entrance is in this section so all sections now bear the suffix R and no distinction is made between left and right. Posts mark the line of the channel. Beware some of the port hand posts which have yet to be painted red which could be very confusing after dark. Opposite the entrance to Meadow Dyke (leading to Horsey Mere) is a stretch of shallow, open water called West Holes. The average depth of the channel at ALW is 1.25m (4.25'). Deep Go Dyke has as much as 1.5m (5') of water in places. Eel setts are sometimes operating in Deep Dyke or Deep Go Dyke on the other side of White Slea. Free 24 hour moorings are available at Deep Go Dyke and White Slea.

HICKLING BROAD AND CATFIELD DYKE.

TH4, 5 & 6R.   The channel is marked with two lines of posts, black with white tops to starboard, red to port, travelling upstream. Swim Coots Mill is to the west of the broad.

Two posts surmounted by a triangle, painted white and in the reeds on the shore are leading marks to find the entrance to Catfield Dyke from Hickling Broad. Turn at the black post with a yellow stripe (confusingly in line with the red port hand posts in the main channel of the broad) and when the leading marks come into line, head straight towards them. If you keep them in line you will find the entrance to Catfield Dyke. The dyke is too narrow for two large motor cruisers to pass but has had some recent maintenance. Larger craft will have difficulty turning. There is a 3 mph speed limit down the whole length. About half way down the dyke, turn to port for Catfield Common Staithe or carry straight on to the Staithe at Catfield. The public staithe has 48 hour moorings.

Catfield Dyke

Hickling Broad has a depth of 1.2m (4') on a hard clay bottom.

On approaching the Pleasure Boat Dyke, keep close to the channel post until in a direct line with the dyke. There is some shoaling on the port side of the dyke entrance. The Pleasure Boat moorings are free to patrons although there is a charge made for mooring and fishing on the Broad. There are public lavatories near the Pleasure Boat. Nearly opposite the Pleasure Boat is Hickling Broad Mill which was used for some years by the artist Roland Green.

This broad is host to two sailing clubs:
Hickling Broad Sailing Club, Sec. Mrs. M.Tate, 127 Taverham Road, Taverham, Norwich. NR8 6SG. Tel: (01603) - 868798. and
Hickling Windsurfing Club. Sec. B. Irving, 220c Unthank Road, Norwich. NR2 2AH. Tel: (01603) - 763229.

Hickling Broad has produced many large pike over a number of years. These pike have a distinctive wide head, said to have developed from feeding on the large shoals of bream.

Nature Trails are open throughout the year, except Tuesdays from 10 am to 5pm.The Norfolk Wildlife Trust run a 2½ hour water trail tour from the Pleasure Boat Staithe in a replica of a local reed boat. The trips run at 10.30 am and 2.00 pm Monday to Friday during July and August and

Tuesdays, Wednesdays and Thursdays during May, June and September. Hickling and Barton offer the best opportunities to see the Swallowtail butterfly which is only now found in this part of East Anglia.

Hamilton's pub is The Greyhound Tel: (01692) - 598306 which has a garden and children's play area and is a short walk to the village, close by the Post Office and a General Store.

The Pleasure Boat (01692 - 598211) which offers bar meals is obviously to be found on Pleasure Boat Staithe.

Boatyard.

Whispering Reeds Boats Ltd.(Hoseasons), slipway and all types of craft for hire. Tel: (01692) - 598314.

HEIGHAM SOUND to HORSEY MERE.

There are no Right and Left distinctions for these sections - all bear the suffix L.

TH 3L   Care must be taken not to cut the corner into Meadow Dyke from Heigham Sound. Round the black post with a yellow stripe to port, if travelling upstream. The speed limit for Meadow Dyke is 4mph until Horsey Mere. Trees are few, but Meadow Dyke is narrow and sailing boats will have to work hard if they have to tack.

TH 4L & R   Moorings can be picked up along the quayheading in TH 4L although the dyke is narrow and care should be taken to leave room for passing craft. Blackfleet Broad is in this section but it is very shallow and unnavigable in anything but a dinghy. Above this broad there is a firm bank to starboard.

HORSEY MERE.

TH 5 & 6L. Speed limit 5 mph. Despite the existence of two public staithes, there are no moorings on Horsey Mere except at the eastern end of the staithe where a mooring fee is charged. Horsey Mere is owned by the National Trust and is considered to be a wildfowl sanctuary of international importance. Its brackish water makes it particularly attractive to a wide variety of migrating sea birds and waders. During the winter when the migrants are here, navigation and fishing are discouraged. Horsey Mill was severely damaged by lightning in 1943. Now owned by the National Trust, it was restored mainly with financial assistance from the now defunct Bradbeer Group of Boat Owners in the early sixties. The mill is open daily from April to September inclusive from 1100 to 1700 hours. Adult admission £1.30. There is a wooden shop alongside together with a lavatory block and boat waste disposal facilities. The pay and display car park makes the area a good venue for walks along both the beach and beside the broad.

There is a telephone kiosk near Hamilton's Pub: The Nelson Head P.H., a half mile stroll into the village. Good food and real ale.

Peter Hancock caught a British record Pike on Horsey Mere in February 1967. The fish weighed 40lb 1oz and was 47" long. It was caught on a wobbled deadbait.

The staithe at Horsey Mere is only 1.25 miles from the sea. When the wind is fresh particularly from the north east to south east, sea bathing may be dangerous. The beach is steep and quickly drops to 3m (9.9') depth. The tide can run strongly along the beach.

TH 7 & 8L To find the entrance to Waxham New Cut, off Horsey Mere, look for the leading marks on the North shore. These are two posts with a triangle and both painted white. The Cut has an average depth at ALW of 1.2m (4')is approximately 1.5 miles long, leading to Bridge Farm. This is the most northerly point of the Broads. In the reign of James 1, Sir William Woodhouse of Waxham Hall built the first duck decoy ever established in England beside Bridge Farm. The Cut is narrow and only very small craft can turn below Waxham Bridge. Craft up to 9.09m (30') have to go through the bridge to turn. Height Clearance on this bridge is 2.03m (6'9")at AHW with a max beam of 4.36m (14'6") It is suggested that boats are turned by hand to save propeller damage. The upper section towards Lound Bridge is no longer navigable. Not far from Waxham New Cut lives a colony of cranes. Brograves Mill, just off Waxham New Cut is derelict.

Waxham New Cut bridge,

SOUTHWOLD.

Southwold is not part of the Broads; but it is very close and a delightfully unspoilt sea side resort, well researched by Hamilton and worth a visit by boat (not Broads hire boats!) or car. Apart from an editorial liking for the town, the only real excuse for including Southwold in a Broads guide is that wherries were built here and worked the once busy River Blyth.

Potential visitors by sea are recommended to make early contact with the Harbour Master (VHF Channel 12, or by telephone on (01502) - 714712.) who can provide both advice on entering the harbour and availability of moorings. The Harbour Office is usually manned for four hours either side of high water.

The harbour entrance into the River Blyth can be very difficult. It is not recommended that it be tackled at much short of high water or in the dark at first attempt. Strong on shore winds can make it a dangerous entrance. The Harbour Master is happy to provide advice on today's positioning of the sand banks and has even been known to talk visitors through the harbour mouth on VHF. Once through the piers in midstream; the channel runs about 10m out from the quay. When the quay ends, resume midstream. These channels can quickly change so be sure to check. In the harbour, the tide runs strongly to about 3.5 knots. Visitor's moorings have about 1.5m depth at chart datum and are found outside Hamilton's pub, The Harbour,

Tel: (01502 - 722381) which has been known to dispense unto Hamilton, the best pint of Adnams ever tasted. The fish and chips aren't bad either. The town of Southwold is charming and about a mile away from the harbour; itself home to a number of small fishing boats, much beloved of local artists. Six old cannon stand guard over Sole Bay from Gun Hill and there are several shops to browse, including the well known Amber Shop. The town has uncommercialised beaches which have been awarded both a European Blue Flag and a Tidy Britain Group, Seaside Award.

Southwold is the home of local brewers Adnams; well known for their real ale which is still delivered locally by horse and dray. They have also been regularly Wine Merchant of the year.

Thoroughly recommended as Hamilton's Restaurants and owned by Adnams are:-

The Swan Hotel, Market Place, Southwold. Tel: (01502) - 722186. Fax: (01502) - 724800. Credit Cards, Visa, Mastercard, Amex., First built in the 17th century and remodelled in the 1820's, the hotel has a relaxed atmosphere with excellent fare available from both bar and dining room. Much feted in the National Press; the bedrooms are more elaborate at The Swan than its sister hotel, The Crown.

The Crown Hotel, High Street, Southwold, Tel: (01502) - 722275. Fax: (01502) - 727263. Credit Cards, Visa, Mastercard, Amex. 18th Century Coaching Inn. Basic bedrooms; good beers brewed in Southwold and a wine list featuring nearly 300 vintages. The Hotel closes for a week in January.

Southwold Museum. Bartholomew Green. Open Easter - September daily 2.30 - 4.30 PM. Free. Tel: 01502 - 722375.

Taxi. Tel: (01502) - 675666.
Southwold Hospital, Casualty Department, Tel: (01502) - 723333.

Boatyard,

John Buckley, Harbour Marine Services Ltd., Blackshore, Southwold, Suffolk. IP18 6TA. Tel: (01502) - 724721. Fax: (01502) - 722060.

Acknowledgments.

The sources used for this detailed publication are many and various. Our thanks are extended to the very large number of people who have helped with a comment or even a chance remark on a change or correction. So many friends have volunteered an anecdote or read a proof. Most grew up with me on these rivers and many similarly failed to reach maturity. Amongst the bodies corporate, The Broads Authority, Waveney District Council, Capt. A. Goodlad of Great Yarmouth Port Authority, Capt. Wooley of Associated British Ports at Lowestoft have all been extremely helpful.

Special thanks are due again to my wife Valerie, who lives with the constant process of updating this publication, exhibiting only remarkable patience and good humour.

Navigation Bye Laws.
1995.

NOTE: NOT FORMING PART OF THE BYELAWS

APPLICATION OF THE BYELAWS - MAP FOR GUIDANCE ONLY

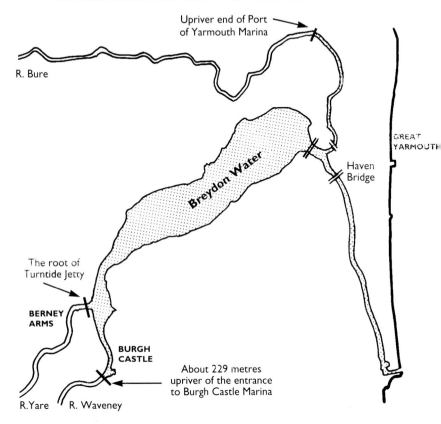

The area of application of the Byelaws is contained in Byelaw 4.

The Byelaws **do not apply** in the Port of Great Yarmouth which is under the jurisdiction of the Great Yarmouth Port Authority and the area of which is shown for the purposes of illustration only shaded on the map.

The boundaries between the Haven and the Broads Authority's Navigation Area are by S25 of Norfolk & Suffolk Broads Act 1988 determined by reference to a notional line drawn -

(a) in the case of the River Bure, between grid references TG 5190 1009 and TG 5193 1012;

(b) in the case of the River Yare, between grid references TG 4700 0511 and TG 4696 0520: and

(c) in the case of the River Waveney, between grid references TG 4722 0379 and TG 4725 0375.

HAMILTON'S BROADS NAVIGATIONS

INDEX
(not forming part of the Byelaws)

1   Citation
2   Commencement
3   Repeal
4   Application
5   Disapplication of The Collision Regulations
6   Interpretation

PART 1:
STEERING & NAVIGATIONAL CONDUCT

7   Responsibility
8   Proper Look-Out
9   Safe Speed
10   Vessels to be Navigated with Care
11   Risk of Collision
12   Action to Avoid Collision
13   Vessels to keep to Starboard/Right Side of Channel
14   Head-on Situation
15   Overtaking
16   Crossing Situation
17   Action by Give-Way Vessel
18   Action by Stand-On Vessel
19   Vessels Crossing/Joining Channel
20   Vessels Entering Navigation Area
21   Letting Go
22   Sailing Vessels
23   Responsibilities between Vessels
24   Sailing Vessels not to Impede Commercial and Passenger Vessels
25   Conduct of Vessels in Restricted Visibility
26   Ferries
27   Towing
28   Person to attend to Towed Vessel
29   Fishing
30   Navigation by Minors
31   Power Vessels approaching Bends or Bridges
32   Speed at Bridges

PART 11:
EXHIBITION OF LIGHTS AND SHAPES

33   Application
34   Visibility of Lights
35   Power-driven Vessels Underway
36   Sailing Vessels, Manually Propelled Vessels and
         Quanted Vessels Underway
37   Towing and Pushing
38   Vessels not under command and Vessels
         restricted in their ability to manoeuvre
39   Vessels constrained by their draught
40   Anchored Vessel
41   Vessels Aground
42   Blue Lights in Official Vessels
43   Visible Signals for Ferries
44   Lights in Moored Vessels
45   Height of Masthead Lights

PART 111:
SOUND SIGNALS

46   Requirement for Whistle
47   Use of Whistle
48   Manoeuvring and Warning Signals
49   Vessels turning Round
50   Sound Signals in Restricted Visibility
51   Signals to Attract Attention

PART IV:
BRIDGE SIGNALS

52   Compliance with Light Signals
53   Signal for Bridge Opening other than Carrow Bridge
54   Signal for Carrow Bridge
55   Signals for Passage of Carrow Bridge
56   Conduct of Vessels not requiring lifting of Carrow Bridge

PART V:
MOORING AND ANCHORING

57   Place of Mooring
58   Moored Vessels to be Properly Secured
59   Mooring Prohibitions to be Obeyed
60   Vessels not to Secure to Navigational Marks
61   Use of Moorings for Specific Periods
62   Vessels to Moor Broadside to Banks
63   Vessels Mooring Abreast
64   Vessels not to Anchor in a Channel
65   Vessels Engaged in Fishing
66   Obstruction of Moorings
67   Working of Engines at Moorings

PART VI:
GENERAL

68   Duty of Master to Comply with Instructions of the Authority
69   Conduct following an Incident
70   Reporting of Sunken Vessels
71   Obstructions
72   Repairs
73   Interference with Vessels
74   Interference with Machinery or Equipment
75   Boarding of Vessels
76   Precautions when Loading or Unloading
77   Security of Anchors and Gear
78   Notice of Lost Anchors
79   Burning of Vessels
80   Bright Lights on Banks
81   Pyrotechnics
82   Firearms and Weapons Prohibited in Navigation Area
83   Drink and Drugs
84   Emission of Smoke or Fumes or the Making of Noise
85   Noise Nuisance
86   Fun Events
87   Indemnity Protecting Officers in Execution of Duty
88   Penalties and Defences

BROADS AUTHORITY NAVIGATION BYELAWS

Byelaws made by the Broads Authority under Section 10(3) and Section 10(5) and paragraph 4 of Schedule 5 of the Norfolk and Suffolk Broads Act 1988.

Citation	1	These Byelaws may be cited as the Broads Authority Navigation Byelaws 1995.
Commencement	2	These Byelaws shall come into operation on the 1st January 1996.
Repeal	3	With effect from the coming into operation of these Byelaws the following are repealed in relation to the navigation area as described in Byelaw 4:

(a) The Rivers Yare, Bure and Waveney Byelaws, 1936;

(b) Byelaw 21 of the Great Yarmouth Port and Haven River Byelaws 1946 as amended by the Great Yarmouth Port and Haven (Amendment) Byelaws 1981;

(c) The River Yare (Carrow Bridge) Byelaws 1938;

(d) The Great Yarmouth Port and Haven (Increase in Fines) Byelaws 1983 in as far as they relate to the Byelaws referred to in paragraphs (a), (b) and (c) above.

Application	4	These Byelaws shall apply to the whole of the navigation area of the Broads Authority as for the time being defined in accordance with Sections 8 and 10(4) of the Norfolk and Suffolk Broads Act 1988 and hereinafter referred to as "the navigation area" and in the case of Byelaws 1-25 and 33-51 and 87 and 88 to all waters navigable by vessels contiguous with the navigation area other than waters within the jurisdiction of the Great Yarmouth Port Authority or Associated British Ports Plc.
Disapplication of The Collision Regulations	5	The Collision Regulations as hereinafter defined shall not apply in any waters to which these Byelaws apply.
Interpretation	6	**(1)** In these Byelaws, unless the context otherwise requires:

"All-round light" means a light showing an unbroken light over an arc of the horizon of 360 degrees.

"Anchor" means any weight, hook, grapnel or similar thing sufficient to hold the mooring line of a vessel to the ground, and "anchoring", "anchored" and "at anchor" shall be construed accordingly.

"The Authority" means the Broads Authority.

"Beam" in relation to a vessel means the full width of the vessel at its widest part and includes fixed fendering.

"By day" means between sunrise and sunset.

"By night" means between sunset and sunrise.

"Channel" means the main navigable part of a river or waterway, or, in broads or similar areas of navigable water, the route generally followed by vessels in transit.

"The Collision Regulations" means regulations made under Section 21 of the Merchant Shipping Act 1979 for the purposes of preventing collisions or under any statutory provisions amending or replacing the same.

"Flashing light" means a light flashing at regular intervals.

"Kedging" means the use by a vessel of an anchor to prevent loss of ground due to unfavourable winds or streams or to prevent the vessel being set into danger, or for hauling off or shifting position.

"Length" in relation to a vessel means the full length of the vessel and includes any fixed fendering, bowsprit or any davits which are not retractable.

"Light sports vessel" means a motor vessel with a block area of no more than 13 square metres which has a planing hull and no permanent covered accommodation and which is capable of towing a water-skier.

"Lighter" means any dumb barge or other like craft for carrying goods or any sailing barge with her masts and gear lowered on deck.

"Manually propelled vessel" means any vessel propelled by oars, sculls or paddles or otherwise by the energy of those on board but excludes a quanted vessel.

"Master" in relation to a vessel means any person whether the owner, master, hirer or other person lawfully or unlawfully having or taking command or charge or management of the vessel for the time being.

"Masthead light" means a white light placed over or as near as practicable over the fore and aft centre line of the vessel showing an unbroken light over an arc of the horizon of 225 degrees and so fixed as to show the light from right ahead to 22.5 degrees abaft the beam on either side of the vessel.

"Navigate" means direct the course of movement of.

"Navigation Officer" means the Navigation Officer of the Broads Authority and any assistant appointed by the Broads Authority.

"Officer of the Authority" means any officer of the Authority employed to secure compliance with these Byelaws.

"Owner" in relation to a vessel includes the person for the time being registered as the owner under the Great Yarmouth Port and Haven River Byelaws 1946 (as amended) or any Byelaw made by the Authority replacing the same.

"Pleasure vessel" means any vessel used for sport or recreation whether hired or privately owned and includes a houseboat.

"Power-driven vessel" means any vessel propelled by machinery.

"Prolonged blast" means a blast of between 4 and 6 seconds duration.

"Quanted vessel" means a vessel whether or not under sail which is being propelled by use of a quant.

"Restricted visibility" means any condition in which visibility is restricted by fog, mist, falling snow, heavy rain storms, sand storms, smoke or similar causes.

"Sailing vessel" means any vessel under sail other than a quanted vessel provided that propelling machinery, if fitted, is not being used.

"Short blast" means a blast of about one second duration.

"Sidelight" means a green light on the starboard side and a red light on the port side each showing an unbroken light over an arc of the horizon of 112.5 degrees and so fixed as to show the light from right ahead to 22.5 degrees abaft the beam on its respective side. In a vessel of less than 20 metres in length the sidelights may be combined in one lantern carried on the fore and aft centre line of the vessel.

"Sternlight" means a white light placed as nearly as practicable at the stern showing an unbroken light over an arc of the horizon of 135 degrees and so fixed as to show the light 67.5 degrees from right aft on each side of the vessel.

"Towed" includes any vessel being propelled by any other and "towing" shall be construed accordingly.

"Towing light" means a yellow light having the same characteristics as a sternlight.

"Underway" when used in relation to a vessel means that it is not at anchor or moored or secured to the banks, shores or bed of a waterway or aground and includes a vessel dropping up or down a waterway with its anchor on the ground.

"Vessel" includes every description of water craft, including a non-displacement vessel, used or capable of being used for transportation on water.

"Vessel constrained by its draught" means a power-driven vessel which because of its draught in relation to the available depth and width of navigable water is severely restricted in its ability to deviate from the course it is following .

"Vessel not under command" means a vessel which through some exceptional circumstances is unable to manoeuvre as required by these Byelaws and is therefore unable to keep out of the way of another vessel.

"Vessel restricted in its ability to manoeuvre" means a vessel which from the nature of its work is restricted in its ability to manoeuvre as required by these Byelaws and is therefore unable to keep out of the way of another vessel. The term shall include but is not limited to:

(i) a vessel engaged in laying, servicing or picking up a navigation mark, submarine cable or pipeline;
(ii) a vessel engaged in dredging, surveying or underwater operations;
(iii) a vessel engaged in replenishment or transferring persons, provisions or cargo when underway;
(iv) a vessel engaged in a towing operation such as severely restricts the towing vessel and its tow in their ability to deviate from their course and/or speed.

"Whistle" means an efficient whistle, siren horn or other sound signalling appliance capable of producing such blasts as are prescribed in the Byelaws.

(2) The Interpretation Act 1978 shall apply for the interpretation of these Byelaws as it applies for the interpretation of an Act of Parliament and as if for the purposes of Sections 15 and 16 of that Act these Byelaws were an Act of Parliament and the Byelaws revoked by Byelaw 3 were Acts of Parliament thereby repealed.

PART 1: STEERING AND NAVIGATIONAL CONDUCT

Responsibility 7 **(1)** Nothing in these Byelaws shall exonerate the master of any vessel from the consequences of any neglect to comply with the provisions thereof or from the neglect of any precaution which may be required by the ordinary practice of watermen in the navigation area or by the special circumstances of the case.

(2) In construing and complying with these Byelaws the master of a vessel shall have due regard to all dangers of navigation or collision or to any special circumstance, including the limitations of the vessels involved, which may make a departure from the provisions thereof necessary to avoid any immediate danger to persons or to property.

(3) In the event of a prosecution for any breach of these Byelaws it shall be for the defendant to prove the existence of any such dangers of navigation or collision or special circumstances necessitating a departure from these Byelaws to avoid any immediate danger to persons or property.

Proper 8 The master of a vessel shall keep or cause to be kept a proper
Look-Out look-out by sight and hearing and shall observe any precaution which may be required by the ordinary practice of watermen in the navigation area or by the special circumstances of the case.

Safe Speed 9 The master of a vessel shall ensure that at all times it is navigated at such a speed that it can take proper and effective action to avoid collision and be stopped within a distance appropriate to the prevailing circumstances and conditions.

Vessels to be 10 The master of a vessel shall navigate the vessel and any
Navigated vessel towed thereby:
with Care
(a) with care and caution; and

(b) at a speed and in a manner which:
(i) avoids injury and the likelihood of injury to the occupants of other vessels;
(ii) avoids damage and the likelihood of damage to other vessels, property, moorings or structures on the banks comprised in the navigation area;
(iii) avoids giving reasonable grounds for annoyance to other persons using the navigation area;
(iv) avoids damage and the likelihood of damage to the banks or bankside vegetation comprised in the navigation area;

(v) shows reasonable consideration for persons fishing from boats or the banks of the navigation area provided that this sub-paragraph shall not be construed as relieving a person fishing of his obligation under Byelaw 29 to ensure that his rod or line does not obstruct the passage of a vessel along a channel.

Risk of Collision   **11**

(a) The master of a vessel shall use all available means appropriate to the prevailing circumstances and conditions to determine if risk of collision exists.

(b) If there is any doubt such risk shall be deemed to exist.

Action to Avoid Collision   **12**

(1) The master of a vessel shall ensure that any action taken to avoid collision shall if the circumstances of the case admit be positive, made in ample time and with due regard to the observance of good seamanship.

(2) The master of a vessel shall ensure that:

(a) any action taken to alter course or speed to avoid collision shall if the circumstances of the case admit be large enough to be readily apparent to another vessel observing visually.

(b) a succession of small alterations of course and/or speed is avoided.

(c) action taken to avoid collision with another vessel shall be:
(i) such as to result in the vessel passing at a safe distance;
(ii) carefully checked by the master until the other vessel is finally past and clear.

(3) The master of a power-driven vessel shall if necessary to avoid collision or to allow more time to assess the situation slacken the speed of the vessel or take all way off by stopping or reversing its means of propulsion.

Vessels to keep to Starboard/Right Side of Channel   **13**

The master of a power-driven or manually propelled vessel proceeding along a channel shall when it is safe and practicable to do so keep to the side of mid channel which lies on the starboard or right hand side of the vessel.

Head-on Situation   **14**   **(1)** When two vessels, whether power-driven or manually propelled, are meeting on reciprocal or nearly reciprocal courses so as to involve risk of collision the master of each vessel shall if it is safe and practicable to do so alter the course of his vessel to starboard so that each vessel shall pass on the port side of the other.

(2) (a) Such a situation as is referred to in paragraph (1) shall be deemed to exist when the master of a vessel sees the other vessel ahead or nearly ahead and by night he could see the masthead lights of the other vessel in a line or nearly in a line and/or both sidelights and by day he observes the corresponding aspect of the other vessel.

(b) When the master is in any doubt as to whether a situation as is referred to in paragraph (1) exists he shall assume that it does exist and act accordingly.

Overtaking   **15**   **(1)** Notwithstanding any provision to the contrary in these Byelaws the master of a vessel overtaking another vessel shall keep his vessel out of the way of the vessel being overtaken.

(2) A vessel shall be deemed to be overtaking when coming up with another vessel from a direction more than 22.5 degrees abaft its beam, that is, in such a position with reference to the vessel it is overtaking that at night the master would be able to see only the sternlight of the vessel but neither of its sidelights.

(3) When a master is in any doubt as to whether his vessel is overtaking another he shall assume that this is the case and act accordingly.

(4) Any subsequent alteration of the bearing between the two vessels shall not make the overtaking vessel a crossing vessel for the purposes of Byelaw 16 or relieve the master of the overtaking vessel of his duty of keeping clear of the overtaken vessel until his vessel is finally past and clear.

Crossing Situation   **16**   When two vessels whether power-driven or manually propelled are crossing so as to involve risk of collision the master of the vessel which has the other on its own starboard side shall keep his vessel out of the way and shall, if the circumstances of the case admit, avoid crossing ahead of the other vessel.

Action by Give-Way Vessel	17	The master of a vessel which is obliged to keep out of the way of another vessel shall, so far as possible, take early and substantial action to keep well clear.

Action by Stand-On Vessel 18

(1) (a) Where pursuant to these Byelaws one of two vessels is to keep out of the way of the other the master of the other shall subject to sub-paragraph (1)(b) keep his course and speed.

(b) The master of the latter vessel may take action to avoid collision by his manoeuvre alone, as soon as it becomes apparent to him that the vessel required to keep out of the way is not taking appropriate action in compliance with these Byelaws.

(2) When for any reason the master of a vessel required under these Byelaws to keep its course and speed finds his vessel so close that collision cannot be avoided by the action of the give way vessel alone he shall take such action as will best aid to avoid collision.

(3) The master of a vessel, whether power-driven or manually propelled, who takes action in a crossing situation in accordance with sub-paragraph (1) (b) of this Byelaw to avoid collision with another vessel whether power-driven or manually propelled shall, if the circumstances of the case admit, not alter the course of his vessel to port for a vessel on the port side of his vessel.

(4) Nothing in this Byelaw shall relieve the master of the give-way vessel of his obligation to keep out of the way of the other vessel.

Vessels Crossing/ Joining Channel 19

(1) Except as provided in paragraph (2) but notwithstanding any other provision in these Byelaws the master of a power-driven or manually propelled or quanted vessel crossing from one side of a channel to the other side or entering a channel from a side dyke or other waterway shall do so at a proper time having regard to any vessels navigating along the channel and shall give way to such vessels.

(2) This Byelaw does not apply to any vessel whilst entering the navigation area from any waterway within the jurisdiction of the Great Yarmouth Port Authority.

Vessels Entering the Navigation Area   **20**

(1) Except as provided in paragraph (2) the master of a vessel entering the navigation area from an adjoining waterway or channel shall carry out that manoeuvre without interfering unreasonably with the passage of any other vessel navigating in the navigation area.

(2) This Byelaw does not apply to any vessel whilst entering the navigation area from any waterway within the jurisdiction of the Great Yarmouth Port Authority.

Letting Go   **21**

The master of a vessel shall ensure that the vessel is not let go from or moved away from a berth or mooring under circumstances where the manoeuvre is likely to interfere unreasonably with the passage of any other vessel in sight.

Sailing Vessels   **22**

(1) When two sailing vessels are approaching one another so as to involve risk of collision, one of them shall keep out of the way of the other as follows:

(a) when each has the wind on a different side, the vessel which has the wind on the port side shall keep out of the way of the other;

(b) when both have the wind on the same side, the vessel which is to windward shall keep out of the way of the vessel which is to leeward;

(c) if a vessel with wind on the port side sees a vessel to windward and cannot determine with certainty whether the other vessel has the wind on the port or on the starboard side, she shall keep out of the way of the other.

(2) For the purposes of this Byelaw the windward side shall be deemed to be the side opposite to that on which the mainsail is carried.

Responsibilities Between Vessels   **23**

(1) Subject to the requirements of Byelaw 15:

(a) The master of a power-driven vessel underway shall keep his vessel out of the way of:

(i) a vessel not under command;
(ii) a vessel restricted in its ability to manoeuvre;
(iii) a sailing vessel;
(iv) a quanted vessel.

(b) The master of a sailing vessel underway shall keep his vessel out of the way of:

(i) a vessel not under command;

(ii) a vessel restricted in its ability to manoeuvre;

(iii) a quanted vessel.

(c) (i) The master of a vessel other than a vessel not under command or a vessel restricted in its ability to manoeuvre shall, if the circumstances of the case admit, avoid his vessel impeding the safe passage of a vessel constrained by its draught, exhibiting the signal in Byelaw 39.

(ii) The master of a vessel constrained by its draught shall navigate his vessel with particular caution having full regard to that constraint.

(2) For the purposes of sub-paragraph (1) (a) (iii) of this Byelaw a Sailing Vessel shall include a wherry under sail notwithstanding that it is also being propelled by machinery; and for this purpose a wherry shall mean a vessel known in the Broads as a wherry or wherry yacht.

**Sailing Vessels 24
Not to Impede
Commercial and
Passenger Vessels**

(1) Notwithstanding any other provision in these Byelaws but subject to paragraph (2) the master of a sailing vessel of length less than 15 metres (49 feet 3 inches) shall not navigate his vessel so as unnecessarily to hamper or delay the passage of:

(a) a power-driven vessel of length greater than 15 metres (49 feet 3 inches) which is being used for or is ordinarily used for the commercial carriage of passengers or goods or for the maintenance or dredging of waterways or for commercial fishing, or

(b) a towing vessel and its tow if the towing vessel is:

(i) towing astern or pushing ahead and the overall length of the tow from the stem of the forward vessel to the stern of the rear vessel exceeds 15 metres, (49 feet 3 inches) or

(ii) towing alongside and the length of either the towing or towed vessel exceeds 10 metres (32 feet 10 inches) or the combined width of towing and towed vessels exceeds 5 metres (16 feet 5 inches)

unless in either case under sub-paragraph (b) the towing vessel is a pleasure vessel of length less than 15 metres (49 feet 3 inches) which is towing a tender or other vessel of length less than 7.5 metres (24 feet 7 inches).

(2) Paragraph (1) shall not be construed as relieving the master of a vessel to which it applies of any obligation under Byelaw 23 to keep out of the way of a sailing vessel.

Conduct of Vessels in Restricted Visibility

25 **(1)** This Byelaw applies to vessels not in sight of one another when navigating in or near an area of restricted visibility.

(2) The master of a vessel to which this Byelaw applies shall:

(a) ensure that it proceeds at a safe speed adapted to the prevailing circumstances and conditions of restricted visibility;

(b) have due regard to the prevailing circumstances and conditions of restricted visibility; and

(c) if it is a power-driven vessel, ensure that the engines of the vessel are ready for immediate manoeuvre.

(3) Except where it has been determined that a risk of collision does not exist, the master of a vessel to which this Byelaw applies who hears apparently forward of the beam of the vessel the fog signal of another vessel, or whose vessel cannot avoid a close quarters situation with another vessel forward of the beam of his vessel, shall:

(a) reduce the speed of his vessel to the minimum at which it can be kept on its course; and

(b) if necessary take all way off his vessel and in any event navigate with extreme caution until danger of collision is over.

Ferries **26** The master of a vessel operating as a ferry shall when crossing a waterway keep out of the way of any vessel navigating along the waterway.

Towing **27** **(1)** Except as provided for in this Byelaw or otherwise with the consent of the Authority the master of a vessel shall navigate singly and shall not cause or permit it to tow or push another vessel.

(2) The exceptions referred to in paragraph (1) are that:

(a) the master of a power-driven vessel may tow one other vessel which is secured alongside provided that no other vessel is at the same time pushed ahead or towed alongside without the consent of the Authority; or

(b) the master of a power-driven vessel may push ahead one other vessel provided:

(i) it is properly equipped for that purpose; and

(ii) no other vessel is towed at the same time; or

(c) the master of a power-driven vessel or a manually propelled vessel may tow not more than two other vessels (or a greater number with the consent of the Authority) in a single line at the same time; or

(d) the master of a power-driven vessel may tow any number of launches, dinghies, skiffs, canoes, punts or similar vessels provided each vessel being towed is less than 7.5 metres (24 feet 7 inches) long; or

e) the master of a sailing vessel or towing vessel may tow a small craft used as a means of gaining access to or going ashore from the vessel which is towing it;

and provided that in each case the conditions referred to in paragraph (3) are complied with.

(3) The conditions referred to in paragraph (2) are that:

(a) If the towing vessel or the vessel being towed is a vessel being used for or ordinarily used for the commercial carriage of passengers or goods or for the maintenance or dredging of waterways or for commercial fishing the overall length of the tow measured from the stern of the towing vessel to the stern of the towed vessel shall not exceed 100 metres (328 feet).

(b) If the towing vessel is a pleasure vessel the overall length of the tow measured from the stern of the towing vessel to the stern of the towed vessel shall not exceed 35 metres (115 feet).

(c) the overall width of a tow including both or all the vessels towed or towing alongside shall not exceed 8 metres (26 feet 3 inches).

(4) In giving their consent under any part of this Byelaw the Authority may impose such conditions as it thinks fit.

(5) Nothing in this Byelaw shall be taken to override the provisions of the Broads Authority Speed Limit Byelaws 1992 in so far as they relate to the towing of waterskiers.

Person to attend to Towed Vessel	**28**	The master of a vessel towing or pushing another vessel which is more than 10 metres (32 feet 10 inches) in length shall ensure that there is always at least one competent person on board the towed vessel for the purpose of its navigation and management.

Fishing   **29**

(1) Subject to paragraph (2) no person shall conduct any fishing or any associated activity from a power-driven or sailing vessel which is underway or cause or permit any net or fishing line to hang from such a vessel into the water whilst the vessel is underway.

(2) Paragraph (1) shall not apply to a vessel which is:

(a) engaged in the handling of licensed eel nets; or

(b) under the control of the National Rivers Authority in connection with its fishery duties.

(3) Any person fishing from a boat or the bank shall show reasonable consideration to any other person using the navigation area and shall ensure that his rod or line does not obstruct the passage of a vessel along a channel.

Navigation by Minors   **30**

(1) Subject to paragraphs (2) (3) and (4) no person below the age of 14 years shall be at the helm of a power-driven vessel.

(2) Subject to paragraph (5) a person who has reached the age of 8 years but is below the age of 14 years may be at the helm of a power-driven vessel provided that the following conditions are satisfied:

(a) The vessel is an open boat of 4.5m (14 feet 9 inches) length or less; and

(b) The vessel if propelled by an outboard motor has engine power of not more than 4.47 kw (or equivalent rating) or if powered by an inboard motor is incapable of attaining a speed greater than 8 mph through the water; and

(c) That person is under the supervision of a person, whether or not in the vessel, over the age of 18 years.

(3) Subject to paragraph (5) a person who has reached the age of 8 years but is below the age of 14 years may be at the helm of a power-driven vessel other than a vessel as described in sub-paragraphs (2) (a) and (b) provided that the following conditions are satisfied:

(a) That person is under the supervision of a person who is in the vessel and who has reached the age of 18 years; and

(b) The person who is providing supervision remains at all times close to the helm so as to be able immediately to take the helm in the event of necessity; and

(c) The person who is providing supervision maintains at all times a proper navigational watch.

(4) A person who has reached the age of 9 years may be at the helm of a power-driven vessel in Oulton Broad at any time whilst the Broad is temporarily closed under paragraph 10(1)(c) of Schedule 5 to the Norfolk and Suffolk Broads Act 1988 provided that the person is an entrant for powerboat racing on Oulton Broad on that day and the vessel has engine power of not more than 11.19 kw (or equivalent rating).

(5) Nothing in paragraphs (2) or (3) shall permit a person who has reached the age of 8 years but is below the age of 14 years to be at the helm of a light sports vessel or at the helm of any power-driven vessel which is travelling at a speed greater than 6 mph over the ground.

(6) A person providing supervision as required by this Byelaw shall be deemed to be the master of the vessel for the purposes of these Byelaws.

(7) No person shall cause or permit another person to be at the helm of a power-driven vessel in contravention of this Byelaw.

Power Vessels approaching Bends or Bridges	**31**	The master of a power-driven vessel navigating against the current or tidal flow shall, if necessary to avoid the risk of collision, ease the speed of or stop the vessel on approaching or rounding a bend or approaching a bridge to allow any vessel navigating with the current or tidal flow to pass clear.
Speed at Bridges	**32**	The master of a vessel passing through a bridge shall navigate the vessel at the lowest practicable speed consistent with safety.

PART II: EXHIBITION OF LIGHTS AND SHAPES

Application   **33**   The master of every vessel shall ensure that:

(a) Byelaws 34 to 45 are complied with in all weathers.

(b) The Byelaws concerning lights shall be complied with from sunset to sunrise, and during such times no other lights shall be exhibited, except such lights as cannot be mistaken for the lights specified in these Byelaws or as do not impair their visibility or distinctive character, or interfere with the keeping of a proper look out or with the safe navigation of any other vessel.

(c) The lights prescribed by these Byelaws shall also be exhibited from sunrise to sunset in restricted visibility and may be exhibited in all other circumstances when it is deemed necessary.

(d) The Byelaws concerning shapes shall be complied with by day.

Visibility of   **34**   The master of a vessel shall ensure that all lights prescribed in
Lights   these Byelaws shall have an intensity sufficient to be visible at the following minimum ranges:

(a) for a vessel of 50 metres (164 feet) or more in length:
-a masthead light, 6 nautical miles (12,150 yards or 11,110 metres);
-a sidelight, 3 nautical miles (6,075 yards or 5,555 metres);
-a sternlight, 3 nautical miles (6,075 yards or 5,555 metres);
-a towing light, 3 nautical miles (6,075 yards or 5,555 metres);
-a white, red, green or yellow all-round light, 3 nautical miles (6,075 yards or 5,555 metres).

(b) for a vessel of less than 50 metres (164 feet) in length:
-a masthead light, 2 nautical miles (4,050 yards or 3,703 metres);
-a sidelight, 1 nautical mile (2,025 yards or 1,852 metres);
-a sternlight, 1 nautical mile (2,025 yards or 1,852 metres);
-a towing light, 1 nautical mile (2,025 yards or 1,852 metres);
-a white, red, green or yellow all-round light, 1 nautical mile (2,025 yards or 1,852 metres).

(c) for an inconspicuous, part-submerged vessel or object:
-a white all-round light, 2 nautical miles (4,050 yards or 3,703 metres).

Power-driven Vessels Underway **35** **(1)** Subject to paragraph (2) the master of a power-driven vessel underway shall cause to be exhibited:

(a) a masthead light;

(b) a second masthead light abaft of and higher than that in (a) except that a master of a vessel less than 50 metres (164 feet) in length shall not be obliged to exhibit such light but may do so;

(c) sidelights;

(d) a sternlight.

(2) Notwithstanding paragraph (1):

(a) the master of a power-driven vessel less than 12 metres (39 feet 4 inches) in length may cause to be exhibited in lieu of the lights prescribed in paragraph (1) an all-round white light and sidelights, and

(b) the master of a power-driven vessel less than 7 metres (23 feet) in length may cause to be exhibited in lieu of the lights prescribed in paragraph (1) of this Byelaw an all-round white light and shall, if practicable, also cause to be exhibited sidelights.

Sailing Vessels Manually Propelled Vessels and Quanted Vessels Underway **36** **(1)** The master of a sailing vessel underway shall cause to be exhibited:

(a) sidelights; and

(b) a sternlight.

(2) The master of a sailing vessel underway may, in addition to but not in substitution for the lights prescribed in paragraph (1) cause to be exhibited at or near the top of the mast, where they can best be seen, two all-round lights in a vertical line, the upper being red and the lower green.

(3) The master of a manually propelled vessel or a quanted vessel underway which is 4.5 metres (14 feet 9 inches) or more in length shall cause to be exhibited the lights in paragraph (1) or shall cause to be exhibited an all-round white light or two white lights giving the same coverage.

(4) The master of a manually propelled vessel or a quanted vessel underway which is less than 4.5 metres (14 feet 9 inches) in length shall ensure that there is ready at hand in the vessel an electric torch or lighted lantern showing a white light and shall cause such torch or lantern to be exhibited in sufficient time to prevent collision.

Towing and Pushing 37 **(1)** The master of a power-driven vessel of greater than 15 metres (49 feet 3 inches) in length shall when it is towing a vessel the length of which exceeds 7.5 metres (24 feet 7 inches) cause to be exhibited:

(a) instead of the lights prescribed in Byelaw 35, two masthead lights forward in a vertical line;

(b) sidelights;

(c) a sternlight; and

(d) a towing light in a vertical line above the stern light.

(2) The master of a power-driven vessel greater than 15 metres (49 feet 3 inches) in length shall when the vessel is pushing ahead or towing alongside, except in the case of a rigidly connected composite unit cause to be exhibited:

(a) instead of the light prescribed in Byelaw 35, two masthead lights in a vertical line;

(b) sidelights; and

(c) a sternlight.

(3) When a pushing vessel and a vessel being pushed ahead are rigidly connected in a composite unit they shall be regarded as a power-driven vessel and exhibit the lights prescribed in Byelaw 35.

(4) The master of a power-driven vessel when towing by night shall cause to be exhibited on the vessel being towed:

(a) when the beam of the towed vessel exceeds the beam of the towing vessel, side lights and a stern light;

(b) when the overall length of the tow exceeds 7.5 metres (24 feet 7 inches) and the beam of the towed vessel does not exceed the beam of the towing vessel, a stern light

provided that any number of vessels being towed alongside the towing vessel or being pushed in a linked group by the towing vessel shall be lighted as one vessel.

(5) Where from any sufficient cause it is impracticable for a vessel or object being towed to exhibit the lights prescribed in paragraph (4) the master of the towing vessel shall ensure that all possible measures shall be taken to light the vessel or object towed or at least to indicate the presence of such vessel or object.

(6) When for any sufficient reason it is impracticable for a vessel not normally engaged in towing operations to display the lights required by paragraph (1) or (2) the master of such vessel shall not be required to ensure that the vessel exhibits those lights when engaged in towing another vessel in distress or otherwise in need of assistance, but shall ensure that all possible measures shall be taken to indicate the nature of the relationship between the towing vessel and the vessel being towed in particular by illuminating the tow line.

Vessels not under command and Vessels restricted in their ability to manoeuvre

38 **(1)** The master of a vessel not under command of 20 metres (66 feet) or more in length shall and the master of a vessel not under command of less than 20 metres (66 feet) in length may cause to be exhibited:

(a) two all-round red lights in a vertical line where they can best be seen;

(b) two balls in similar shapes in a vertical line where they can best be seen; and

(c) when making way through the water, in addition to the lights prescribed in this paragraph, sidelights and a sternlight.

(2) The master of a vessel restricted in its ability to manoeuvre of 20 metres (66 feet) or more in length shall and the master of a vessel restricted in its ability to manoeuvre of less than 20 metres (66 feet) in length may cause to be exhibited:

(a) three all-round lights in a vertical line where they can best be seen. The highest and lowest of these lights shall be red and the middle light shall be white;

(b) three shapes in a vertical line where they can best be seen, the highest and lowest of these shapes shall be balls and the middle one a diamond;

(c) when making way through the water, a masthead light or lights, sidelights and a sternlight in addition to the lights prescribed in sub-paragraph (a); and

(d) when at anchor, in addition to the lights or shapes prescribed in sub-paragraph (a) and (b), the lights or shapes prescribed in Byelaw 40.

(3) The master of a vessel engaged in a towing operation such as renders it unable to deviate from its course and/or speed shall, in addition to the lights or shapes prescribed in sub-paragraphs (2) (a) and (b) of this Byelaw cause to be exhibited the lights prescribed in Byelaw 37.

(4) The master of a vessel engaged in dredging or underwater operations, when restricted in its ability to manoeuvre shall cause to be exhibited the lights and shapes prescribed in paragraph (2) and shall in addition, when an obstruction exists, cause to be exhibited:

(a) two all-round red rights or two red balls in a vertical line to indicate the side on which the obstruction exists;

(b) two all-round green lights or two white diamonds in a vertical line to indicate the side on which another vessel may pass;

(c) when making way through the water, in addition to the lights prescribed in this paragraph, masthead lights, sidelights and a stern light.

(5) The master of a vessel engaged in dredging or underwater operations when at anchor shall cause to be exhibited the lights or shapes prescribed in sub-paragraphs (4) (a) and (b) of this Byelaw instead of the lights prescribed in Byelaw 40.

(6) Notwithstanding the provisions of paragraph (4) of this Byelaw the master of a dredger or vessel engaged in underwater operations in the navigation area which is less than 20 metres (66 feet) in length may in place of the lights and shapes prescribed in that paragraph ensure that the vessel exhibits the following signals:
(i) by night a red light visible all round the horizon at a distance of 1 kilometre (1,100 yards) or such other light signals as are approved by the Authority;
(ii) by day, a red flag on the side where there are obstructions to navigation.

(7) The master of a vessel engaged in diving operations shall cause to be exhibited a rigid replica of the International Code Flag A of a size and in such a position as to be clearly visible to other vessels in the vicinity. Measures shall be taken by the master to ensure all-round visibility.

(8) The signals prescribed in this Byelaw are not signals of vessels in distress and requiring assistance.

Vessels constrained by their draught 39 The master of a vessel constrained by its draught may in addition to the lights prescribed for power-driven vessels in Byelaw 35 cause to be exhibited where they can best be seen three all-round red lights in a vertical line, or a cylinder.

Anchored Vessels 40 **(1)** Subject to paragraph (2) and paragraph (c) of Byelaw 65 the master of a vessel at anchor shall cause to be exhibited where they can best be seen:

(a) by night an all-round white light which shall be visible at a distance of 1 kilometre (1,100 yards);

(b) by day one ball.

(2) Notwithstanding paragraph (1) the master of a pleasure vessel of less than 25 metres (82 feet) in length when at anchor otherwise than in or near a channel shall not be required to exhibit an anchor light or shape.

Vessels Aground 41 The master of a vessel aground of 50 metres (164 feet) or more in length shall and the master of a vessel aground of less than 50 metres in length may in addition to the lights prescribed in Byelaw 40 cause to be exhibited where they can best be seen:

(a) two all-round red lights in a vertical line;

(b) three balls in a vertical line.

Blue Lights in Official Vessels 42 Except with the consent of the Authority the master of a vessel shall not cause or permit the vessel at any time to have fitted to it or to show a blue flashing light unless it is a vessel operated by the Authority, the Armed Forces, any other navigation or harbour authority or a public or local authority acting in a law enforcement or emergency role.

Visible Signals for Ferries 43 The master of a vessel plying as a ferry and crossing from one side of a waterway to the other shall:

(a) by day exhibit at the forward end of the vessel at such height as to be visible all round two black shapes not less than 0.6 metres (2 feet) in diameter in a vertical line one over the other not less than 1 metre (3 feet 3 inches) apart of which the upper shall be a ball and the lower a cylinder; and

(b) by night ensure that the vessel exhibits in the same position two lights in a vertical line not less than 1 metre (3 feet 3 inches) apart and visible all-round at a distance of 1.6 kilometres (1 mile). The upper of these lights shall be red and the lower light white.

Lights in 44 Moored Vessels

(1) Subject to paragraph (2) a moored vessel, any part of which extends 15 metres (49 feet 3 inches) or more into a channel or more than a quarter of the width of the channel (whichever is the less) shall by night exhibit an all-round white light at the outer extremity of the vessel. Such a light must be visible at a distance of one kilometre (1100 yards).

(2) This Byelaw does not apply to any vessel having a beam of less than 3.8 metres (12 feet 6 inches) moored alongside the bank of a waterway.

Height of 45 Masthead Lights

A power-driven vessel which navigates under fixed bridges at a time when required to exhibit lights shall be required to carry a masthead light above the level of the vessel's sidelights but otherwise not at such a height as will prevent safe clearance beneath any such bridge.

PART III: SOUND SIGNALS

Requirement for Whistle   **46**

(1) The master of a vessel of 25m (82 feet) or more in length shall ensure that the vessel is provided with an operative fixed or portable whistle capable of producing the blasts prescribed by these Byelaws and audible at a distance of one half of a nautical mile (2,025 yards or 1,852 metres).

(2) The master of a vessel of length more than 7.5m (24 feet 6 inches) but less than 25 metres (82 feet) shall ensure that the vessel is provided with a whistle or some other means of making an efficient sound signal.

Use of Whistle   **47**

(1) All sound signals prescribed by these Byelaws shall be given on the whistle.

(2) The master of a vessel shall not cause or permit the whistle of the vessel to be sounded for any purposes other than the safe navigation or management of the vessel.

Manoeuvring and Warning Signals   **48**

(1) When vessels are in sight of one another the master of a power-driven vessel under way when manoeuvring as authorised or required by these Byelaws may indicate that manoeuvre by the following signals on its whistle:
-one short blast to mean "I am altering my course to starboard" (i.e. to the right);
-two short blasts to mean "I am altering my course to port" (i.e. to the left);
-three short blasts to mean "I am operating astern propulsion".

(2) The master of a vessel may supplement the whistle signals described in paragraph (1) of this Byelaw by light signals, repeated as appropriate, whilst the manoeuvre is being carried out:

(a) these light signals shall have the following significance:
-one flash to mean "I am altering my course to starboard";
-two flashes to mean "I am altering my course to port";
-three flashes to mean "I am operating astern propulsion".

(b) the duration of each flash shall be about one second, the interval between flashes shall be about one second, and the interval between successive signals shall not be less than 10 seconds.

(3) When vessels in sight of one another are approaching each other and for any reason the master of either vessel fails to understand the intention or actions of the other, or is in doubt whether sufficient action is being taken by the other to avoid collision, the master of the vessel in doubt may immediately indicate such doubt by giving at least five short and rapid blasts on the whistle. Such signal may be supplemented by a light signal of at least five short and rapid flashes.

(4) The master of a vessel nearing a bend or an area of a channel or fairway or a bridge or other place where other vessels may be obscured by an intervening obstruction may, if the circumstances require, sound one prolonged blast. Such signals may be answered with a prolonged blast by the master of any approaching vessel that may be within hearing around the bend or behind the intervening obstruction.

Vessels Turning Round

49 The master of a power-driven vessel of 15 metres (49 feet 3 inches) or more in length and underway when about to turn round shall if circumstances require signify the same by four short blasts of its whistle followed after a short interval if turning with its head to starboard by one short blast and if to port by two short blasts. Whilst turning the vessel the master shall repeat such to any approaching vessel the master of which shall take any action necessary to avoid collision.

Sound Signals in Restricted Visibility

50 In or near an area of restricted visibility, whether by day or night, the signals prescribed in this Byelaw shall if the circumstances require be used as follows:

(a) a power-driven vessel making way through the water shall sound at intervals of not more than two minutes, one prolonged blast;

(b) a power-driven vessel underway but stopped and making no way through the water shall sound at intervals of not more than two minutes, two prolonged blasts in succession with an interval of about two seconds between them;

(c) a vessel not under command, a vessel restricted in its ability to manoeuvre, a vessel constrained by its draught, a sailing vessel and a vessel engaged in towing or pushing another vessel shall instead of the signals prescribed in sub-paragraphs (a) or (b) of this Byelaw sound at intervals of not more than two minutes, three blasts in succession, namely one prolonged blast followed by two short blasts;

(d) when a pushing vessel and a vessel being pushed ahead are rigidly connected in a composite unit they shall be regarded as a power-driven vessel and the master of the pushing vessel shall cause to be sounded the signals prescribed in paragraphs (a) or (b) of this Byelaw;

(e) the master of a vessel at anchor or aground shall at intervals of not more than one minute cause to be sounded three blasts in succession namely one short, one prolonged and one short blast or ring a bell rapidly for five seconds to give warning.

Signals to Attract Attention **51** Where it is necessary for the purpose of the safe navigation or management of a vessel for its master to attract the attention of another vessel he may make light or sound signals that cannot be mistaken for any signal authorised elsewhere in these Byelaws, or may direct the beam of his vessel's search light in the direction of the danger in such a way as not to embarrass any vessel.

PART IV: BRIDGE SIGNALS

Compliance with Light Signals 52 (1) Where light signals control the approach to, or passage through, a bridge the master of a vessel shall:

(a) not navigate the vessel past the light signals while red is displayed; and

(b) keep clear of the bridge so as to avoid obstructing the passage of any oncoming vessel.

(2) Sub-paragraph (1) (a) of this Byelaw does not apply to any fixed or permanently displayed red light the purpose of which is to give warning of the existence of a bridge.

Signal for Bridge Opening other than Carrow Bridge 53 The master of a vessel requiring any bridge (other than Carrow Bridge) to be lifted or swung open to permit the passage of the vessel may signify the same by three prolonged blasts of its whistle.

Signal for Carrow Bridge 54 The master of a vessel requiring Carrow Bridge to be lifted may signify the same by one prolonged blast followed by five short blasts.

Signals for Passage of Carrow Bridge 55 The master of a vessel requiring Carrow Bridge to be lifted shall not pass or attempt to pass through the opening span of the Bridge until authorised to do so by an authorised officer of the Authority.

Conduct of Vessels not requiring the lifting of Carrow Bridge 56 The master of a vessel which does not require Carrow Bridge to be lifted for the passage of the vessel shall not navigate or attempt to navigate the vessel through the opening span at any time or in such a manner as would hamper or inconvenience the passage through the bridge of a vessel which requires the bridge to be lifted.

PART V: MOORING AND ANCHORING

Place of Mooring   **57**   Subject to Byelaw 62(2) the master of a vessel:

(a) shall ensure that the vessel is not anchored, moored, berthed or stopped in such a position or manner as to impede the clear and free passage of any other vessel, or otherwise to obstruct the navigation of a waterway or channel or the use of a right of way on the banks thereof;

(b) shall not anchor, moor, berth or secure the vessel in any place or position where, because of any bridge or other permanent or temporary structure or obstruction to navigation or because of tidal or wind conditions in that place there exists permanently or temporarily a significant risk that any vessel navigating or manoeuvring in the channel may come into collision with the vessel.

Moored Vessels to be Properly Secured   **58**   (1) The master of a moored vessel shall ensure that the vessel is properly, safely and effectively secured and fendered so as to hold the vessel to the mooring and to prevent the risk of avoidable damage to the vessel or any other vessel or to the place of mooring or to any mooring equipment provided therein.

(2) The master of a vessel shall not without the consent of the Authority moor that vessel stern-on or bow-on except

(a) at a place where stern-on mooring or bow-on mooring (as the case may be) is approved by the Authority and

(b) in accordance with such conditions and during such times as the Authority may have by Notice displayed at or near that place.

Mooring Prohibitions to be Obeyed   **59**   (1) The master of a vessel shall not moor the vessel at any place where the Authority has prohibited mooring by a Notice displayed at or near that place.

(2) The master of a power-driven vessel shall not moor the vessel at any place where the Authority has by Notice displayed at or near that place indicated that such place is reserved for the mooring of sailing vessels.

Vessels not to Secure to Navigational Marks   **60**   The master of a vessel shall not secure the vessel to any buoy, beacon, post, sign or similar mark the purpose of which is to indicate hazard or channel or to give navigational direction.

Use of Moorings for Specific Periods 61

(1) This Byelaw applies where, by a notice displayed at or near any place, the Authority has prohibited mooring for more than a limited period or has restricted the number of times a vessel may use that place for mooring in a limited period.

(2) The master of a vessel shall not cause or permit the vessel to be moored in a place in contravention of any prohibition or restriction contained in a notice referred to in paragraph (1).

(3) A 'place' in this Byelaw includes, in relation to any restriction on the number of times a vessel may be moored in a place in a limited period, any other place within 500 metres (550 yards) thereof which is also subject to a notice displayed under the Byelaw.

Vessels to Moor Broadside to Banks 62

(1) Unless otherwise permitted by the Authority, the master of a vessel moored to a quayhead or bank shall ensure that either the vessel is made fast to the quayhead or bank at each of its ends and is laid so close as possible to and along the side of that mooring place or, if the vessel is moored alongside another vessel, it is not moored in contravention of Byelaw 63.

(2) Notwithstanding Byelaw 57 and paragraph (1) of this Byelaw a sailing vessel may lie secured to a quayhead or bank head to wind provided that in so doing:

(a) the master of the vessel takes all reasonable steps to avoid impeding the navigation of other vessels; and

(b) the vessel does not extend into the channel by more than a quarter of the width of the channel except whilst raising or lowering a mast or sail.

(3) Paragraph (2) shall apply also to a vessel equipped with sails notwithstanding that its sails are not for the time being set provided the vessel is lying head to wind preparatory or incidental to mooring or unmooring or in the course of a manoeuvre made or to be made under sail.

Vessels Mooring Abreast 63

(1) The master of a vessel shall not without the permission of the Authority moor that vessel alongside another vessel:

(a) at any place where the Authority has by notice displayed a prohibition of double mooring or the mooring of vessels alongside other vessels; or

(b) in contravention of any condition relating to double or multiple mooring which the Authority may by notice display at or near that place; or

(c) outside such times as the Authority may by notice permit for double or multiple mooring.

(2) Notwithstanding paragraph (1) the master of a vessel shall not moor alongside another vessel if by so doing any part of his vessel extends more than 10 metres (32 feet 9 inches) into the channel or extends into the channel more than one quarter of the width of the channel whichever is the less.

Vessels not to Anchor in a Channel

64 **(1)** Except as provided for in paragraph (3) or as may otherwise be permitted by the Authority the master of a vessel shall not cause or permit it to be anchored in a channel except to avoid immediate danger to the vessel or any other vessel, the bank or anything in or near the waterway.

(2) As soon as the danger referred to in paragraph (1) has passed the master of the vessel shall cause the anchor to be raised and the vessel to get under way.

(3) Nothing in paragraphs (1) and (2) shall prevent the master of a sailing vessel from anchoring the vessel

(a) whilst lowering or raising a mast or sail; or

(b) whilst kedging; or

(c) in order to control the progress, speed or direction of the vessel whilst moving under the influence of wind or stream. Provided that in each case:
(i) it is reasonably necessary to do so because of prevailing conditions of wind or stream and
(ii) in so doing he takes all reasonable steps to avoid impeding the navigation of other vessels.

(4) Paragraph (3) shall apply also to a vessel equipped with sails notwithstanding that its sails are not for the time being set.

Vessels Engaged in Fishing

65 The master of a vessel anchored for the purposes of fishing shall ensure that:

(a) no part of the vessel shall extend more than 3.8 metres (12 feet 6 inches) into the channel; and

(b) no part of the vessel shall obstruct the passage of any other vessel; and

(c) notwithstanding Byelaw 40 the vessel shall exhibit by night an all-round white light, the indirect illumination of which is visible for at least 100 metres (110 yards) but which will not interfere with the safe navigation of any other vessel.

Obstruction of Moorings   **66**   No person shall prevent, obstruct or hinder the lawful mooring of any vessel.

Working of Engines at Moorings   **67**   The master of a moored vessel shall not cause the engines of the vessel to be worked or the vessel to be operated in such a way that damage is, or is likely to be, caused to any part of the mooring place to which the vessel is secured.

PART VI: GENERAL

**Duty of Master 68
to Comply with
Instructions
of the
Authority**

The master of a vessel shall:

(1) Obey and conform to all lawful directions given by the Navigation Officer or other authorised Officer of the Authority.

(2) Not hinder or obstruct any such Officer in the execution of his powers or duties.

(3) Permit any such Officer to board and enter the vessel in such a manner and at any time as is reasonable for the purpose of:

(a) ascertaining whether or not these Byelaws are duly observed;

(b) ensuring compliance with these Byelaws.

**Conduct 69
following an
Incident**

(1) On the occurrence of any incident resulting in personal injury or serious damage to property or to any other vessel, the master of each vessel involved therein shall:

(a) stop the vessel as soon as practicable; and

(b) inform in writing the Navigation Officer or other Officer of the Authority and any other person having good reason to request it of his full name and address, the name and address of the owner of the vessel and its registration details.

(2) On the occurrence of any incident resulting in damage to property or to any other vessel not being an incident described in paragraph (1) the master of each vessel involved therein shall:

(a) Stop the vessel as soon as practicable; and

(b) Inform in writing any person having good reason to request it of his full name, address and the name and address of the owner of the vessel and its registration details; and

(c) Promptly take all reasonable steps to ascertain the identity of the owner of any property or other vessel involved therein and inform in writing such person or persons of his full name and address, the name and address of the owner of the vessel and its registration details.

Reporting of Sunken Vessels	**70**	The master of a vessel which for any reason has sunk or become stranded shall as soon as reasonably practicable report the occurrence to the Authority giving full written details including the position of the vessel.

Obstructions   **71**   (1) Subject to paragraph (3) the master of a vessel or owner of any thing shall:

(a) not cause or permit it to be stopped, grounded or sunk or placed so as to impede the free and clear navigation of any part of the navigation area;

(b) cause the vessel or thing to be re-moored or re-positioned without any delay, if required to do so by any person impeded or obstructed thereby or by an Officer of the Authority.

(2) If any person refuses, fails or neglects to remove a vessel or thing under paragraph (1) (b) an Officer of the Authority shall be entitled to cause it to be removed and, if necessary, to be unloaded and the cost of such removal or unloading shall be paid in full by the owner of the vessel or thing.

(3) Paragraphs (1) and (2) shall not apply to the stopping of a sailing vessel for so long as is reasonably necessary to lower or raise any sail or mast on the vessel provided that in any case the master of the vessel takes all reasonable steps to avoid impeding the navigation of other vessels.

Repairs   **72**   The master of a vessel shall not permit the vessel to lie in the navigation area while disabled or under repair for a period exceeding 28 days without written permission from the Authority unless the vessel is within a boatyard.

Interference with Vessels   **73**   No person other than the Navigation Officer or an Officer of the Authority acting in the execution of his duty shall without reasonable excuse let go or attempt to let go or part the mooring line or lines of any vessel except with the permission of the master of the vessel.

Interference with Machinery or Equipment   **74**   No person shall start or attempt to start any machinery or the equipment of a vessel without the permission of the master of the vessel.

Boarding of Vessels   **75**   (1) Subject to paragraph (2) no person shall board or attempt to board a vessel without the consent of the master of the vessel.

(2) Paragraph (1) does not:

(a) prevent the reasonable boarding of a vessel in order to gain lawful access to another vessel moored alongside or access to the bank from a vessel on an outside berth; or

(b) apply to an Officer of the Authority acting under Byelaws 68 or 71.

Precautions **76**
when Loading or
Unloading

The master of a vessel and a person undertaking the loading or discharging of any cargo, ballast, fuel, refuse or any other material into or from the vessel shall:

(a) use or cause to be used such methods as the Authority may direct for preventing any such matters from falling or escaping into the navigation area;

(b) in cases where such material is likely to fall into the navigation area, ensure that sufficient precautions are taken to prevent such material from so falling.

Security of **77**
Anchors and
Gear

The master of a vessel shall ensure that the anchor or anchors and all spars and gear of the vessel (whether moored or underway) shall when not in use be stowed in such a position as not to injure or damage any person or other vessel or property on or by the waterway.

Notice of **78**
Lost Anchors

(1) Subject to paragraph (3) the master of a vessel which has slipped or parted from or lost any anchor, chain, cable or propeller, shall:

(a) as soon as reasonably practicable inform the Navigation Officer thereof and, if possible, give him details of the position of the anchor, chain, cable or propeller; and

(b) if the Navigation Officer so directs, cause it to be recovered as soon as practicable.

(2) Subject to paragraph (3) the master of a vessel slipping or parting from an anchor or propeller shall leave a buoy to mark the position thereof.

(3) Paragraphs (1) and (2) shall not apply in any case where a failure to comply with the requirements of those paragraphs is unlikely to lead to any interference with the safe navigation of another vessel.

Burning of Vessels   **79**   **(1)** No person shall set fire to any vessel without the consent of the Authority.

(2) In giving its consent under this Byelaw, the Authority may impose such conditions as it thinks fit.

Bright Lights on Banks   **80**   No person shall cause or permit to be exhibited within or on any land adjoining the navigation area any bright light or lantern which is capable of:

(a) impairing the vision of any person navigating a vessel within the navigation area; or

(b) otherwise interfering with the safe navigation of such a vessel.

Pyrotechnics   **81**   **(1)** No person shall light, discharge or detonate any fireworks, flare or pyrotechnic within the navigation area or on its banks, except for the purpose of signalling distress, without the express consent of the Authority.

(2) In giving its consent under this Byelaw, the Authority may impose such conditions as it thinks fit.

Firearms and Weapons Prohibited in Navigation Areas   **82**   **(1)** Subject to paragraph (2), no person shall use any firearm, air weapon or any bow, catapult or sling or any projectile weapon without the consent of the Authority.

(2) This Byelaw shall not:

(a) affect any common law rights of any owner of land adjoining the navigation area;

(b) prohibit the use of a firearm or projectile solely for the purpose of signalling or saving life, or the use of any firearm or projectile by a member of the Police or Armed Forces in the execution of his duty;

(c) prohibit the use of a catapult in connection with the projection of bait into the water for the purposes of fishing provided that the person using the catapult does so in a manner which is not likely to cause danger or annoyance to any person or damage to any vessel.

(3) In giving its consent under this Byelaw, the Authority may impose such conditions as it thinks fit.

Drinks and Drugs	**83**	A person shall not navigate a vessel whilst under the influence of drink or drugs to such an extent as to be incapable of taking proper control of the vessel.
Emission of Smoke or Fumes or the Making of Noise	**84**	The master of a vessel shall not permit the vessel to emit smoke or fumes or make any noise or nuisance which gives reasonable grounds for annoyance to any other person.
Noise Nuisance	**85**	The master of a vessel shall ensure that no musical instrument, television or radio receiver or any other apparatus aboard the vessel is used in such a way that it causes nuisance or gives reasonable grounds for annoyance to any other person.
Fun Events	**86**	**(1)** Except with the written consent of the Authority no person shall organise or participate in any function or event in connection with the recreational use of any waterway which includes the use of any raft, tub vessel or other floating object not registered with the Authority pursuant to Byelaws made under paragraph 5 of Schedule 5 to the Norfolk and Suffolk Broads Act 1988.
		(2) In giving its consent under this Byelaw the Authority may impose such conditions as it thinks fit.
Indemnity Protecting Officers in Execution of Duty	**87**	An act necessary for the proper execution of his duty by an Officer of the Authority (or by any person acting on the instructions of an Officer of the Authority) shall not be deemed an offence against these Byelaws.
Penalties and Defences	**88**	**(1)** Every person contravening any of these Byelaws without reasonable excuse shall on summary conviction for every such breach be liable to pay a penalty not exceeding level 3 on the standard scale.

(2) In any proceedings for an offence under these Byelaws it shall be a defence for a person charged to prove:

(a) that he/she took all reasonable precautions and exercised due diligence to avoid the commission of such an offence; or

(b) that he/she had a reasonable excuse for the act or failure to act.

HAMILTON'S BROADS NAVIGATIONS

THE COMMON SEAL OF THE BROADS AUTHORITY was hereunto affixed in the presence of

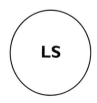

Given under the Common Seal of the Broads Authority the day of 3rd April 1995

Nicholas Hancox
Solicitor to the Broads Authority

Signed by Authority of the Secretary of State for Transport

P R Smith
(Assistant Secretary in the Department of Transport)

Date 11 August 1995

Speed Limit Byelaws.
1992

BROADS AUTHORITY SPEED LIMIT BYELAWS

Byelaws made by the Broads Authority under Section 10(3) and Section 10(5) and paragraph 4 of Schedule 5 of the Norfolk and Suffolk Broads Act 1988.

Citation	**1**	These Byelaws may be cited as the Broads Authority Speed Limit Byelaws 1992.
Commencement & Revocation	**2**	These Byelaws shall come into operation on 1st November 1992.
	3	With effect from the coming into operation of these Byelaws the following are repealed:

a The Norfolk Broads Speed Limit Byelaws 1978.

b Great Yarmouth Port and Haven (River Speed Limits) (Vessels) Byelaws 1989.

c Byelaws 4 and 8 of the Byelaws made by the Oulton Broad Joint Committee on 10th May 1934 and confirmed by the Minister of Transport on 10th December 1934.

Interpretation 4(1) In these Byelaws unless the context otherwise requires:

"The Authority" means the Broads Authority;

"Motor Vessel" means any ship, boat, lighter, yacht, houseboat, launch or craft of any kind propelled by any form of power whether mechanical or otherwise and includes any craft propelled by a detachable outboard engine, but excluding any sea-going vessel used as a tug or exclusively for the carriage of animals, fish or goods;

"Light Sports Vessel" means a motor vessel with a block area of no more than 13 square metres which has a planing hull and no permanent covered accommodation and which is capable of towing a water-skier;

"Coaching Vessel" means a motor vessel which is being used for the purpose of coaching one or more rowing crews.

"Boatyard Vessel" means a motor vessel which is being used by a boatyard for the purpose of trial or demonstration or testing after repair and whose navigator is an employee of the boatyard, having charge of the vessel in the course of his duties;

"Navigator" means any person who whether as owner or with the permission of the owner or without authority, has charge or control of any motor vessel and includes any person who is (a) present in the vessel and who gives orders to the person having charge or control of the vessel or (b) the hirer of the vessel;

"Owner" means the person who for the time being is registered as the owner of any vessel under the Authority's Byelaws for the time being in force;

"Prescribed Annual Toll" means the appropriate annual toll within the scale of tolls, currently in force in any year, as prescribed by the Authority pursuant to Section 26 of the Harbours Act 1964;

"Km/h" means kilometres per hour; "Mph" means statute miles per hour.

(2) Except as herein otherwise provided words and expressions to which a special meaning is assigned in the Norfolk and Suffolk Broads Act 1988 shall have the same meaning in these Byelaws as they have in that Act.

Application of Speed Limits

5 1 No person, being the navigator of a motor vessel, shall cause or permit such a vessel to be navigated on any stretch of water specified in Schedule 1 to these Byelaws at a speed over the ground greater than that specified in the said Schedule in relation to that stretch of water.

2 This Byelaw shall not apply to:

(a) the use of a light sports vessel while it is being used for the purpose of towing a water-skier, in accordance with Byelaw 6, on any of those stretches of water specified in Schedule 2 within the times specified in the said Schedule in relation thereto.

(b) The use of a boatyard vessel while it is being used, in accordance with Byelaw 8, on any of those stretches of water specified in Schedule 3 within the times specified in the said Schedule in relation thereto.

Water-Skiing 6   The use of a light sports vessel for the purpose of towing a water-skier shall be permitted subject to the following conditions:

a   The owner of the vessel shall have first complied with Byelaws 9, 10 (b), and 11 (b), 11 (c) and 11 (d).

b   The navigator of the vessel shall comply with Byelaw 12.

c   The navigator of the vessel shall have on board one person to provide assistance during towing.

d   The navigator of the vessel shall at no time tow more than two water-skiers.

e   Each water-skier shall remain in or on the water during towing.

f   The navigator of the vessel shall use tow-ropes of equal length when towing two water-skiers and the two water-skiers shall not cross in front of, or behind, each other.

g   The use of the vessel under this Byelaw shall be confined to those stretches of water specified in Schedule 2 within the times specified in the said Schedule in relation thereto.

h   In this Byelaw the purpose of towing a water-skier shall be deemed to include the act of recovering a water-skier who has been separated from the vessel during towing.

Coaching Vessels 7   Any person navigating a coaching vessel while coaching one or more rowing crews shall, subject to compliance with Byelaws 10(b) and 12, be exempt from Byelaw 5 on:

(i)   that part of the River Yare from the confluence of the River Wensum to a point 275 metres (300 yards) downstream of the upstream dyke leading to Surlingham Broad (Birds Dyke) between sunrise and 1400 hours on Sundays and between sunrise and sunset on all other days.

(ii) River Waveney, Oulton Dyke and Oulton Broad, on Sundays between 1000 hours and 1300 hours and Wednesdays during the summer (i.e. from 1st March to 1st November) between 1800 hours and sunset.

Boatyard Vessels 8 The use of any motor vessel as a boatyard vessel shall be permitted subject to the following conditions:

a The boatyard shall have first complied with Byelaws 10 (a) and II(a).

b The boatyard shall have paid the prescribed annual toll for the set of registration marks to be used on the said motor vessel.

c The navigator of the boatyard vessel shall comply with Byelaws 10 (a) and 11(a).

d The use of the boatyard vessel shall be confined to those stretches of water specified in Schedule 3 within the times specified in the said Schedule in relation thereto.

Water-ski Permit 9 a The owner of any light sports vessel shall before using, or permitting the use of, the vessel to tow a water-skier, pursuant to Byelaw 6, first obtain a permit which shall be issued by the Authority in accordance with this Byelaw. Provided that any light sports vessel has been registered in accordance with the Authority's Byelaws and provided that payment of the prescribed annual toll for the vessel has been made, the owner of the vessel may apply for a permit to the Authority.

b In the case of any application for a permit under this Byelaw, the Authority shall satisfy itself that the vessel concerned complies with the definition of a light sports vessel under Byelaw 4, before granting the owner a permit to use that vessel to tow a water-skier.

c The owner of any light sports vessel shall be required, as a condition of the grant of a permit under this Byelaw, permanently to remove from the vessel any wording which indicates that the vessel was formerly an authorised sports vessel.

d Any permit issued under this Byelaw shall expire on the 31st day of March next following the date of issue or on the date of the transfer of ownership of the vessel (whichever is the sooner).

e During the currency of any permit issued under this Byelaw the owner shall display on the light sports vessel registration marks in accordance with Byelaw 10 (b) and in any case where a permit expires or is not renewed the owner shall remove the said registration marks.

Registration Marks   10   a Any boatyard wishing to operate a boatyard vessel in accordance with these Byelaws shall first apply to the Authority for a set of registration marks, of a height, type, colour and material to be approved by the Authority, and the said marks shall be displayed on each side of the bow and at the after end so as to be visible from astern on any vessel being navigated as a boatyard vessel.

b In addition to any other byelaws requirements of the Authority, registration marks of a minimum height of nine inches and of a type, colour and material to be approved by the Authority shall be permanently displayed on each side of the bow and at the after end, so as to be visible from astern, on any light sports vessel which is used for towing a water-skier or on any coaching vessel.

Log Books   11   a Any boatyard to which a set of registration marks has been issued under Byelaw 10 (a) shall be issued with a log book by the Authority in respect of the said set of marks and during the use of the said marks shall keep it on the vessel being used and shall at all other times keep it with the said marks and shall on request present it for inspection to any officer of the Authority.

b The owner of any light sports vessel for which a permit has been issued under Byelaw 9 shall be issued with a log book by the Authority in respect of the said vessel and shall keep the log book on the vessel and shall on request present it for inspection to any officer of the Authority.

c On any occasion on which any light sports vessel is used in accordance with Byelaw 6 or any boatyard vessel is used in accordance with Byelaw 8 the navigator shall immediately before and immediately after such use make a record of the use in the log book issued under this Byelaw and shall on request present the log book for inspection to any officer of the Authority.

d On the transfer of ownership of any light sports vessel for which a log book has been issued the log book shall be immediately returned to the Authority by the former owner.

Wash **12** No person while navigating any light sports vessel in accordance with Byelaw 6 or any coaching vessel in accordance with Byelaw 7 shall cause the vessel to make a sustained wave, against a bank, of more than 300mm (12 inches) in height from trough to crest.

Penalties **13** Any person who commits a breach of any of these Byelaws shall be guilty of an offence and liable on summary conviction to a fine as follows:

a for a breach of Byelaws 8, 10 and 11, not exceeding level 2 on the standard scale.

b for a breach of any other byelaw, not exceeding level 3 on the standard scale

Defences **14** In any proceedings for an offence under these Byelaws it shall be a defence for the person charged to prove:

a that he took all reasonable precautions and exercised all due diligence to avoid the commission of such an offence; or

b that he had a reasonable excuse for his act or failure to act.

Definition of reasonable excuse **15** For the purpose of Byelaw 14 hereof "reasonable excuse" shall include:

a That the speed at which the motor vessel was navigated was reasonably necessary having regard to the fact that the navigator was assisting or offering to assist in an emergency arising from illness, accident, collision, fire or other circumstance which might reasonably be expected to involve danger to persons or property.

b That the navigator being employed in the service of the Authority, the Great Yarmouth Port Authority, the National Rivers Authority, or any Authority in whom their powers and duties may from time to time be vested, navigated the motor vessel at a speed which was reasonably necessary to perform his duties or any of them.

c That there was no sign conspicuously posted to mark the limit on that stretch of river and that the vessel had been navigated at a speed and in a manner not likely to endanger safety of other vessels or the banks of the rivers.

THE COMMON SEAL OF THE BROADS AUTHORITY was hereunto affixed in the prescence of

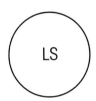

Given under the Common Seal of the Broads Authority the Eleventh day of December 1990.

T D W Molander,
Solicitor to the Broads Authority

The Secretary of State for Transport hereby confirms the foregoing byelaws as modified.

Signed by Authority of the Secretary of State for Transport,
M W Jackson
(An Assistant Secretary in the Department of Transport)
Date 30 September 1992

Annex A
Speed Limits Schedule

Byelaw 5 (Application of Speed Limits)
Schedule 1 Speed Limits

River Wensum

6.4km/h (4mph)   From the head of navigation at New Mills to the confluence with the River Yare.

River Yare

8.0km/h (5mph)   Trowse to Postwick - From Trowse Road Bridge to a point 800 metres (875 yards) below the sewage outfall at Whitlingham, including the Old Reach of the River Yare at Thorpe.

9.6km/h (6mph)   Postwick to Bramerton - From a point 800 metres (875 yards) below the sewage outfall at Whitlingham to the upstream end of the frontage of the Woods End Public House at Bramerton.

8.0km/h (5mph)   Bramerton - From the upstream end of the frontage of the Woods End Public House at Bramerton, to 274 metres (300 yards) downstream of the downstream end of Bramerton Common.

9.6km/h (6mph)   Bramerton to Surlingham - From 274 metres (300 yards) downstream of the downstream end of Bramerton Common to 1006 metres (1100 yards) upstream of the site of Surlingham Ferry.

8.0km/h (5mph)   Surlingham Ferry - From 1006 metres (1100 yards) upstream to 91 metres (100 yards) downstream of the site of Surlingham Ferry.

9.6km/h (6mph)   Surlingham to Brundall - From 91 metres (100 yards) downstream of the site of Surlingham Ferry to 274 metres (300 yards) downstream of the upstream dyke leading to Surlingham Broad (Bird's Dyke).

8.0km/h (5mph)   Brundall - From 274 metres (300 yards) downstream of the upstream dyke leading to Surlingham Broad (Bird's Dyke) to 91 metres (100 yards) downstream of Hobro's Dyke.

9.6km/h (6mph)   Brundall to Buckenham Ferry - From 91 metres (100 yards) downstream of Hobro's Dyke to 402 metres (a quarter of a mile) upstream of the Old Ferry Dock at Beauchamp Arms Hotel.

8.0km/h (5mph)	Buckenham Ferry - From 402 metres (a quarter of a mile) upstream to 402 metres (a quarter of a mile) downstream of the Old Ferry Dock at the Beauchamp Arms Hotel.
9.6km/h (6mph)	Buckenham Ferry to Cantley - From 402 metres (a quarter of a mile) downstream of the Old Ferry Dock at the Beauchamp Arms Hotel to 183 metres (200 yards) upstream of the Red House at Cantley.
8.0km/h (5mph)	Cantley - From 183 metres (200 yards) upstream, to 91 metres (100 yards) downstream of the Red House at Cantley.
9.6km/h (6mph)	Cantley to Reedham Ferry - from 91 metres (100 yards) downstream of the Red House at Cantley to 350 metres (383 yards) upstream of Reedham Ferry.
8.0km/h (5mph)	Reedham Ferry - From 350 metres (383 yards) upstream to 183 metres (200 yards) downstream of Reedham Ferry.
9.6km/h (6mph)	Reedham Ferry to Reedham - From 183 metres (200 yards) downstream of Reedham Ferry to 1207 metres (three quarters of a mile) upstream of the confluence of the River Yare with the Haddiscoe New Cut.
8.0km/h (5mph)	Reedham - From 1207 metres (three quarters of a mile) upstream of the confluence of the River Yare with the Haddiscoe New Cut to 91 metres (100 yards) downstream of that confluence.
9.6km/h (6mph)	Reedham to Berney Arms - From 91 metres (100 yards) downstream of the River Yare confluence with the Haddiscoe New Cut to 805 metres (half a mile) upstream of Turntide Jetty.
8.0km/h (5mph)	Berney Arms - From 805 metres (half a mile) upstream of Turntide Jetty to Turntide jetty.

River Yare Tributaries

4.8km/h (3mph)	Surlingham Broad - The whole of the Broad including Bargate Water, Birds's Dyke and Surlingham Fleet Dyke.
8.0km/h (5mph)	Rockland Broad - The whole of the Broad.
4.8km/h (3mph)	Rockland - The Whole of the Boat Dyke, Fleet Dyke and Short Dyke.
4.8km/h (3mph)	Langley - Langley Dyke in its entirety.

4.8km/h (3mph)   Hardley - Hardley Dyke in its entirety.

River Chet

6.4km/h (4mph)   From the head of navigation at Loddon to the confluence
                  with the River Yare at Hardley Cross.

Haddiscoe New Cut

8.0km/h (5mph)   The whole of the Haddiscoe New Cut from Haddiscoe to
                  Reedham.

River Waveney

4.8km/h (3mph)   Ellingham to Geldeston - From Shipmeadow Lock,
                  Ellingham to the confluence with and including Geldeston
                  Dyke.

8.0km/h (5mph)   Geldeston to Beccles - From the confluence of the River
                  Waveney and Geldeston Dyke to 1350 metres (1476
                  yards) upstream of the Town Road Bridge spanning the
                  River Waveney at Beccles.

6.4km/h (4mph)   Beccles - From 1350 metres (1476 yards) upstream of
                  the Town Road Bridge spanning the River Waveney at
                  Beccles to 1207 metres (three quarters of a mile)
                  downstream of the Town Road Bridge Spanning the River
                  Waveney at Beccles.

9.6km/h (6mph)   Beccles to Burgh St Peter - From 1207 metres (three
                  quarter of a mile) downstream of the Town Road Bridge
                  spanning the River Waveney at Beccles to 100 metres
                  (110 yards) upstream of the Boat Dyke at Burgh St Peter.

8.0km/h (5mph)   Burgh St Peter Staithe - From 100 metres (110 yards)
                  upstream to 302 metres (330 yards) downstream of the
                  Boat Oyke at Burgh St Peter Staithe.

9.6km/h (6mph)   Burgh St Peter to Somerleyton - From 302 metres (330
                  yards) downstream of the Boat Dyke at Burgh St Peter
                  Staithe to 366 metres (400 yards) upstream of
                  Somerleyton Ferry Pier.

8.0km/h (5mph)   Somerleyton - From 366 metres (400 yards) upstream to
                  183 metres (200 yards) downstream of Somerleyton Ferry
                  Pier.

9.6km/h (6mph)	Somerleyton to St Olaves - From 183 metres (200 yards) downstream of Somerleyton Ferry Pier to 1207 metres (three quarter of a mile) upstream of the Road Bridge spanning the River Waveney at St Olaves.
8.0km/h (5mph)	St Olaves - From 1207 metres (three quarters of a mile) upstream to 402 metres (a quarter of a mi l e) downstream of the Road Bridge spanning the River Waveney st St Olaves.
9.6km/h (6mph)	St Olaves to Seven Mile House - From 402 metres (a quarter of a mile) downstream of the Road Bridge spanning the River Waveney at St Olave's to 183 metres (200 yards) upstream of Seven Mile House (Pettingills Mill).
8.0km/h (5mph)	Seven Mile House - From 183 metres (200 yards) upstream to 183 metres (200 yards) downstream of Seven Mile House (Pettingill's Mill).
9.6km/h (6mph)	Seven Mile House to Burgh Castle - From 183 metres (200 yards) downstream of Seven Mile House (Pettingill's Mill) to the boundary with the navigation jurisdiction of the Great Yarmouth Port Authority 229 metres (250 yards) upstream of the entrance to Burgh Castle Marina.

Oulton Dyke and Broad

9.6km/h (6mph)	Oulton Broad - The whole of Oulton Broad
8.0km/h (5mph)	Oulton Dyke - The whole of Oulton Dyke from Oulton Broad to the River Waveney.

River Bure

4.8km/h (3mph)	Coltishall - From Horstead Mill to 914 metres (1000 yards) downstream of the Rising Sun public house and from Coltishall Lock to the confluence of the Lock Cut with the River Bure.
6.4km/h (4mph)	Coltishall to Belaugh - From 914 metres (1000 yards) downstream of the Rising Sun public house to 229 metres (250 yards) upstream of Belaugh Staithe.
4.8km/h (3mph)	Belaugh - From 229 metres (250 yards) upstream to 229 metres (250 yards) downstream of Belaugh Staithe.

6.4km/h (4mph)	Belaugh to Wroxham - From 229 metres (250 yards) downstream of Belaugh Staithe to the Northern entrance to Wroxham Broad.
8.0km/h (5mph)	Wroxham to Horning - From the Northern entrance to Wroxham Broad to the dyke leading to Hoveton Little Broad.
6.4km/h (4mph)	Horning - From the dyke leading to Hoveton Little Broad to Cockshoot Dyke.
8.0km/h (5mph)	Horning to Thurne - From Cockshoot Dyke to 1150 metres (1258 yards) upstream of the confluence with the River Thurne.
9.6km/h (6mph)	Thurne to Acle - From 1150 metres (1258 yards) upstream of the confluence with the River Thurne to 805 metres (half a mile) upstream of Acle Bridge.
8.0km/h (5mph)	Acle - From 805 metres (half a mile) upstream of Acle Bridge to 170 metres (186 yards) downstream of the confluence with Hermitage Dyke.
9.6km/h (6mph)	Acle to Stokesby - From 170 metres (186 yards) downstream of the confluence with Hermitage Dyke to 402 metres (a quarter of a mile) upstream of the site of the Ferry at Stokesby.
8.0km/h (5mph)	Stokesby - From 402 metres (a quarter of a mile) upstream to 402 metres (a quarter of a mile) downstream of the site of the Ferry at Stokesby.
9.6km/h (6mph)	Stokesby to Stracey Arms - From 402 metres (a quarter of a mile) downstream of the site of the Ferry at Stokesby to 402 metres (a quarter of a mile) upstream of the Stracey Arms projecting quay.
8.0km/h (5mph)	Stracey Arms - From 402 metres (a quarter of a mile) upstream to 402 metres (a quarter of a mile) downstream of the Stracey Arms projecting quay.
9.6km/h (6mph)	Stracey Arms to Great Yarmouth - From 402 metres (a quarter of a mile) downstream of the Stracey Arms projecting quay to the point where the boundary between Caister Parish and Great Yarmouth crosses the left bank of the River Bure.

River Bure Tributaries

4.8km/h (3mph)	Bridge Broad and access channels.
6.4km/h (4mph)	Salhouse - The whole of Salhouse Broad.
6.4km/h (4mph)	Ranworth - The whole of Malthouse Broad and Ranworth Dyke.
6.4km/h (4mph)	South Walsham - The whole of the Inner and Outer Broads and Fleet Dyke.
4.8km/h (3mph)	Upton - Upton Dyke in its entirety.
4.8km/h (3mph)	Acle - Hermitage Dyke in its entirety.

River Ant

4.8km/h (3mph)	Dilham Dyke from Brick Kiln Bridge to its confluence with the River Ant.
6.4km/h (4mph)	The whole of the River Ant and its navigable branches from a point 320 metres (350 yards) upstream of Wayford Bridge to its confluence with the River Bure, excepting Barton Broad, Dilham Dyke and Lime Kiln Dyke.
8.0km/h (5mph)	Barton Broad - The whole of Barton Broad.
4.8km/h (3mph)	Lime Kiln Dyke - From Neatishead Staithe to Gays Staithe.

River Thurne

6.4km/h (4mph)	From West Somerton to 1884 metres (one mile and 300 yards) downstream of the old Road Bridge at Potter Heigham.
8.0km/h (5mph)	Potter Heigham to Thurne - From 1884 metres (one mile and 300 yards) downstream of the Old Road Bridge spanning the River Thurne at Potter Heigham, to the confluence of the River Thurne and the River Bure.

River Thurne Tributaries

8.0km/h (5mph)	Hickling Broad - The whole of the Broad as far as the northwest end of Deep Dyke.
4.8km/h (3mph)	Catfield Dyke - From Catfield Staithe to Hickling Broad and the dyke leading to Catfield Common Staithe.

HAMILTON'S BROADS NAVIGATIONS

8.0km/h (5mph)	Deep Dyke to Candle (Kendal) Dyke - From the northwest end of Deep Dyke to the confluence of Candle (Kendal) Dyke with the River Thurne.
4.8km/h (3mph)	Waxham Cut - From Bridge Farm Waxham to Horsey Mere.
8.0km/h (5mph)	Horsey - The whole of Horsey Mere.
6.4km/h (4mph)	Meadow Dyke - The whole of Meadow Dyke to the confluence with Heigham Sound.
6.4km/h (4mph)	Womack Water and Dyke - From the head of navigation (Staithe House) to the confluence with the River Thurne.

Byelaw 6 (Water Skiing)
Schedule 2 Water Skiing - Light Sports Vessels

Stretch of Water

River Yare

1 From a point 800 metres (875 yards) downstream of the outfall of the Norwich sewage treatment works at Whitlingham to the upstream end of the frontage of the Woods End Public House at Bramerton.

Times

a Between the 21st March and the 30th September in any year:between 1600 hours and sunset on Wednesdays, Fridays, Sundays and public holidays.

b Between the 1st October and the 20th March in any year:between 1300 hours and sunset on Sundays and public holidays.

2 From a point 400 metres (437 yards) downstream of Hobro's Dyke to a point 400 metres (437 yards) upstream of the old Ferry Dock at the Beauchamp Arms Hotel at Buckenham Ferry.

3 From a point 400 metres (437 yards) downstream of the old Ferry Dock at the Beauchamp Arms Hotel to a point 400 metres (437 yards) upstream of the Red house at Cantley.

a Between the 21st March and the 30th September in any year:between 1000 hours and 1400 hours on Saturdays and between 1600 hours and sunset on any other day.

4 From a point 1210 metres (1323 yards) upstream of the confluence of Hardley Dyke and the River Yare to a point 90 metres (98 yards) upstream of that confluence.

b Between the 1st October and 20th March in any year:between 1300 hours and sunset on Sundays and between 0900 hours and sunset on any other day.

5 From a point 400 metres (437 yards) downstream of the confluence of Haddiscoe New Cut and the River Yare to a point 400 metres (437 yards) upstream of Upper Seven Mile House.

Stretch of Water

Times

River Waveney

1 From a point 230 metres (252 yards)downstream of the confluence of Oulton Dyke and the River Waveney to a point 1840 metres (2012 yards) downstream of that confluence.

2 From a point 1610 metres (1761 yards) upstream of Somerleyton Ferry Pier to a point 800 metres (875 yards) upstream of that pier.

3 From a point 400 metres (437 yards) downstream of Somerleyton Ferry Pier to a point 1410 metres (1542 yards) upstream of the road bridge spanning the River Waveney at St Olaves.

a Between the 21st March and the 30th September in any year:between 1000 hours and 1400 hours on Saturdays and between 1600 hours and sunset on any other day.

b Between the 1st October and 20th March in any year:between 1300 hours and sunset on Sundays and between 0900 hours and sunset on any other day.

4 From a point 1210 metres (1323 yards) downstream of the road bridge spanning the River Waveney at St Olaves to a point 400 metres (437 yards) upstream of Seven Mile House (Pettingill's Mill)

5 From a point 400 metres (437 yards) downstream of Seven Mile House (Pettingill's Mill) to a point 2010 metres (2198 yards) upstream of the lower limit of the River Waveney being 460 metres (503 yards) upstream of the base Turntide Jetty.

a Between the 21st March and the 30th September in any year:between 1000 hours and sunset on Saturdays and between 1600 hours and sunset on any other day.

b Between the 1st October and the 20th March in any year:between 0900 hours and sunset on any day.

Byelaw 8 (Boatyards)
Schedule 3 Boatyard Vessels

River Yare

1 From a point 800 metres (875 yards) downstream of the outfall of the Norwich sewage treatment works at Whitlingham to the jetty at Postwick Hall Farm between sunrise and 1600 hours on any day excluding Saturdays, Sundays and public holidays.

2 From a point 90 metres (98 yards) downstream of the site of Surlingham Ferry to a point 275 metres (301 yards) upstream of Riverside House at Brundall Gardens between 0900 hours and 1500 hours on Saturdays and between 0900 hours and 1700 hours on any other day excluding Sundays and public holidays between the 25th March and the 24th October in any year.

3 From a point 400 metres (437 yards) downstream of Hobro's Dyke to a point 460 metres (500 yards) upstream of Rockland Fleet Dyke between sunrise and 1500 hours on Saturdays and between sunrise and sunset on any other day excluding Sundays and public holidays between the 25th March and the 24th October in any year.

4 From a point 400 metres (437 yards) downstream of the confluence of the Haddiscoe New Cut and the River Yare to a point 400 metres (437 yards) upstream of Upper Seven Mile House between sunrise and 1500 hours on Saturdays and between sunrise and sunset on any other day excluding Sundays and public holidays between the 25th March and the 24th October in any year.

River Waveney

1 From a point 500 metres (547 yards) upstream of Carpenter's Dyke at Gillingham to that dyke between 0800 hours and sunset on any day excluding Sundays and public holidays between 1st May and 30th September in any year.

2 From a point 400 metres (437 yards) downstream of the confluence of Oulton Dyke and the River Waveney to a point 1610 metres (1761 yards) downstream of that confluence between sunrise and 1500 hours on Saturdays and between sunrise and sunset on any other day excluding Sundays and public holidays between the 25th March and the 24th October in any year.

3 From a point 1210 metres (1323 yards) downstream of the road bridge spanning the River Waveney at St.Olaves to a point 400 metres (437 yards) upstream of Seven Mile House (Pettingill's Mill) between sunrise and 1500 hours on Saturdays and between sunrise and sunset on any other day excluding Sundays and public holidays between the 25th March and the 24th October in any year.

River Bure

1 From a point 595 metres (651 yards) downstream of Wroxham Castle Staithe to a point 920 metres (1006 yards) downstream of that staithe between sunrise and 1500 hours on Saturdays and between sunrise and sunset on any other day excluding Sundays and public holidays between 1st May and 30th September in any year.

2 From a point 275 metres (301 yards) downstream of the southern entrance to Wroxham Broad to a point 550 metres (601 yards) downstream of the said entrance between 0900 hours and 1500 hours on Saturdays and between 0900 hours and 1700 hours on any other day excluding Sundays and public holidays between the 25th March and the 24th October in any year.

3 From a point 550 metres (601 yards) downstream of Cockshoot Dyke to a point 1000 metres (1094 yards) downstream of the said dyke between 0900 hours and 1500 hours on Saturdays and between 0900 hours and 1700 hours on any other day excluding Sundays and public holidays between the 25th March and the 24th October in any year.

River Thurne

1 From Womack Dyke to a point 920 metres (1006 yards) upstream of the confluence of the River Bure and the River Thurne between sunrise and 1600 hours on any day excluding Sundays and public holidays between 25th March and 24th October in any year.

Broads Authority Vessel Dimension Byelaws. 1995

These byelaws came into effect on 1 January 1997
The byelaws impose a maximum beam restriction of 3.8 metres (12.6") on vessel navigating on certain waters, viz:

River Wensum	Upstream of Foundry Bridge
River Yare	Upstream of Trowse Eye
	Bird's Dyke & Surlingham Fleet Dyke
	Rockland Boat Dyke, Fleet Dyke & Short Dyke
	Langley Dyke
	Hardley Dyke
River Chet	The entire waterway
River Waveney	Geldeston Boat Dyke
River Bure	Upstream of "The Rising Sun", Coltishall
	Upton Dyke
	Hermitage Dyke, Acle
River Ant	The entire waterway and its navigable branches including Barton Broad
River Thurne	Upstream of Dungeon Corner
	Catfield Dyke and its branches
	Waxham Cut
	Meadow Dyke
	Candle Dyke
	Womack Dyke & Womack Water

The beam restrictions do not apply to dredging and maintenance craft or sailing wherries. Vessels first registered in the Broads before October 1991 are exempt, as are vessels undergoing boatyard testing.

Vessels of length greater than 14 metres (46') are also prevented from using the above listed waterways. in the case of length, vessels first registered in the Broads before April 1992 are exempt.

Vessel of beam over 3.8 metres (12'6") or length over 14 metres (46') may make up to four passages each year in restricted waters provided at least seven days written notice of each passage has been given to the Broads Authority specifying the start and finishing places.

There are further restrictions on vessels having beam greater than 4.27 metres (14'). Further Information should be sought from the Broads Authority, 18 Colegate, Norwich NR3 1BQ. Tel: (01603) 610734

Hamilton's Broads Tide Calculator.

1. Look up the time of Low Water at Yarmouth Yacht Station. If you are not using Hamilton's Tide Tables, be sure to ensure that these are given in British Summer Time, if appropriate. If your tide tables give times at Yarmouth Bar, then add one hour to forty five minutes to the times given. If you are at all unsure of the times of tides or feel that weather conditions may, for example, have caused them to run late; then for the sake of accuracy and peace of mind, telephone Yarmouth Yacht Station to check how the tides have been running. (01493 - 842794).

2. For simplicity, time is shown on the outer dial in the form of a 12 hour clock. Low Water is marked in red on the inner dial. For an example, move the red line with an arrow on the inner dial line, marked " Yarmouth Yacht Station Low Water" to point at 12.15 on the outer dial, which we will assume is the time given for Low Water at Yarmouth Yacht Station.

3. Times of high and low water can be read off the calculator for other locations given on the inner dial. In our example above:- High Water at Great Yarmouth is given at 5.15, the water would be Slack till very nearly 1.45 whilst Low Water at Wroxham and Norwich can be read off as 3.45. The time can be either am. or pm. it makes no difference.

4. To make a passage at slack water through Great Yarmouth all that is necessary is a calculation of the distance involved (Distance tables are given from page 24 onwards of Hamilton's Navigations), times your average speed. Do not forget that this should be your average speed over ground. You should be travelling with the current and this would normally be greater than your average speeds on the upper reaches of any of the rivers which have significantly less tide.

Hamilton's Slack Water Calculator.

Hamilton's Yarmouth Slack Calculator is designed as an easy reference to help skippers judge exactly the right departure times from a range of locations, to make a passage through Great Yarmouth at Slack Water, without resorting to mental arithmetic.

1. First, look in your tide tables for the time of Low Water at Yarmouth Yacht Station. Comments on timing of tides for the Broads Tide Calculator above, apply equally to the Slack Water Calculator.

2. Turn the "clock face" on the inner dial to the correct time to bring the time of Low Water Yarmouth Yacht Station next to the red arrow on the outer dial marked Low Water YYS.

3. Look on the outer dial for your departure point or nearest location.

4. The time given beside this location on the inner dial will be the latest time you can hope to depart and hope to make passage through Great Yarmouth at Slack Water.

Useful Telephone Numbers

Norfolk Central Police	01603 - 768769
Suffolk Central Police	01986 - 835300
Ambulance.	01603 - 424255
Broads Authority	01603 - 610734
River Inspectors	01603 - 625091
Information Centres.	
Beccles	01502 - 713196
Hoveton (Wroxham)	01603 - 782281
Loddon (inf. only)	01508 - 520690
Potter Heigham	01692 - 670779
Ranworth	01603 - 270453
Toad Hole Cottage, How Hill.	01692 - 678763
Environment Agency	01603 - 662800
East Anglian Tourist Board	01473 - 822922
Gt. Yarmouth Information Centre	01493 - 846345/842195
Lowestoft Information Centre	01502 - 523000/565989
Norwich Information Centre	01603 - 666071
Beccles Yacht Station	01502 - 712225
Gt. Yarmouth Port Authority	01493 - 335500
Gt. Yarmouth Yacht Station	01493 - 842794
Lowestoft Harbour (ABP)	01502 - 572286
Norwich Yacht Station	01603 - 622024
Oulton Broad Yacht Station	01502 - 574946
Church Services Information	01263 - 82263
(South Walsham)	
British Rail Information (Central)	0345 - 484950
Bus information Centre	01603 - 613613
Gt. Yarmouth Bus Station	01493 - 842341
Norwich Bus Station	01603 - 622800
Lowestoft Bus Station	01502 - 565406
RSPCA Norfolk & Suffolk	0990 - 555999
RSPB Norwich	01603 - 661662
Norfolk Wherry Trust	01603 - 505815
Norfolk Wildlife Trust	01603 - 625540
Norfolk Windmills Trust	01603 - 222222
Suffolk Wildlife Trust	01473 - 890089
Weather call	0891 - 500764
Weather centre	01603 - 660779
Marinecall	0891 - 500765
Metfax. Marine.2 day forecast. Anglian Coast	0336 - 400455

NOTES